LEVINAS ON THE PRIMACY OF THE ETHICAL

Northwestern University
Studies in Phenomenology
and
Existential Philosophy

General Editor Anthony J. Steinbock

LEVINAS ON THE PRIMACY OF THE ETHICAL

Philosophy as Prophecy

Jeffrey Bloechl

Northwestern University Press
Evanston, Illinois

Northwestern University Press
www.nupress.northwestern.edu

Copyright © 2022 by Northwestern University. Published 2022 by Northwestern
University Press. All rights reserved.

Printed in the United States of America

10   9   8   7   6   5   4   3   2   1

Library of Congress Cataloging-in-Publication Data
Names: Bloechl, Jeffrey, 1966– author.
Title: Levinas on the primacy of the ethical : philosophy as prophecy / Jeffrey
    Bloechl.
Other titles: Northwestern University studies in phenomenology & existential
    philosophy.
Description: Evanston, Illinois : Northwestern University Press, 2022. | Series:
    Northwestern University studies in phenomenology and existential philos-
    ophy | Includes bibliographical references and index.
Identifiers: LCCN 2022023762 | ISBN 9780810145443 (paperback) | ISBN
    9780810145450 (cloth) | ISBN 9780810145467 (ebook)
Subjects: LCSH: Lévinas, Emmanuel. | Lévinas, Emmanuel—Ethics. | Phe-
    nomenology. | Philosophy and religion. | BISAC: PHILOSOPHY / Move-
    ments / Phenomenology | PHILOSOPHY / Ethics & Moral Philosophy
Classification: LCC B2430.L484 B56 2022 | DDC 194—dc23/eng/20220524
LC record available at https://lccn.loc.gov/2022023762

Let justice flow like a river,
And righteousness a never-ending stream.
　　—Amos 5:24

In the beginning there is ethics, and
then there are problems.
—Emmanuel Levinas

Contents

Acknowledgments

An early draft of the first three sections of chapter 1 of this work was given as a lecture at a conference on "Religion and Violence" organized by Michael Staudigl at the University of Vienna. Parts of chapter 2 were given as invited lectures at the Catholic University of America and at the Universidad de Alberto Hurtado in Santiago, Chile. Chapter 4 originated from a line of questioning opened up after my plenary lecture at the first annual "Psychology of the Other" conference, organized by David Goodman at Lesley University. An early draft, again only of parts, of chapter 5 was given as a plenary lecture at the 2015 annual meeting of Simposio Hermeneia, organized by Roberto Wu at the Federal University of Santa Catarina, Brazil. I am grateful to my hosts and interlocuters at these events. Chapter 3 is an expanded and modified version of an essay published by Kevin Hart and Michael Signer (eds.) in *The Exorbitant: Emmanuel Levinas between Christianity and Judaism*. I am grateful to Fordham University for permission to republish it here.

My interpretation of Levinas here originated in my graduate studies at the KU Leuven, already a long time ago, among careful readers such as Rudolf Bernet, Roger Burggraeve, Paul Moyaert, Ignace Verhack, and, above all, Rudi Visker, though he is certain to be dissatisfied with these results. The philosophy of Levinas is also read and taught with interest at Boston College, where I have learned a great deal, especially from my friends Richard Kearney and the late William J. Richardson, and from the questions, resistance, and occasional agreement of our good students.

I don't often enough state my particular debt to the works of an entire range of scholars, only some of whom I have had occasion to cite along this particular trajectory. I am pleased to mention their names here: Bettina Bergo, Robert Bernasconi, Rudolf Bernet, Roger Burggraeve, Richard A. Cohen, John Drabinski, Didier Franck, Claire Katz, James Mensch, Paul Moyaert, Adriaan Peperzak, Jacques Taminiaux, Alan Udoff, Rudi Visker, and Bernhard Waldenfels. I am also pleased to state my gratitude for the fine work of my copy editor, Paul Mendelson, which has made my text much more lucid and readable.

Boston College is a generous institution. This book was completed while on sabbatical for the 2020–2021 academic year. I wrote nearly all of its final draft during eight weeks of complete solitude in Umbria, sustained by the support and encouragement of my wife, Catherine, and our three children, Tessa, Nicholas, and Julia. What goes into this book, like a great deal else, is first and last for them.

LEVINAS ON THE PRIMACY OF THE ETHICAL

Philosophy and Prophecy: An Internal Reading of Levinas

The following study proposes an internal reading of Emmanuel Levinas's philosophical work centered on the relationship between two central features. On one hand, his argument is most generally pursued through claims that are phenomenological in nature. On the other hand, the horizon for those claims is always finally religious. The patient reader is generally led from one to the other when it turns out that some of Levinas's phenomenological claims become considerably more plausible when traced to the religious concepts that ground them, or when it turns out that some of the religious concepts cannot be assessed until one attends to the examples that would verify them. The former path opens up in front of any doubt one may feel at Levinas's claim that the face of the neighbor is the self-expression of an otherness that is strictly unqualified and yet commands responsibility. How can what is unqualified have any intelligible effect at all? In various ways, Levinas suggests that we are in fact prepared for such an event. Subjectivity is hollowed out in advance, prior even to its closure into itself, and it already desires more than the limited goods that it pursues under the domination of self-interest. We find that the "hollowing out" (this is his own expression) is entailed by the relation with Infinity, which Levinas does not hesitate to characterize as a philosophical name for "God."[1] We also find out that the desire that transcends self-interest aims at a Good that is again a philosophical name for "God." Infinity is God as primordial condition, and Good is God as most desirable. If these concepts are withdrawn or overlooked, the face might signify nothing more than the approach of a rival, and the desire that Levinas calls "metaphysical desire" might not rise above what Sartre, very much in the course of dismantling religion altogether, calls "useless passion."[2]

Having said all of this, and now thinking in the contrary direction, it will not do for one to start from Levinas's religious concepts and simply extrapolate. If one wants to know what it means that ethics is a spiritual optics, that the ethical relation is a religious relation, or that the breach of totalization by the face of the other person is also the opening up of the dimension proper to the divine—all of which Levinas claims more than once—there is no avoiding a close inspection of the phenomena that he must contend are unaccountable in any other terms.

These challenges are not unique to a reading of Levinas, but in his case they are made especially urgent by the extravagance of his argument. There is no mistaking it: in order to respect the structure of the ethical call and response, it will be necessary to recognize that ethics and not ontology or epistemology is first philosophy, and this requires a departure from the basic claims of Western philosophy as such. Of course, one will rightly object that it appears that for Levinas "Western philosophy" in fact means, for the most part, classical metaphysics as interpreted by Heidegger in the course of defining the fundamental ontology that is the real target of criticism. The implications of this position are among the unstated concerns of the present study, but the aim is not to suggest that Levinas has been ungenerous in his reading of a particular author or has overlooked features in a particular text that might be more favorable to his contention. I have taken that approach elsewhere, in other works, which have concentrated on tracing the outer limits of his position. Without entirely disavowing that work and its approach, the present study instead traces certain inner limits, or perhaps better, highlights the force of a thinking that negotiates—not only better than one sometimes hears, but also, it seems to me, better than many other impressively capacious philosophies—an extraordinary range of intellectual debate. I have said that it is centered on the relationship between phenomenology and religion. This in fact says little, since Levinas has his own conceptions of both of them. Without going into those matters here, let it only be said, by way of anticipation, that a properly Levinasian phenomenology begins to take shape already before he has come fully to his understanding of religion. And as for religion, it is philosophical rather than cultic or theological, ethical without reducing God or the other person to one another, and has a root in what it will be necessary to call Jewishness or being Jewish but nonetheless claims a universal extension.

Levinas did not always hold the views we associate with his major texts, but he came to them along a steady line of reflection that was prompted first by a need to think through the questions of violence and peace. He was hardly alone in this, even among his contemporaries, during the interwar years. What already set him apart from the others was his combination of great personal sensitivity to the rise of an especially virulent antisemitism advocated by German National Socialism, a profound understanding of the phenomenological methods he would bring to bear on that theme, and a tortured sense that a prominent exponent of the latter was implicated in the former. In chapter 1 of the present work, I take as my point of departure an extended look at Levinas's anguished early essay, "Reflections on the Philosophy of Hitlerism." At that time and for just a short while longer, he is moved by a need to understand a political problem at the level of subjectivity favored by Husserl and, after a fashion, Heidegger. This is not at all to say that there is no historical context in Levinas's analysis of fascism and antisemitism, but only that he is most intent on grasping the thing itself—the violence of suppression and exclusion, and the pain that it inflicts—as it appears in lived experience. To be sure, the entire tradition is found wanting on the question of how to respond to what Levinas judges is the root of the problem, and this gives rise to a new conception of our being that opens the way to the polemic with "Western philosophy" that has alternately thrilled and dismayed his readers. This is where a "religious" solution enters his thinking. One already finds strong indications of it in the long essay published as *De l'évasion*, and ample reason to take great care with what the word "religion" will always mean to him. Chapter 1 draws mainly on elements of these two essays in order to mark Levinas's distance from Heidegger and Sartre on his chosen themes of violence and peace. The philosophers of being and situation are charged by him with providing conceptual license for the violence that emanates from self-determination and self-interest. Against this, Levinas proposes that philosophy does have access to a goodness and a peace that transcend violence, even if philosophy must nonetheless recognize that we are never without a propensity to violence. Because such a philosophy thus accepts for itself the task of calling us to a peace and a goodness that are always more than we can accomplish, it must be characterized as *prophetic*. The philosopher enters into the public sphere, engaging us in our relations with one another, with a vision that sees beyond anything that appears within the horizon of being and history.

Chapter 2 takes up Levinas's reflection on his experiences as a prisoner of war. During this time, he clarifies for himself the nature and range of his disagreement especially with Heidegger. The early postwar books that we have in English as *Existence and Existents* and *Time and the Other* work out what we must recognizes as a proposed correction of the analysis of Dasein found in *Being and Time*. They also take important steps toward Levinas's argument that ethics and now fundamental ontology are first philosophy, and they indeed at least prefigure the phenomenology of intersubjectivity that becomes prominent in *Totality and Infinity*. These things have long been well known. This is not the case for some of what appears in fragments, short essays, and transcripts from the wartime and early postwar years, but unpublished in Levinas's own lifetime. The essay on Hitlerism attends closely to the pain of suppression and exclusion. *Existence and Existents* characterizes being as suffering. Between these two works, some of the wartime texts interpret the persecution of the Jewish people, most intensively those who were actually imprisoned, as both the key to understanding their proper identity and the content of a teaching that they have to offer humanity as such. This theme brings Levinas directly to an encounter with the God of ontotheology and providence, whose supreme will would ground an order in which suffering is necessary. It is doubtful that Levinas ever believed in such a God, and it is certain that his philosophy has never had room for it.

These various claims are refined and unified at the heart of *Totality and Infinity*. Chapter 3 finds that text to turn around the mutual implication of infinity and plurality, which grounds Levinas's understanding of the ethical relation as a religious relation. Ethical metaphysics, in which desire for the good is concretized as responsibility for the other person, at once grounds an account of intersubjectivity as asymmetrical and exhibits a relation with God that has escaped theological understanding. In his interpretation of Descartes's "Third Meditation," Levinas finds a philosophical way to God in the idea of infinity which, present in consciousness without being contained there, holds us open to the call for help that is expressed in the face of the other person. In his interpretation of the Platonic notion of a good beyond being, he discovers a second philosophical way to God. As infinity, God is that by which we are ordered to one another prior to recognition and freedom. As the supreme good, God is most desirable, above and beyond anything only for ourselves. In the former case, God is implicated in ethical plurality. In the latter case, God is implicated in the fact that we choose the good. Both conceptions of God are raised in due course by an analysis of what transpires in and through the face of the other person.

Chapter 4 brings Levinas's conceptions of desire, good, and finally God in contact with corresponding conceptions in Freudian and Lacanian psychoanalysis. Though these accounts of subjectivity and the relation with the other person have an important structural similarity with that of Levinas, their positions are directly opposed to his on virtually all of their key claims. Freudian psychoanalysis, certainly including it as understood by Lacan, is a materialism or, if one prefers, a vitalism. The goodness promoted by Levinas is for Freudians a danger, and ethics is born in the possibility of maintaining distance from it. Precisely from this difference, psychoanalysis raises important questions about Levinas's efforts to keep responsibility, metaphysical desire, and the very relation with what he calls "God" free of any investment by the subject of affect or interest. This tendency is already well known when it is a matter of the relation with the other person. A close reading of the phenomenology of eros that makes up section IV.B of *Totality and Infinity* will bring to the surface every necessary question or doubt. In this chapter, I follow Levinas's position on that matter back to the position on God that sustains it. We find there that he is under no illusions about what he asks—and in fact, it occurs to me now that one could generate an excellent reading of Levinas simply by taking seriously his extraordinary radical claims. At the end of chapter 4, we find him adopting the word "psychosis."

Chapter 5 resumes the question of God, but now as a way into Levinas's philosophy of language. After showing that there is a turn to language underway already in *Totality and Infinity*, and indeed showing why, I revert to some of his unpublished work on metaphor that is roughly contemporaneous with the great book. On the one hand, what one finds there is recognizably close to important features of the theory of language he developed in his published works not long afterward, but around a distinction between saying (*le dire*) and the said (*le dit*). On the other hand, those texts also raise the question of the word or name "God" specifically as a problem for finite speech. By this point in my investigation, and now with added emphasis from Derrida, I hope to have made it clear that such a problem would shake the entire account of ethics that appeals to it. Levinas's unpublished work on metaphor takes on the difficult theme of a God who, prior to any speech, is at once the condition for everything we say and yet unspeakable. Only philosophy can hold this in view, and only philosophy can speak the name that is not a name like any other. This secures the religious task of philosophy, which is part and parcel with its ethical task, and is beyond not only ontology but also theology. This also invests philosophy, as prophecy, with a specific teaching.

Chapter 6 finds Levinas committing much of his philosophical work to offering this teaching most immediately to a culture that is still predominantly Christian. His engagement with theology is not at all episodic, as one might think if one only counted the explicit occasions (though there are more than a few of these). A form of thinking that identifies itself as philosophical is seeded with theological concepts, all of which are given new ethical definitions, and does not cease to invoke "God" even while excoriating other definitions of that word. Yet this is not without appreciation of the discourse under correction. Levinas knows, for example, that mystical theology is alive with an authentic desire for the true God. Yet his assessment of religion is unfailingly negative, when in the end there appears a claim to comprehend and to take comfort or feel enthusiasm, all of which are for Levinas symptoms of the return of ontology and thus violence. In order to free religion, or ethics as religion, from all of this, it is necessary to think that we are ordered to one another and to God, and indeed respond to one another and desire God, before and beyond our relation to being. In *Otherwise Than Being, or Beyond Essence*,

Levinas calls this ordering a "plot" and a "matrix" established without resting on any ontology of theology. This is both his last word, inasmuch as his mature philosophy depends entirely on it, and his first word, since it will have held open the space within which everything else, for a very long time (though we did not know it), has been argued in the name of a peace and goodness that are not defeated by violence.

Levinas was prolific. He was also insistent about a single powerful argument. Few of his many texts move far from it, and the great majority of them retrace it in one or another way. Rather than cite many texts in support of a single claim, or worse, range among his texts indiscriminately, I have for the most part tried to stay as close as possible to what I judge to be his most important works: *Existence and Existents*, *Totality and Infinity*, *Otherwise Than Being, or Beyond Essence*, and a small set of essays. There are exceptions, but I hope the reasons for them are made evident: "Reflection on the Philosophy of Hitlerism," "The Spirituality of the Jewish Prisoner," "Being Jewish," and works on metaphor published only after Levinas's death.

I have occasionally modified or, I venture to say, corrected translations. These changes are in all cases acknowledged. When a text is translated without mention of a translator, I am responsible for the English. I have also sometimes engaged in some reflection on the advantages of different possible translations of an exceptionally difficult notion, hoping thereby to familiarize the reader with what I take to be an important question or issue. I have generally avoided capitalizing key terms like "being," "other," "infinity," and "saying" and "said," because it is my sense that the context of their use generally makes clear their specific meaning, and because I prefer to avoid appearing to suggest that those words mean more in some instances or passages than in others. In the case of "infinity," I have also with occasional exceptions preferred that term over "the infinite," only because the latter expression can appear to ontologize what is clearly taken to transcend any such thing. These practices sometimes place me at odds with Levinas's own procedures as well as those of his publishers. I am content to let the reader judge whether I have made the text more vivid and intelligible, or less so.

1

Situation and Violence: Levinas, Heidegger, and Sartre

Force and Exclusion

It is often overlooked that Levinas's first original work was in political philosophy. One might well be intrigued by its title, from the hand of an author whose profound meditations on good and evil are well known to have been marked by the rise of modern fascism. Of course, this would occur only in retrospect. Considered in its original context, the turn in his early work appears considerable. After important studies of Husserl and Heidegger, Levinas turns in 1934 to "Reflections on the Philosophy of Hitlerism."[1] This essay is complicated. What one finds there is an attempt not so much to provide an extensive account of the thinking that provides German National Socialism with a worldview and social program, as a case for the idea that none of the prominent philosophies from which one might expect a grounded and effective response to the phenomenon have proven up to that task because they have not recognized its deepest roots—and indeed, also not recognized that their own roots are entangled with them.

According to Levinas, this is in both cases a matter of an old and abiding disturbance in the European conception of human freedom. This is plain to see in the case of Nazism, which plays on the fear and aggression that lurk at the margins of genuine thought by promising the complete security that would come with a stable and unqualified identity. To belong to a *Volk* would be to know without any doubt who one is, what one wants, and how one may seek it. Of course, this kind of drive for identity must come at the cost of suppressing every element or figure that would interrupt it, whether in the robust form of those "others" who are said to live and think in a wholly different manner, or in the subtler form of impulses, emotions, and thoughts that belong to the inner complexity of any human being, oneself included. Barely a decade later, Levinas will be among those who have reminded us that such tendencies have always been present in antisemitism, long before exploding in the Shoah.[2] But before that, before the unthinkable had come to pass, he is focused especially on the contradictory state of a freedom that would move as if one has escaped personal insecurity by abandoning oneself entirely to an identity that comforts precisely by absorbing one. For that is the condition and the consequence of a commonality, like the *Volk*, that emerges from a particular heritage only to progressively erase that very particularity—or rather, elevate it over all others, which for their part are to be excluded by any available means. The discourse that accompanies this process is properly called *ideological*, and to the extent that it succeeds, it severs those who adhere to it from a positive sense of the material conditions of life where, after all, their particularity lives and breathes.[3] One is enveloped in what might by contrast be called "sheer spirituality" and which, on the condition that one truly doubts that human beings can ever be in any meaningful sense strictly immaterial, might be accused of distortion. In Nazi ideology, all of this is there to be seen in the contradiction by which the questions of blood and race, themselves material and thus particular, are raised over all of human society. To Levinas, this shows that Nazism does not pursue the straightforward universality of transparent ideas but only the relentless expansion of its provenance, to be achieved necessarily by force.[4] We have already invoked the horrors awaiting those who would soon be crushed by this. Let us now recognize their terrible counterparts, as Levinas would have us see them. For those who instead embrace and belong to the expanding tide of Nazi violence, there is only a vacuous anonymity in which everyone is equal and nothing of importance truly depends on any creative act. One either submits to the force of the idea, confirming its progress in everything one is and does, or else finds oneself in its way.

It is this metaphysics of force that would define the "philosophy of Hitlerism." As a matter of fact, as a form of thinking it is much closer to crude rhetoric than it is to philosophy, insofar as its success lies in provoking a movement from fear to aggression and pride.[5] And if indeed there is success, as there surely was in large numbers, we are required to think that at least the fear will have been real. Yet one cannot say the same thing of the absolute security that is promised, as one suspects already when noticing, as our historians assure us, that the expansion to assert mastery over others appears to have been practically endless. For his part, Levinas concentrates on the implications of a basic phenomenological insight: fear is given as our interpretation of our own vulnerability,[6] and the dark genius with which Nazi ideology exploits the former is compromised by its willingness to believe, or at least pretend, that the latter can be overcome.

It is this that the prominent philosophies of the day did not truly understand. In order to grasp Levinas's claim in its proper depth, it is necessary to understand that in his judgment the site of human vulnerability is specifically the body.[7] There is immediate sense in this claim.

The body, after all, is where we have immediate contact with material reality and indeed are immersed in it for better and for worse. Yet the body is not therefore strictly our insertion in a destiny, since there is also a spiritual dimension to being human, by which we can stand back from material conditions, withdrawing from and sometimes even rejecting the claims they make on us. If "spirit" (*l'esprit*) is therefore the possibility of our freedom, body is the condition of our material entanglement.[8] Moreover—and Levinas never pretends otherwise—the two cannot be separated.[9] In a human life, what may appear as body without spirit in fact signals the degradation or perversion of spirit, and what only appears as spirit without body is in fact spirit in denial of the roots by which it has access to much of reality. Levinas's manner of conceiving their true relation can make one think of some features of Husserl's phenomenology: in affects such as pain and fear, we see a living relation with the material world emanating from our physical contact with it, but also the beginning of a spiritual (*geistige*) capacity to understand and respond to their perceived causes. It is true, of course, that spirit may find the body foreign to its endeavors, and may aspire to get free of it, but these would be the marks of a contradiction, or more precisely, a movement to forget what one truly is. One's primordial relation with one's own body, Levinas observes, accomplishes an original positioning in the world, prior to any free choice for a place or a stance. "Do we not affirm ourselves in the unique warmth of our bodies long before any blossoming of the Self [*le Moi*] that claims to be separate from the body?"[10] If this is so, the body is not an impediment to the flight of spirit but, understood within proper limits, its constant condition. "To separate the spirit from the concrete forms with which it is already involved is to betray the originality of the very feeling from which it is appropriate to begin."[11] Body, then, is access and exposure to material conditions which inevitably impress themselves on spirit. Spirit, for its part, must recognize and address those conditions as such.

What does this mean? To begin with, we know that one's basic feeling for oneself, as oneself, cannot be escaped or handed off to others. Descartes furnishes us with an excellent example from which to see this in full: my pain, even when it occurs in a dream, is entirely my own and undeniable.[12] In this sense, what Heidegger says of death may thus be said of affectivity in general—it singularizes, touching on and bringing forth what of me is most mine: my intimacy with myself, such that body has always already touched on spirit and spirit is already answerable to it.[13] With these few thoughts in mind, we may now reformulate Levinas's understanding of "the philosophy of Hitlerism." The thinking that exploits fear and promotes aggression withdraws the spiritual dimension of its adherents entirely into the orbit of the body, which becomes the source of impulses that actively determine the course of reason, rather than submitting to rational inspection and a free response. This may explain some of the success of a discourse which, as we have already noted, asks that one surrender one's freedom to the alleged security of conditions in which, however, every vestige of personal freedom is put under constant pressure. It is not only that Hitlerism addresses a vulnerability which large numbers of German people evidently felt, but also that its manner of doing so taps directly into forces emanating from the body, which is "closer to us and more familiar than the rest of the world."[14]

Beyond Liberalism and Marxism

Which are the philosophical alternatives that Levinas finds wanting at this level? Writing in the interwar period in France, he considers these to be liberalism and Marxism. The charge is simple enough. Liberalism, precisely in its exaltation of a consciousness that would stand clear of every claim made on it from outside, underestimates the power of claims that are instead made from within, which is to say from the body. Levinas does not specify his target here, but it cannot be Locke, founder of political liberalism, whom he has already charged, in his doctoral dissertation, not with exalting consciousness but instead with subsuming it in the natural order.[15] He much more likely has in mind the rationalist liberalism of Leon Brunschvicg, whose lectures at the Sorbonne he had recently been following.[16] Brunschvicg's philosophy of history responds especially to the advance of modern science, in which we are to recognize the steady and ordered unfolding of reason, and by which general human progress would be assured. It is then the twofold task of philosophy to recognize the evidence for this in the "laws of spirit" that structure humanity through time, and to urge a morality and politics that embrace their movement.[17] Levinas cannot have been the only one for whom such optimism was unsustainable in view of the rise of Nazism. But more than this, his early insistence on an account of the body as a source of unruly passion capable of invading our capacity for rational decision suggests a much deeper reservation at the very idea of unbroken progress in our collective human endeavor.[18] To take seriously our embodiment, in short, is to recognize the real and inextinguishable possibility that fear and aggression, and not courage and peace, will define our relations with one another. Neither our politics nor its underlying anthropology can afford to think otherwise.

In Levinas's estimation, Marxism makes a more promising start, with its realization that "[spirit] is prey to material need."[19] And indeed, though he does not say so, there is in Marx's own writings a robust theory of the vital body. In the *Grundrisse*, Marx famously goes so far as to understand human being as a "totality of needs and drives"[20] that we are powerless to satisfy entirely or for long. The body thus registers both demand for objects and distance from them, and in that sense, it represents the material condition of human suffering. It would not be exaggerating much to propose that Marx's political writings try to hold this insight constantly in view. The accompanying historical-political vision is well known: critical intervention will emancipate consciousness from the external forces that threaten it, all the way down to the unjust distribution of the basic goods that would satisfy material demand. We have seen enough of Levinas's critique of liberalism to be confident that his response now to Marxism will concentrate especially on two of its features. In calling for reflection on the structures of oppression and alienation, Marx flirts with exempting philosophy from the conditions it wishes to correct, which would raise the specter of a freedom no longer encumbered by a relation with the body and its impulses. As a characterization of Marx's thinking, this seems to go much too far, but if one considers the fact that his critique unfolds in view of a conviction, quasi-eschatological, that history moves necessarily toward the achievement of an economy capable of sustaining the equitable distribution of goods, then the thinking does seem to approach the thesis of a body without unsatisfiable need. Simply put, if one eye is constantly on human suffering, the other is constantly on its near-total eradication in the communist state. Needless to say, it is this that enables Levinas to criticize Marxism alongside liberalism, despite its better attention to the body. Marx has understood that material conditions impress themselves on spirit, but he tends strongly to suggest that they may be overcome by a sufficiently clear-eyed political economy (and, if we are to believe certain of his followers, an equally unflinching willingness to insist on it at any cost). Whatever one makes of this thesis as a real possibility, it does exhibit appreciable confidence—or as Levinas might prefer it, dubious optimism—about our prospects for achieving peace over and against whatever disruption may otherwise be wrought by forces lurking in the body.

If a frank look at the manner in which Hitlerism exploits fear and promotes aggression dispels much optimism about our prospects for sustained peace, and if that is predicated on a rather unromantic conception of the body, this does not yet mean either that peace is an untenable proposition or that the body is simply and exclusively the principle of violence. And we do not need philosophy to see this. Who does not know of people who act firmly and courageously against violence without necessarily believing that it can be brought to a permanent end? Who does not recognize in the human body, one's own and others, impulses leading us toward the good, alongside others that would lead elsewhere? One cannot imagine Levinas overlooking any of this. But then one wants to know what truly are the conditions of our commitment to peace. What, if anything, truly elevates good over evil, for even a moment, if at the level of the body we are driven equally, or perhaps intermittently, to both?

Levinas's early position on these matters is nuanced, if not exactly novel. It is not that the body itself is strictly evil, but that some impulses that animate it call for guidance that would qualify as fully evil should we submit to them. This may likewise be said of other impulses that we would recognize as good. Evil, for Levinas, in this text and in fact throughout his subsequent works, is aligned closely with oppression and exclusion. As we have seen—and this, too, will become an abiding principle—at the heart of the latter would be a commitment to the view that one's concern is necessarily first and fundamentally for oneself. This conception of evil, associated closely with the anthropology of self-interest, necessarily implies that goodness must involve service and welcome, and that to work at them is to reverse the direction of one's being. What Levinas calls "spirit" (*l'esprit*) is a name for the mental life that includes a capacity to recognize and choose for or against these different sorts of impulses. The experience in Nazi Germany remains darkly instructive. It is always possible that we will choose for oppression and violence, and convince ourselves that this is for the good.

Yet this is not at all to say that we are without the means to ground the pursuit of a realistic peace. Levinas looks again at the body, now as the site of exposure to offense. This is necessarily more than an appeal to understand the victim, since pain and fear, which signals the approach of pain, have already been identified as the antecedent condition of aggression. One registers an offense in pain. But if we look closely at pain, we see that it does not simply undergo the offense; rather, there is already in pain a spontaneous recoil in which Levinas would have us recognize primitive opposition—or, as he will propose more forcefully in a later text, "outrage"—that signals the violation of more primal attachments.[21] Phenomenologically, then, pain is at once wound and protest. Ontologically, it is exposure to certain conditions and yet also refusal to succumb to them. To be in pain is already to desire escape from its causes, toward what one knows or else projects to be a better situation. There is in much of this a nascent desire for the good, though often enough one that is too rushed for careful identification of what might truly define it. Unfortunately, history—and the everyday life that is not often enough recorded there—is replete with instances in which the refusal that belongs to pain becomes a pursuit of goodness in actions that do not go beyond self-interest. We are thus reminded that peace is generally precarious because human nature is volatile so long as we are both *body*, in all of its complexity, and *spirit*, in its ambiguous exposure to body—and indeed, Levinas takes care to state that this adherence of body and spirit is no mere "happy or unhappy accident," but one that we are powerless ever to escape.[22]

All of this furnishes philosophy with a specific task. It must hold in view the fact that the body is not only the source of violence but also the contour of our protest at offense. In the phenomenology of pain, we are to see a crucial indication of our deep attachment to conditions that leave us exposed to the violence that preys on us. This both leaves us exposed to those who are intent on a violence that they believe is in their own interest, and tempts us to the same thing in ourselves. It is not difficult to work out the general solution to this problem in the terms that Levinas has offered. One must protect spirit from the encroachment of impulses emanating from the body that urge constantly to resolve the difficulties of life by violence, and instead direct human desire toward the good-ness that lies in seeking peace. Between the offense and the response, philosophy must intervene in the name of the good, and this consists of teaching us where to seek it and, of course, where *not*.

Pain and Evasion

"Reflections on the Philosophy of Hitlerism" should be tested against the thought of Heidegger, though that name never appears in the essay. We have already observed that Levinas's brief phenomenology of pain may be settled in a more general account of affectivity that has a noticeably Hei-deggerian resonance. Pain, we have said, singularizes. It brings forth what is uniquely and inescapably one's own. When in *Being and Time* Heidegger develops this as a primordial condition of Dasein, his interest is in show-ing that when Dasein finds itself affected—that is, when it becomes aware of itself as this one who is permeated by fear or anxiety—it may thus catch sight of its full self, such as otherwise goes unnoticed when one is absorbed in the practical concerns of everyday life. In short, Heidegger's interest is in securing the possibility of grasping oneself in the unicity of one's being. Without strictly opposing this notion, Levinas's account of pain has a slightly different inflection. In pain, one does not only undergo the offense, but also the impossibility of definitive escape. We have not said enough, phenomenologically, if we state only that the experience of pain is lacking in pleasure, or perhaps contentment. To be in pain is also to feel an anchor to the conditions in which this is possible, so that one suffers from the offense and from one's exposure to its possibility. The cry of pain, then, protests not only the unpleasurable event, but also the very weight of destiny.

Perhaps this thought also informs Levinas's translation of Heidegger's *Geworfenheit* as *déréliction* in his nearly contemporaneous essay, "Martin Heidegger and Ontology."[23] If so, the choice of translation indicates a reservation of some importance, for there is an important difference between the sense of these two words. To the point when Levinas presents Dasein as "thrown into and struggling with its possibilities," he is strictly faithful to a central thesis of *Being and Time* which holds that the worldhood of the world and the implementality of tools are imbued with a care for our existence that is itself motivated by underlying anxiety at death. This says nothing more and nothing less than that there is no ulterior basis for the meaning of our possibilities other than that care itself. Yet Levinas does go slightly further than this when claiming also to detect in this thrownness a trace of "abandonment," which is heavy with a sense of loss or a lack of some greater fulfillment. It is one thing to say that our possibilities are projected from anxiety, but something else to say that they are haunted by our dissatisfaction with them, and in that sense have precisely fallen into them—it is one thing to think that we embrace our possibilities all too eagerly, but another to think that even while we do so, we already chafe against the limits that they would impose. The latter thought is not to be found in *Being and Time*, which after all only portrays Dasein as going out ahead of itself either in flight from its own death or in resolute acceptance of it. Of course, one cannot be sure that Levinas has this fully in mind in a text that strives only to explicate a difficult work, but as it happens, it is broadly consistent with the approach to affectivity taken in the account of pain that we have found in his essay on "Hitlerism": we are at once exposed to conditions that violate our well-being, and animated by an urge to escape their grip.

Whatever its importance in these short essays, this thought lies squarely at the heart of *De l'évasion—On Escape*—a much longer, highly original essay from the same period.[24] This essay is rich and suggestive, and contains elements clearly consistent with what has already been lain down. A year after Levinas's first incursion into political philosophy—it is now 1935—the subtler implications of what has been said especially about pain now belong to an interpretation of subjectivity as a struggle that calls for an entirely different ontology than one finds in the pages of *Being and Time*. Against the Heideggerian emphasis on being as the nothingness whose approach renders Dasein breathless with anxiety, Levinas now, and indeed henceforth, sees a brute plenitude in which the living subject may drown or suffocate the moment it ceases to assert itself as itself. This difference, moreover, is consistent with the difference that Levinas has already opened up between the Heideggerian account of our being in the world and his own account of the life of the subject. Whereas Dasein maintains itself as itself in its care for the existence that is suspended over an abyss, the effort of the living subject to stand out from undifferentiated fullness exhibits a desire that Levinas is unwilling to characterize as futile or misguided. Once again, this raises a thought for which Heidegger has no room, since on his terms our relation with being has the first and final word on what we are. The ontology developed in *Being and Time* deprives us of any reason to expect the discovery of any condition for our existence that would surmount a finitude that is both fundamental and, in the phenomenological sense, irreducible. To the contrary, everything comes down to the question of how one relates to one's own mortality, from which there is no meaningful escape. In this sense, Heidegger's philosophy must appear as essentially tragic, and Levinas's emerging resistance as the mark of another sort of philosophy which, since Plato, has taken the view that we are more than the fate that is nonetheless handed down to us.

At this juncture, and indeed for a good long time afterward, Levinas applies himself not to the task of simply overturning or rejecting ontology altogether, but only of proposing significant corrections.[25] And this leaves room to grant that the tragic vision is attuned to an experience of life that is both real and plausible, even if it is also incomplete. Such a thought runs throughout the texts that we have been reviewing. Just as in the essay on Hitlerism Levinas has found in pain an experience of inescapable adherence to oneself, in the essay on Heidegger he says that Dasein is "riveted to [*voué à*] its possibilities," which in their sum are "imposed" on it,[26] and in *On Escape* he evokes an acute feeling of being "held fast" (*rivé*) to being.[27] If Levinas's word "évasion" adds anything at all to what is indicated by these observations, it must designate a desire that moves toward a good that genuinely transcends these conditions, a desire that will eventually be called "metaphysical" in order to set it off from anything that Heideggerian ontology has caught sight of. And with this, Levinas reaches claims that resemble those of religion: one desires a goodness that the world itself does not provide, and thus is moved from within the world to transcend the world. Indeed, Levinas does not shrink from the expected language. In the very temporality of our being, he writes, there is "an unspeakable savor for the absolute [*la saveur indicible de l'absolu*]."[28] But as for what to make of such a claim, there is always the possibility of therefore opening philosophy to theology. This has been the tendency of some of Levinas's Catholic contemporaries, especially Maurice Blondel, Joseph Maréchal, and Karl Rahner, for whom philosophy and theology are distinct yet inseparable, so that the philosophy which would be conducted without theology could know only nature, without any means to recognize the grace that infuses and completes it.[29] It is well known that Levinas's later texts refuse any such appeal to theology, but even without consulting them it can be said of these earlier texts that they propose to think only philosophically, which is to say phenomenologically. This means that he is intent only on finding in a careful account of our subjectivity, strictly as it gives itself to be seen, evidence of a relation that cannot be contained within the horizon of our relation with being. The implication is startling, at least when considered in the context of what his teachers, Husserl and Heidegger, had already said on the matter:[30] for Levinas, phenomenological rigor leads necessarily to a positive sense of religion, understood as a primordial feature of our subjectivity. Any other conception is precisely a limited conception, one that suspends or suppresses the non-horizon beyond all horizons that is the religious relation with an absolute good. To defend some such conception is necessarily to confine it within what is henceforth, with the religious relation now in view, the sphere of immanence. And this, he does not hesitate to say, is a philosophical commitment to what is properly called "paganism."[31]

This conception of paganism, we should immediately note, is consistent with what the essay on Hitlerism has led us to understand about violence. The mode of life that starts and ends in self-relation, without proposing to act on a desire for more than the world that is projected from its own cares, is one that is always disposed to react in fear and aggression when confronted by otherness. In his foray into political philosophy, Levinas interprets the forms of active violence (exclusion, oppression) according to a phenomenology of affection (fear, aggression); in his move toward religion, he begins to define a perspective from which to look critically on their original possibility: "being" is a name for the self-relating that projects objects and a world that serve one's effort to continue as oneself—without opening to a transcendent good, and thus without grounding one's identity in anything that it cannot presume to give to itself. But then—we have already implied it—this critique holds up only on the condition that such a higher appeal is truly within reach, or at least that an authentic life can take shape in commitment to it. There is no doubt that a great deal of this still lies ahead of the early Levinas. Up to and including *On Escape*, he is intent mainly on achieving a proper understanding of the movement of our being. There is, of course, an entire tradition that interprets this as a restlessness that wants only comfort with the basic conditions that define our relation to the world and everything in it, as if there could only be the lack that is experienced as discord and the fulfillment that comes in serene acceptance. Levinas has already said more than this. "Religion," if we may invoke the word in this most general sense, is grounded in the desire for immeasurably more, and—again, unless it is simply futile—it would be fulfilled in acts that proceed in confidence that this may nonetheless enter into human lives. In thus opening themselves to a good that is more than any that may be grasped according to an insistence first upon oneself, such lives would instead be committed to a self-emptying that anticipates salvation from a violence that is no longer the evident condition of our shared humanity. It is difficult not to witness in these few thoughts the first steps toward a philosophy that comes fully into possession of itself only decades later, in *Totality and Infinity*. To escape from paganism, holding a desire for the supreme good steadily in view, is to realize that the first fact of relations among subjects is not difference and the likelihood of rivalry, but instead plurality and the possibility of peace.[32]

Community without Heritage or Heroes

It is no longer possible to postpone the question of whether Levinas has yet found the means to specify a realizable path toward the good and the peace that he has in view. By what means or according to what cause would we turn from a primary concern for our own being into an active pursuit of the good that would also be the way to peace? One need not be familiar with Levinas's eventual conceptions of the face of the other that calls to us from beyond being and of the responsibility that is also love of the good, in order to come upon the thought that this opening may be ethical (and which, we may already surmise, any thought of the primacy of our relation with being will suppress). Nor would Levinas be alone in observing that the presence of another subject can awaken and call us forth from brute self-interest.[33] But this thought does not appear in his earliest works, even as they seek the existential grounds for a conception of community that the politics of identity and exclusion violate. Only the bare outline has come into view. To the extent that our being would be animated by a desire for the absolute, it would also be defined by a relation with what cannot be grasped by images or ideas that are subject to the limits of our own understanding. After all, it belongs properly to the absolute that it exceeds and therefore withdraws from the relation that would hold it there. With this, a significant portion of Levinas's work as a phenomenologist is set: movement toward the absolute cannot become access to the absolute; in this sense, the desire that would move us toward it cannot be fulfilled. This would necessarily define our finitude. The subject who desires what surpasses anything it can hold by its own powers is a subject who is radically itself in a manner that is lost or covered over when it takes itself to stand with others on a same knowable ground, as if it were made up first and foremost by participating in what is also available to the others. It would be the plurality of those who have nothing substantive or essential in common that would come into view through a rigorous account of the opening to goodness and peace. And this is, in the strict sense set forth here, a religious plurality.

A plurality of subjects animated by desire for the absolute is not the same thing as a community of members who have certain things in common. It has already become clear that Levinas suspects that the latter rests on and indeed enforces a fundamental exclusion. But if this is to be the thought, then it will be necessary in turn to reconsider the nature and role of a great deal that binds us together in a manner that the real prospects for peace must depend on: at minimum a language by which our lack and need of peace become intelligible, and a practical morality from which to receive initial guidance for our actions. Are we to consider even these, and in all their forms, to support violence? Before this is a matter of contesting the ontology, broadly Heideggerian, that interprets all speech and conduct as the actions of a being who is motivated by concerns that are originally his or her own—so that a different interpretation of our being may support a different conception of speech and conduct—it is simply a question of our relation to the claims of our own past. It is true, as close readers of Levinas know very well, that in order to make a case for the real chances of what he is willing to understand as genuine peace, he will have to break decisively with what the philosophy of Heidegger has said about these things. And this is essentially a matter of claims made about our self-relation and existential movement in the best-known pages of *Being and Time*. But it is also true that each of us finds herself or himself already among possibilities for speech and action that have been given prior to any question of choosing or refusing them. In a word—it is written by Heidegger, later in the same text—one starts out on terms that make up a "heritage" (*Erbe*).[34]

It should be said that the question of quite what makes up a heritage matters less to Heidegger than the question of how we may relate to it. Let us suppose, for example, that among what has been handed down to Dasein is a set of moral values. Undeniably, one often has them and feels answerable to them without being aware of it. In the terms of Heidegger's analysis of Dasein, in such a mode one relates to them inauthentically, which is to say in a manner that is turned away from one's true condition as being turned toward one's own death. One accepts them, as Heidegger likes to put these things, in the mode of what "one does," and if one speaks of them, this occurs likewise in the mode of what it is commonplace or standard to say. Inauthentic Dasein is Dasein under the influence of values that it has inherited without its having taken them on reflectively for itself. As such, those values exercise a latent claim of the past on its present and indeed, so long as this remains unchanged, its future. But in anxiety, arising in sensitivity to the inescapable fact of one's own death, Dasein is thrown out of inauthenticity altogether, and this includes its values.[35] By catching sight of itself as itself and nothing else, anxious Dasein thus becomes authentic Dasein, which is to say Dasein that freely chooses for or against possibilities that had previously only been assumed. It is important to recognize that this does not in any sense mean that Dasein's freedom is exercised from wholly outside of either its possibilities or the heritage to which they belong. Instead, Dasein achieves a new relation with them—or, if one prefers, comes back to the original relation that has been covered over by the veil of inauthenticity. In other words, possibilities that were already available—we have taken the example of moral values—now come into view as a set or range from among which authentic Dasein is now capable of making resolute choices for its comportment in the world, with others and toward its own death.

For present purposes, two features of this way of thinking are especially important. First, it ought not to pass notice that the analysis of Dasein is of course universal in its scope. This means not only that each of us is in the world toward death, but also that our passage from inauthenticity to authenticity is in each and every case worked out in relation to a set of possibilities received from a heritage—conditions, in other words, that would be historical, cultural, moral, and perhaps ethnic. It cannot plausibly mean either that all heritages hand down the same possibilities to all Daseins, or that among recipients of a same heritage the authentic relation to one's possibilities will therefore be the same except in the formal sense of taking them up resolutely. No one would argue that the moral values instilled by different heritages are essentially the same, and there is no reason to think—including none given by Heidegger— that when two Daseins who in ordinary life are possessed of the same moral values each becomes resolute in the face of death, they therefore also take up the same moral vision and course of actions. With the new relation to possibilities that have been handed down can also come a distinct manner of understanding, embracing, and acting on them—and indeed, perhaps only some of them. And so secondly, for all of the force behind Heidegger's conception of inauthentic and authentic possibilities, it is difficult to find in it any allowance for the advent of genuinely new possibilities. It thus comes as no surprise to find that when he develops a vision of authentic life that would transcend Dasein's relation to itself, he speaks of a destining that must be received, understood, and advanced *in common.*

> But if fateful [*schicksalhafte*] Dasein, as Being-in-the-World, exists essentially in Being-with-Others, its historizing is a co-historizing and is determinative for it as [*bestimmt als*] destiny [*Geschick*]. This is how we designate the historizing of the community [*Gemeinschaft*], of the people [*des Volkes*]. Destiny is not something that puts itself together out of individual fates [*Schicksalen*], any more than Being-with-one-another can be conceived as the occurring together of several Subjects. Our fates have already been guided in advance, in our Being with one another in the same world and in our resoluteness for definite possibilities. Only in communicating and in struggling does the power of destiny become free.[36]

Now one can scarcely accept these proposals without soon wondering—since it is a matter of resoluteness, which is also to say authenticity—how "the people" might make their way forward in a manner that neither denies the conditions of heritage nor merely replays them. How might what Heidegger here calls "resolute possibilities" prove to rest on anything more than impassive commitment? Still within the later passages of *Being and Time,* this difference is said to require the choice of a hero (*ein Held*) whom one might loyally follow in a manner that takes up what is handed down without merely actualizing all over again what has already come to pass.[37] This appeal to a hero, which presumably is to the figure of a creative and insightful example, at once recognizes the freedom of singular Daseins, before and apart from their belonging to a people and a community whose conditions are given in advance, and directs us to identify its proper meaning with adherence to a unifying vision.

A great deal might be said about the political implications of this claim and about the correct interpretation of the concepts that underlie it. The early Levinas does not weigh in on this.[38] Yet there certainly are seeds of the serious critique that we know would soon come. Already in his essay on "Hitlerism," there is an opening to the charge that Heidegger, to the degree that he remains in continuity with his own German tradition, has an inadequate grasp of freedom. There is also no mistaking the possibility of a strong link between what Levinas has said there about identity, exclusion, and violence and some features of Heidegger's suggestion that authentic Dasein finds its resolute possibilities in the footsteps of a hero, and his attendant conception of a community whose members would seek a common destiny along that way. These worries have in the meantime become familiar, so that those who entertain them might be tempted now to enlist Levinas to their side. But there is in his thinking another element that resists this, and indeed complicates the charges he might otherwise have been inclined to make already in the 1930s. One finds its source in Heidegger's own emphasis on the manner in which Dasein's relation with its death throws it back on itself. Needless to say, within the confines of the existential hermeneutics staked out in *Being and Time*, where the facticity and historicity of Dasein are never in question, this cannot become more than a radical interruption by which authentic repetition is possible.[39] As we have just seen, for Heidegger, it is evident that the latter does not break with everything that has been handed down so much as understands it in a manner that is enriched by the new perspective in which one takes it up. We do not need Levinas to imagine that in the interval of this interruption, bathed in anxiety, one might find genuine openness unbearable. And flight into the They is not the only possible form of closure.

Levinas supplies us with something like a Heideggerian objection to Heidegger himself: the commitment to a hero can look suspiciously like a flight from the truth that is disclosed in anxiety. But this objection could be sustained only by radicalizing the phenomenology of anxiety beyond what Heidegger himself has professed to see there. It would be necessary to think that in anxiety, Dasein is thrown fully out from all contact with its own possibilities—they would be given neither tacitly nor resolutely—so that its return to itself among them is delivered by a freedom that does not itself fully belong there. Heidegger envisions only a repetition that enacts them anew. Has the early Levinas claimed more than this? It is difficult to be certain. When in his essay on Heidegger he reaches the crucial juncture, he proposes that anxiety "renders impossible the understanding of the self in terms of possibilities that relate to innerworldly [*intramondaine*] objects," and in this way brings Dasein back to itself.[40] This commentary does not evidently break with Heidegger's conception. But shortly after this, having emphasized the manner in which Dasein's care for its own existence calls it to itself in a manner that unifies its structures, Levinas proposes to find there the "root of personality and of freedom," and of a temporality that is bound to return to its entanglement in the "trivial and innocuous" time that we call the past, the future, and the present.[41] Let us not overwork the final lines of an essay that plainly intends only to present. But let us also not overlook at least some hesitation at the thought that we have only our fate and the freedom to work out a relation with it, and in turn at least the appearance of the thought that we do not belong wholly to the interplay of being and beings such as lies at the center of Heidegger's interests. Perhaps this hesitation belongs together with the understanding of "thrownness" as "abandonment," in which we have already suspected a trace of longing for fulfillment that would be alien from Heidegger's philosophy (and which we have found robustly present in *On Escape*). Perhaps it also resonates with a tendency, hardly unique in Levinas, to suggest that Heidegger characterizes Dasein's everyday mode—"trivial," "innocuous"—as if it were impoverished or superficial in comparison with a more elevated mode, which once again is at odds with what we have learned to find in *Being and Time*.[42] Together, these thoughts imply that our subjectivity would be more than the comprehension of a world and things, more than the relation to our death that conditions it, and indeed more than the relation to being that occurs in anxiety at death. It is not at all certain that the early Levinas already harbors these thoughts, even if we have found considerable reason to think that he is on his way toward them. What is certain is that they are at some distance from any thoughts that inform the universe of fundamental ontology. They cannot be pursued without submitting philosophy to an entirely different orientation.

Situation and Prophecy

Whether or not the early Levinas has Heidegger specifically in mind as he criticizes notions of identity and community that are predicated on exclusion and violence, even a brief review of Heidegger's position provides an important perspective from which to recognize the difficulty that this will imply. We have wondered about the possibility of newness among Dasein's resolute possibilities, and about the real difference between those who follow in the steps of the same hero of their tradition. In the terms already set forth in Levinas's nascent political philosophy, this becomes a question of admitting a plurality without exclusion. And from the beginning, as we have noted, he appends this to a disturbance in the modern understanding of freedom. Under what conditions might we hold in view the possibility of exercising our freedom not from the fear and aggression that strike out against others, but instead from a receptivity that grounds respect and even care? Having seen clearly that the former, fear and aggression, can take hold of our freedom, Levinas knows well that there is a basic vulnerability about it, and that respect would constitute the achievement of considerable autonomy. And indeed, this theme is more than a little Kantian, insofar as Levinas here approaches the idea that freedom truly attends to others only insofar as it suspends any adherence to the particular categories or criteria of moral life, such as he has come to view with considerable suspicion. What then of this? Kant's observation already in his first *Critique* can be taken as a warning: "it is in the power of freedom to pass beyond any and every specified limit,"[43] but in that case destruction is always possible.

To be sure, it would not be difficult to show that Levinas's later argument that absolute freedom is necessarily the freedom of service, and thus freedom for the Good, is influenced by a keen awareness of this very possibility.[44] Among his most important interlocutors, Sartre in fact comes close to advocating it. Between Levinas and Sartre there is at once the appearance of remarkable proximity and a substantial underlying distance.[45] Let us therefore turn to some thoughts on Sartre's position, anticipating an opportunity to better understand the construal of freedom, respect, and justice that emerges in Levinas's later texts.

· We might begin by recalling a number of basic claims. In his ontology, Sartre considers that what distinguishes us from anything else—what makes us the sole exception to the metaphysical principle of identity—is our consciousness of self across an interval that can never be closed. This means, at one and the same time, that our first condition is restlessness and that the only way to find peace would be to grasp one's full self without interruption or remainder. But this is not possible for beings who are conscious of themselves in time. I am only my identification with my self, but without possibility of becoming fully one with myself. Or, as Sartre puts it, I am present to my self in the mode of not being one with it.[46] Now these matters do not exist in general form. Consciousness always has a history and its own desire. Sartre's predilection for examples is thus an essential part of his argument. According to a familiar one, the waiter may wish to be the perfect waiter, and may even achieve considerable success with this wish, yet his identity with himself will never be that of a stone which is not qualified by any such dynamic differentiation. A stone is only a stone, impenetrably so, but a subject always lags behind, and seeks to catch up with, an image or ideal. This, of course, is what it means for Sartre to characterize the subjectivity of the subject as *pour-soi*, which furnishes his conception of our freedom.[47] One is originally and ineluctably the movement of one's own being, so that the only question worth asking is whether one will recognize it and act with it fully in mind. The passage from freedom to responsibility, then, is conditioned by our capacity for transparency to self. On this line of reasoning, one may even go so far as to say that responsibility, which for Sartre is always in the end *self*-responsibility, depends on it (on self-transparency).

This knot of freedom and self-responsibility produces the well-known emphasis on rivalry in Sartre's account of intersubjectivity that makes up nearly one-third of his *Being and Nothingness*. Each of us pursues our own ideal—Sartre says "project"—in the good or bad faith that are expressions of a capacity or incapacity to know what we are truly doing, and thus when any two of us meets, there necessarily arises a struggle in which each attempts to grasp and subdue the other. These pages are too well known to require elaboration here. We need only recall their conclusion that not even the most insistent masochism (love) or sadism (hatred)—essential figures of intersubjective relations—finally succeed in possessing the other, to then recognize the presence of a nascent morality. The presence of the other whom I love or desire leads me finally to realize what in bad faith I will have forgotten: my freedom, as the movement to identify fully with myself, rises again and again from the ashes of every failed escape toward perfect identity—which is to say, again, that I am my own project, and must take responsibility for it.

It is Sartre's notion of good faith that leads him to political concerns that are unexpectedly close to those of Levinas in his essay on "Hitlerism." Fundamentally, this is a matter of what Sartre would have us think of as authentic community. The long essay *Réflexions sur la question juive* (1945/46), which we have in English as *Anti-Semite and Jew*, comes after the foregoing accounts of being, freedom, and responsibility have been worked out, so it is relatively unsurprising, though perhaps disappointing, to find that the rise of fascism and its incitement of antisemitism altered his thinking almost not at all. Sartre nonetheless begins from an interpretation of antisemitism that is in broad agreement with what Levinas has detected in German fascism: the antisemite projects and pursues an identity that would be secured in the abolition of the Jewish other. One shudders, of course, to consider how far the Nazi antisemites went toward achieving this in real terms, but for Sartre the problem is in the first instance ontological, and that is also where its solution must be sought. Antisemitism is a form of hatred of the sort he has described at length in *Being and Nothingness*: it is a passion to dominate and make use of the other in the service of securing oneself; to this, antisemitism adds only a choice to actually *think* from this passion that Sartre considers, as we have already noted, to be impossible. This is plainly the mark of bad faith,[48] and bad faith on this scale calls for political intervention.

How is this to be undertaken? Sartre's proposal has in full view a complication which has important things in common with the Heideggerian conception of heritage that we mobilized in order to bring into relief the radicality of Levinas's position. This is to say that Sartre does not suppose that one can act directly on individual freedom, as if to awaken individuals to self-responsibility, as it were, by personal appeal, because the bad faith of a community that has lost its sense of self-responsibility—

choosing instead the violence of possession or exclusion—is embedded in a complex weave of historical and cultural factors informing any number of social structures which together he calls "situation."[49] In short, a subject is always situated, and there is no shortcut around that fact. For Sartre, this is first of all a matter simply of his own insistence, broadly Heideggerian, that consciousness is always already exposed to any number of claims on its movement. But whereas for Heidegger the danger that those claims will simply stifle our freedom is mitigated by the possibility that we might find guidance to a deeper understanding, for Sartre, who appears to have Levinas on his side in this, there is only the danger. And the danger is subtle. Not only do the elements of what he calls "situation" provide legal and moral justification for exclusion and perhaps even suppression, but they also constitute a familiar, even comforting environment to which the solitary individual may always return after encounters with others who have called into question the stable identity he is intent on preserving. One thus understands Sartre's growing enthusiasm for a "concrete liberalism" in which each citizen works vigilantly against any grounding of law, policy, or social norms in conditions that would be particular to a place, a nation, or a people.[50]

We have seen enough to be sure that a commitment to authentic community would yield a social program—would promote specific concrete interventions—on an understanding of injustice essentially as the limitation of human freedom. As far as this goes, Levinas could hardly be opposed, since respect for all people for who they are in themselves must necessarily include insistence on their freedom. Yet for all of that, Levinas is not Sartre—not in his early work, which has not yet defined for itself a clear position on freedom and respect, and not in the later work that roots freedom in responsibility for the other person who faces me here and now. Between these two moments in his thinking is Sartre's argument that freedom is essentially freedom for oneself, over and against any and all claims that are made on it from elsewhere. The freedom outlined in Sartre's account of our being is a freedom that appears to transcend the dangers of "heritage" or "situation" according to a capacity to move through and beyond any limit, or rather, in his own terms, to choose for or against them by a decision that he calls authentic insofar as it would have to be made entirely by one's own accounting. Here again, as with the latter passages of Heidegger's *Being and Time*, one cannot be sure that Levinas has closely studied a text whose position he clearly opposes, but there is no mistaking the neuralgic point of Sartre's essay on antisemitism: if, as Sartre seems bound to hold, stable identity of any kind is both ontologically false and politically violent, then—he does not conceal it—the critique of "situation" applies not only to the various forms of antisemitism but also to Judaism itself.[51] Of course, no one would for long contest the idea that communities can settle into an attitude by which a concern for security clogs their lifeline to an original inspiration, but the charge reaches farther than this: a tradition, a set of practices, and the institutions that support them would by definition call for immediate critique in their very instantiation. It is incumbent on philosophy, which for Sartre returns ceaselessly to being as nothingness and thus to the irreducible contingency of every claim for truth and value, to sustain the necessary politics of ceaseless revolt in the name of a freedom that is always on the verge of suppression by the forms of life in common. The authentic community is the community without anything fundamentally in common except this freedom, its peril, and whatever insistence on itself may flow into concerted action.

This brings into view a second difficulty with the authentic exercise of freedom, in addition to the potential for destruction that Kant has helped us to see in a capacity to throw off every limit: whatever the moral authority that we may grant to those who would accept full responsibility for it, in fact its meaning rests on a premise that in the final account it lies before and outside reproach by any other agency—a premise which says that one accepts any such reproach only in what must be yet again a free act—so that arbitrariness in morality and indeed politics can never be ruled out. In short, it is from his purported radical freedom that Sartre can claim that situation as such is also suppression and exclusion, and at the same time this can only mean that that freedom transcends situation. And so, with regard to that freedom, one has equal reason to suspect that it is arbitrary, fear that it is destructive, and wonder whether it is truly accountable to anything higher than itself.

Now unless Levinas were to simply moderate his position on community, identity, and violence—softening his view that the elements of our historical and social worlds comprise a destiny that only includes or excludes—it will be necessary to show that (a) in fact our freedom is grounded, but not according to any fixed commitment to what is handed down to us, (b) this grounding is also an ordering to what is genuinely good and valuable, and (c) this ordering does represent a positive limit insofar as any turn to other goods or values must constitute deviation or corruption. As will later become clear, this formula anticipates much of Levinas's mature position. It also rejoins the effort to sketch a generally religious conception of subjectivity that we have discovered in *On Escape*. Without proposing now to do more than advance one more step in that direction, we may ask, where is the subject who is attuned to the absolute and even desires the absolute without belonging to a religious "heritage" or "situation"? And we may suspect that the critique of the latter (heritage, situation) leads precisely there, as if any success in showing that a particular religious community is self-justifying and exclusive in the same way that a particular ethnic or political community is self-justifying and exclusive thereby uncovers the religious subjectivity that is our most profound condition. Yet Levinas here engages in no such myth of original purity, but instead argues only that rigorous attention to the affective and erotic dimensions of our existence recognizes that we are at once thrown into a range of claims upon our understanding and commitments, and are unable to come to rest among them. But because this restlessness is already interpreted as absolute desire, there can be no question of addressing it by a call only for free creativity in negotiating these various claims and the institutions behind them—no question of stopping at what the Brazilian philosopher and legal theorist Roberto Unger calls our "negative capability" to deny "whatever in our contexts delivers us over to a fixed scheme of division and hierarchy," in favor of new syntheses forged from the conflict between distinct sources of meaning and value.[52] From Levinas's perspective, such a stance would be provisional at best, and the pleasure that it may seem to offer cannot run especially deep. And so, it becomes increasingly clear that what he begins to conceive as religious subjectivity is also tormented subjectivity, since it is always already handed over to conditions that necessarily frustrate any movement toward what one wants most. What thus comes into view is at least the outline of a philosophy that is at once phenomenological, religious, and political. The plurality of subjects who at once inhere in a world of concrete claims and limits and yet also desire a good that positively exceeds all of that, would be a plurality that is anterior to every form of identity and exclusion, though without existing apart from their meaning and influence. Each subject, in its concrete inherence, is in the world and exposed to its dangers. But each singular subject, in its religious attunement, is also more than this.

It scarcely needs to be said that this conception of the subject is radically at odds with that of Sartre, and thus that the resulting critique of institutions and practices, and indeed the historical, social, and cultural conditions that support them, will also be significantly different. For Levinas, what defines the subjectivity of the subject, that by which we do not belong wholly either to what is included by any identity or to what is excluded by any identity, is not simply the freedom by which we take up or refuse what is handed down to us, but the desire for a good that transcends anything that is within the reach of that freedom. It is above all this desire that is suppressed and eventually forgotten by ways of living and thinking which are motivated in the first instance by a desire for security, and which may become aggressive toward those whose way of being reminds us that no one belongs wholly to any sum or totality. Of course, violence surely does strike directly against individual freedom, yet in Levinas's understanding true freedom is freedom that is fulfilled by entering into accord with the desire that binds it to what is highest. Violence is already afoot in the world wherever the simple freedom of self-determination is curtailed, but its damage is most lasting wherever it destroys the very possibility of moving freely toward the good. This damage, moreover, is in fact twofold: there are above all the victims themselves, on whom alienation and suffering are imposed until the very notion of a highest good may become inaccessible, but just as surely there are the oppressors, who either have also lost a sense for any such good or else have come to seek it in something else entirely.

Is it possible for a tradition and its institutions to effectively promote peace? If, following Sartre, we identify peace with the unconditional movement of radical freedom, any argument in favor of particular values, norms, or practices is necessarily a harbinger of violence. What he understands as authentic subjectivity is discovered and maintained in commitment to this freedom as the source and criterion for any choice that one makes, and thus is vigilantly opposed to any other authority. Perhaps this is the moment to recognize that from Levinas's perspective, Sartre's critique of the oppression licensed by the resources of a totalizing "situation" exhibits some of the same tendencies and some of the same blind spots or deficiencies that Levinas himself finds in modern liberalism and Marxism. Both the critique and the intervention that it produces appear grounded in the possibility of thought and action capable of suspending every influence, so that in fact it may be contended against Sartre that his political theory only replaces the conflict that everyone recognizes between different social and political orders with one that must always define the relation between the authentic community and all others. The idea of a transcendent good is never raised. If instead, following Levinas, we identify peace with movement toward such a good, it is always conceivable that arguments in favor of particular values, norms, or practices are in some qualified manner properly supportive. What he understands as religious subjectivity is discovered and maintained in the confluence of freedom with the desire for the highest good, and is therefore capable of assenting, no doubt with great care, to a teaching. At the same time, it must therefore also be asked, and asked often, whether religious communities, no less than communities of any other kind, offer a teaching that has any other effect than to shore up an established identity. This would define the very nature of political intervention, which would always be in the service of liberating the free movement of religious desire. There is room in this vision for at least a hope that the original religious impulse discovered by phenomenological attention to affects and desire can remain alive in the doctrine of a tradition, the practices that it enjoins, and the institutions that offer them to us. There is also room to think that a rigorous critique of any social order can become a religious act of recollection.

This is often clearly Levinas's perspective on his own Judaism. Judaism, he avers, has need of a political identity, which in this case means a nation-state, in order to ensure its survival against the violence witnessed in the rise of Nazism. But this political Israel is not the real, ethical Israel which is defined by the idea that everyone is a neighbor and thus by a vision of community in which everyone belongs.[53] There is no reason to think that what is the case most particularly for the religion that must go all the way to establishing a nation should not hold itself to the same test it imposes on others: fidelity to our original condition requires ceaseless vigilance, if not constant revolt, against the various forms of community that are meant to be supportive but may easily begin to suppress and forget.[54] But this claim applies equally to what we today call "faiths" and "denominations." Philosophy discovers for us a vision of the human community as a plurality of neighbors from which no one is excluded. This plurality can become the proper basis for a notion of justice that would be universal insofar as it is for everyone, but without becoming abstract so long as it is informed by a sense that each of us has his or her own needs, interests, and, as we have seen, desire. This is what it means for Levinas to call for "revolt against [the] injustice which begins the moment that an order is founded."[55] And indeed, moral norms must have the same ambivalent status. If the possibility of fear and aggression is never ruled out, there can be no doing without social order and moral norms. This may sometimes impose a certain violence on the freedom and desire that would otherwise move without encumbrance, but then a vivid sense and frequent reminders of the deeper community of neighbors that it serves may ensure that this necessary violence will always be a humane violence, a violence that must be exercised in order to direct consciences properly to the good.

These claims are hardly absent from Levinas's major philosophical works, though they often touch on them only in passing. *Totality and Infinity* is unintelligible without its conceptions both of a Good "beyond being" that is the sole and proper object of our desire, and the fundamentally metaphysical nature of that desire. Moreover, that great book begins with a call to reconsider our commitment to politics and to morality not at all to overthrow and reject them, but only to recall them to a sense of the relation to the good that opens genuine plurality.[56] The theme of violence, including the form that is necessary for the work of peace, appears in the first pages of *Otherwise Than Being, or Beyond Essence* before it deepens Levinas's account of subjectivity, and then expands at some length on the religious orientation of the latter. But these books are directed by a conviction which the early works have not yet fully realized. If philosophy has fallen under the spell of tragedy, of a commitment that in the final account there is only conflict and the rule of destiny, then the effort to awaken it to another vision will require the identification of some new word, a kerygma, that philosophy no longer hears yet can be taught to hear again (or perhaps for the first time). This word would have to have come first, before destiny, or else it would always be understood in terms that already hold sway. Urged on by a keen sense of real dangers, philosophy must free itself from its modern prejudice, and recall us to another, higher teaching. The proper name for this teaching is prophecy.[57]

2

The Spirituality of Captivity: Being Jewish

Our true condition is covered by the spontaneous movement away from it that makes up the dynamism of our being. So long as we accede to this movement, we do not know who we truly are. In order to come to ourselves, we must fall out or be shaken out of a tendency so familiar to us as to seem unquestionable. The most basic facts of life are difficult to come by. Self-knowledge requires insight that one cannot achieve by efforts that are still consistent with that tendency, but must instead arise from challenges arriving from beyond expectation.

There is more than a little of this thought in the philosophy of Heidegger, whose analysis of Dasein draws its most important insights from experiences that befall us. It is also in the postwar philosophy of Levinas, though he works out his position in sharp rejoinder to Heidegger and with appeal to experiences that are all but absent from Heidegger's works. There are two important strands in this taut line between them. The first concerns the subjectivity of the subject, or of what Heidegger calls, taking exception to those terms, "Dasein." The second concerns the original givenness of things and indeed of the world that phenomenology teaches us is the subject's proper horizon. Ever since *Husserl* showed that there is no object not already given to a subject and no subject not already conscious of an object, phenomenology has known that one cannot make a claim about either the subject or objects without also, at least implicitly, also suggesting something about the other. Also since Husserl, phenomenology has wished—and in fact, has not ceased renewing its effort—to get as close as possible to the concrete occurrence of meaning, in which, to remain with Husserl's preferred terms, things are given as objects in the consciousness of the subject. For all of *Heidegger's* well-known insistence on the primacy of the question of Being and the claim that Husserl has not truly seen it, he still takes himself to be advancing these cardinal phenomenological pursuits.[1] The interpretation of Dasein as caring for its own existence under the approach of its own death not only establishes the primacy of our relation with Being and not merely beings, but also opens the way for an account of beings as tools in the service of that caring before they may be taken as objects present to a subject. In turn, for all of *Levinas's* insistence, from early on, that the goodness of the Good transcends the violence of being and the idea that neither Husserl nor Heidegger have truly seen it, he too spends considerable time showing that this makes an important difference for how we understand both the subjectivity of the subject and the givenness of things. The subject who is prevented from access to the Good by the very fact of its own existence, anchoring it in Being, is a subject that cannot give to itself what it wants most, and is thus a subject that is strangely, essentially incomplete. The fact that this desire is unfulfilled marks us with an openness that the very movement of our being ceaselessly covers over. Levinas finds this dynamic already at work in sensory contact with the material world, or what he calls "the elemental." Sensibility is a porosity (and in later terms, a passivity) unresolved by the subject's relation with itself. In one's body, as the organ of sensation, one is already an openness, and yet this is always covered over by the very act of living from the sensed.[2] Since this act, however incipient, could not occur except at one's own initiative, we must add to the notion that our subjectivity is a desire for the Good beyond being the seemingly opposed notion that it is also a tendency to claim position here and now in a world. In order for these claims to hold up under phenomenological inspection, it will be necessary to find evidence of the conditions that they describe even in our most primitive relations. To live from the elements would be to enjoy them as nourishment, before any turn to make use of them as tools. Such would be the leading edge of a response to Heidegger that may be conducted without prior reference to the matter of ethics and religion.

The case for this is originally made in texts that announce a break with fundamental ontology that is not so much argued in detail as it is justified by the interpretation of a series of examples giving form to an entirely new conception of our relation to existence.[3] As Levinas understands them, the experiences of fatigue, indolence, and eventually insomnia suggest an account of human being that can no longer be submitted to the principles set forth in *Being and Time*. He therefore refuses the idea that we are moved first by the approach of our own death.[4] Let us follow this thread into the heart of his distinctive position.

Revising the Existential Analytic

Levinas's point of entry might at first be taken only to complement some well-known claims in *Being and Time*. Our being, he observes, is not only haunted by its own end but is also burdened by its own beginning. To exist is to begin anew from instant to instant, or rather, each instant is the very achievement of this beginning. For all of Heidegger's insistence on the priority of our relation to the end, death, he could not entirely disagree with this. If, according to his analysis of Dasein, one relates ceaselessly to one's own death, then the relating is renewed in each new act, or in his preferred terms, each new movement of our being. And whether one is in flight from that death or resolute in the face of its eventuality, being is effort. *Existence and Existents* is substantially a phenomenology of birth,[5] and although Heidegger is not entirely silent on the matter of birth,[6] the very little that he does say stops short of developing the matter with any precision. What matters most in the theory of time that accompanies his analysis of Dasein is that Dasein goes out ahead of itself toward possibilities taken up in view of its own death. Levinas would have us suspend the question of being-toward-death, and look more closely at the movement itself. Movement involves renewal, and renewal requires effort. Again, one wonders whether this is entirely alien to the Heideggerian notions of flight and resoluteness, but even if not, when we pause to consider the effort, we soon enough pick up on the various signs of exhaustion that are already familiar to us in the everyday experiences of walking, lifting, leaning, and supporting that go into it. This is expressed, unprompted by any reflection and prior to any judgment, in the weariness of the breath that flutters as one applies oneself to the task. Levinas would have us take this physical weariness as our cue to recognize the ontological case in which it is the whole of one's subjectivity that trembles. He advances this observation early in the development of his analysis, and only later applies himself to an important clarification: the subjectivity of the subject is asserted against the constant possibility that it will otherwise dissolve into the unmeasured plenum that Levinas calls "there is" (*il y a*).[7] The effort that this requires is expressed in what he calls the "hypostasis" of the subject, whereby one stands forth amid existence while also belonging to it (hence Levinas often calls it the *existent*).[8] For after all, the subject who exists necessarily remains anchored to existence even while struggling to maintain itself as its own self. The drama of a life is played out there, and exhibits a constant need of respite.

Phenomenology has always known that our existing does not move by some pure energy, whether mental or spiritual, but is always embodied. The hypostasis of the subject moves initially in flesh and bone, and it is there that it first feels itself as burden. To live and move within the fullness of being is no ethereal matter. The fullness of being is felt first and most closely in the materiality that our interests transform into an environment. All of this marks only the farthest reach of an effort that is no sooner completed than it must immediately begin again. This does not mean that the subject and its environment are without history, but only that that history, too, must be taken up ceaselessly in the accomplishment of each new instant. What it does mean is that subjective time is disjointed, just as the subject itself is evanescent. And if all of this occurs, as we have already said, in the flesh-and-blood experience of one who must be here and yet desires persistently to escape the grip of any "here," it finally also means, contrary to the letter of Levinas's own text, that space is the irreducible condition of time.[9]

Levinas characterizes the weariness that is prior to reflection and judgment as a "refusal" (*le refus, ce refus*).[10] This is to say that existing, already in its temporal becoming, is held back from the end that it seeks, and plainly not that it is diverted by some knowing decision. The effort to secure oneself as oneself against the possibility of dissolving, or unraveling, is already held back from fulfillment in the effort, as a weight that urges against us. This is the weight of existence, to which each of us is bound so long as he or she exists. Again, it is not that a free subject, principally capable of satisfying its desires, strikes up against external limits, but rather that the subject is weighted, and thus limited, from within. The existence of the existent yields free flight, but it also exerts gravity. The tension between flight and gravity is felt in weariness.

Levinas is already far from Heidegger, who seems never to have meditated on being/existence as fullness and to whom the idea of sinking or vanishing into being/existence would have been unintelligible. Dasein's relation to being is constituted by its relation to its own death, and, according to some of the most widely discussed passages of *Being and Time*, when the relation to death is no longer flight but "anticipatory resoluteness" (*vorlaufende Entschlossenheit*), one at last responds freely to the possibilities that are properly one's own and thus truly make up one's relation with being.[11] Levinas is closer to the view that it is our relation to existence that threatens to pull us toward something akin to death, at least if we think that this is what the end of the subject would truly entail. And nowhere in Levinas's philosophy, either early or late, is there the thought that one might prove capable of taking onto oneself the mortality of one's temporal being in all that that would entail. To the contrary, he takes great pains to observe that whereas for Heidegger taking ownership of one's own death opens the way to authentic activity and freedom—authentic because conducted in a lucid grasp of one's existence and one's possibilities—for him, Levinas, death marks the limit of possibility as such, since it is "never present" until we no longer are, and is thus "absolutely unknowable" and "foreign to light."[12] For Levinas, to exist is always and already to bear a burden and thus to suffer. Death comes upon these conditions from beyond their final range, which is to say without possibility of providing a new vantage point on their meaning. It is the burden and the suffering that must be recognized and taken up, and the subject, the existent anchored in existence, is without means to get outside of them.

These, then, are the conditions in which Levinas would have us consider our experiences of "fatigue" and "indolence" (*la lassitude, la paresse*). It goes without saying that his interest runs deeper than what moral philosophy will make of them. It is true, of course, that we sometimes weary of particular tasks, including some that are unquestionably noble, and it is true that we even weary of friends who are of good character and will. And for these things, one may rightly be censured. But we have already seen that Levinas has in view a weariness that would be prior to any question of moral evaluation because it afflicts the very existence of the existent who would act or else fail to act. This is the weariness felt at the primordial necessity that one must do something, must assert and reassert oneself or else cease to be. In fact, there is no other weariness at all, but only different forms and occasions in which to catch sight of it. The tired resistance I sometimes feel at having to do my duty or answer reasonable expectations is in the first instance an expression of the weight simply of existing, and only secondarily, for example, what moralists may call sloth. Something in me urges against existing, even while something in me also seeks the impossible liberation that could only come in transcending existence altogether. It has never been otherwise—neither in the history of any single subject nor in the trajectory of any single instant. For if fatigue troubles the act itself, indolence clings to its very beginning. Consider another familiar example: one feels fatigue in the entire course of rising from a chair, but before that one feels some resistance even to beginning. "Indolence," writes Levinas, still entirely in the register of ontology, "is an impossibility of beginning, or, if one prefers, it is the effecting of the beginning."[13] And, as he goes on to observe, this more than anything else assures that lived time must be disjointed. In the experience of indolence, existence refuses to let go even as the existent aims to break free. If Levinas has been right to suggest that we are always weary, and in that sense always suffer, because existing is a necessary yet futile effort, indolence is its presence at the root of every movement. The weight of existence that one feels in weariness is also a stumbling block that one encounters in indolence. Each instant is the expression of a struggle to act that must always be won out against it.

Levinas would have us understand that these things belong among the most basic conditions of our subjectivity, and no doubt permeate our most elevated capacities. It is true, of course, and fortunate, that some activities cause us to forget this (play, lovemaking, the arts), but in fact there is no respite from the effort of existing. So then what of the energy that this necessarily requires? This question hangs over the entirety of this kind of analysis, and yet Levinas uses the word "energy" only rarely in his entire oeuvre. When applying himself to fatigue, his counterpart is generally *l'élan*,[14] which suits his attempt to highlight the tension at the heart of effort. A simple insight determines the analysis: fatigue is not merely lack of the force required for initiative, but works in opposition to it. In fatigue, a force arises that is contrary to the thrust or upsurge that is required for action. The tension between these contrary forces is the proper locus for the question of energy. It is also the very life of the existent, since unlimited upsurge, breaking entirely with existence, would mean death, whereas absolute submission to fatigue, sinking entirely into existence, would mean, if not quite death, something quite like catatonia. Levinas has given us considerable reason to think that the former of these two is strictly impossible.[15] The possibility of the latter is a real and important concern. What would be our condition, if we were to succumb to the weight that is felt in weariness and impressed on us in fatigue? And what might it say about our subjectivity more generally, if this might befall us?

Levinas once again proceeds by way of an example. In taking up insomnia at some length, he is not entirely alone even in his own time. Sartre and Emil Cioran also come to mind.[16] Sartre's novel *Troubled Sleep* (*La mort dans l'âme*) is populated with characters who long for a sleep that would be undisturbed by the questions of shame, responsibility, and dignity that preoccupy them after the end of the Second World War. Cioran suffered all his life from insomnia, and although by his own account it was the crucible for many of his deepest reflections, he failed to cure himself of it by philosophical work, and so was more than dubious of any effort to provide a lucid account of it, let alone a positive place within an analysis of our existence. Unlike Sartre, Levinas does not restrict himself to the insomnia that would be an effect of historical or political disturbances troubling individual consciences, and instead he seeks its general conditions in our most profound experience of it. Unlike Cioran, he does think that philosophy, as phenomenology, has access to it, though insomnia proves to lie at the limit of its reach. Once again, let us consider the experience of insomnia in its most familiar form. It is difficult to identify the onset of insomnia, but one can be sure that it has arrived when one feels equally that one would like to sleep and that one is powerless to make that happen. It says very little to observe that in this much the insomniac has only struck up against the peculiar fact that one cannot conduct oneself into sleep but must instead be overtaken by it. It says just slightly more to claim that only human beings suffer from insomnia (though this is not evident to everyone who has been around other animals). Nor are we able to do justice to the entire question of sleep and sleeplessness by trying to situate it, in Heideggerian fashion, within the horizon of our relation with our own death. The most that one might claim along this line is that when one sleeps, such a relation is suspended, which is not at all the same thing as saying that one sleeps either *in order to* suspend that relation or, absurdly, as a form of resolutely accepting it. Still less is the incapacity to sleep a form of either flight or acceptance. Insomnia is a form of the failure of all capacities, or rather, it is an experience of that failure. As every insomniac knows, its ultimate form consists in paralysis. In extreme cases, one finds not merely that no solution turns out to work, but even that one cannot even begin to act on any one of them. And none of this is caused simply by some obstacle or intervention. True insomnia is not an effect of loud noises or an uncomfortable bed, but steals over the would-be sleeper even in the best of beds on a peaceful night. It is first and last a feature of the solitary existent, in which one is withdrawn from engagement with the world and everything in it until reduced almost completely to the relation with oneself: whatever sights and sounds remain have become unmoored from the order of a lived world, so that they are swept along in the anonymous rustle that is deepest night. This is no longer thematizing intentionality, no longer the attending to (*veiller à*) object that Levinas's later texts neatly distinguish from the blank vigilance or watchfulness (*veiller*) that sees without seeing anything in particular.[17] By the same token, it is also no longer seeing from a perspective, because the insomniac has lost the mooring in a world that would ground a perspective. If there is seeing in such a state, it occurs without distinction or focus, and according to a temporality that is no longer that of the effort of existing. Of that effort, moreover, all that remains is the mute discomfort that signals minimal resistance. Levinas calls this discomfort "horror," and reserves the term for our protest at the approach of a suffocation felt most insistently in the night. The horror of insomnia is the helpless pain of only *going on*, without the possibility of initiative.[18]

One cannot read these descriptions without recognizing a key justification for Levinas's claim to have broken with Heidegger. Naturally, insomnia is not death itself, since the existent has not entirely ceased to be itself. Nor is it the anxiety at death that Heidegger interprets as an attunement to nothingness, since horror responds instead to the approach of an undifferentiated fullness (one is not suspended over an abyss, but menaced by surplus).[19] More notably, and as the real stake in this difference, this horror, befalling us as the energy of existing declines, would include the impossibility of everything that Heidegger still ascribes to anxious Dasein. In the face of its own death, Dasein is strictly and only its care for its own existence, and this care is still capable of either embracing authentic freedom or falling back away from it. The existent overtaken by horror can do neither. What Levinas calls "horror" is a paroxysm of care, bringing us to the verge of sheer helplessness.

Nowhere in all of this is there any indication that the subject might somehow save itself from such a downward spiral. Indeed, we learn from a close look at our own experiences of insomnia that it is not by one's own efforts that one escapes. When it has passed, this is because one has either finally succumbed to biological exhaustion, taken medicine, or been taken care of by someone else. Of course, not everyone suffers from insomnia, but in insomnia there appears what Levinas takes to be an indispensable insight into our being: the various powers that tend naturally to self-care are not in themselves enough to overcome our vulnerability to the burden of existence, and so vulnerability must be understood as our fundamental condition. It makes no difference that we are seldom conscious of this. It is nonetheless what we truly are, more radically than Heidegger seems to have understood, already beneath any course of action or projected life we may embark on, whatever its vitality.

These determinations open the way to a criticism of fundamental ontology that is significant in its own right, before any encounter with Levinas's claim, made robustly in *Totality and Infinity*, that the entire problem must be understood to arise from forgetfulness of the ethical relation.[20] For even without making such a claim, it is already possible to bring some embarrassment upon the ontology that considers the relation with being/existence to be fundamental and thus takes the effort of existing as our primary concern. If Levinas is right, this can only lead to a self-understanding that does not truly recognize the depth of our vulnerability and thus flirts constantly with the exhaustion that awaits those who would instead live as if the powers of their existence are enough to provide security and happiness. Levinas's conception of our existence is to this point tragic. We cannot help wanting what we cannot have, and our natural manner of pursuing it seems precisely wrong. Yet in response to this great problem, the ontology that knows only being and beings teaches only that this is how things must be—that there will be unrequited striving in individual lives, and no doubt unavoidable violence when individuals meet. Levinas's friend Gabriel Marcel detects the arrival of this thinking in popular consciousness, which in the absence of transcendent values settles into a stoicism that brings great "spiritual fatigue."[21] This is not far from Levinas's concern, though for reasons we have already found in his earlier works, he is often reticent about the word "spirit," and only seldom surfaces from rigorous analysis in order to address himself to current affairs. We have also already found, again in his earlier works, the evident basis for his own approach set forth in his claims that we are animated by a desire for the absolute.[22] The subsequent non-Heideggerian account of our existence contributes to this effort by enriching our sense of just how much in us actually runs against that desire—while in the meantime also warning us against the philosophy that would have us overlook these matters entirely.

Restlessness and Enjoyment

No one will deny that suffering may strike at any given moment, and it will strike each of us sooner or later. Levinas has argued considerably more than this. To find in the movement of our being a fatigue and indolence whose meaning becomes clear finally in horror, in which the very subjectivity of the subject is at risk, is to understand that suffering gnaws at our every moment. This thought casts doubt on Heidegger's vision of a Dasein that can face up to its own death well enough to freely embrace the possibilities that are disclosed there. On one hand, Heidegger will have failed to fully recognize the original vulnerability that belongs to our Dasein, or as Levinas has put it, the existing of the existent. On the other hand, and perhaps more surprisingly, Heidegger also appears to have underestimated the alterity of death, which according to Levinas is not only a nothingness that is foregrounded by our real possibilities, but an eventuality that strikes from wholly beyond anything we could ever make of it, arriving from a future that remains a profound "mystery."[23] Between vulnerability and mystery there is a suffering that one may call "existential" (Levinas himself does not use this expression) because it belongs inescapably to our very existing. And for the being who suffers, there can be no salvation delivered by his or her own hands. Salvation, too, must come, if it comes at all, from the future, and indeed from mystery.

From here, one has little difficulty recognizing the increasing importance Levinas ascribes to the relation with the other person. His first original works have already sought a way to derive from the very presence of others the opening to a peace that the subject itself, so often insecure and aggressive, seems unable to achieve. The early postwar texts have only understood the problem better: if we find ourselves ready for insecurity and prone to aggression, this is because we are necessarily preoccupied with our own existence. In *Existence and Existents* and its close companion, *Time and the Other*, Levinas proposes that the other person, in his or her very approach, might call me to a service and offer me a good that do not receive their meaning or value from my own efforts, and in this way liberate me from the conditions belonging to self-absorption.[24] Still, the association of the other person with the possibility of peace is not yet well-developed in those texts. What we do find clearly defined, though only in the final chapter of *Existence and Existents*, is the evidence of our desire for peace where the gravity of suffering produces a hope for the salvation that is still to come. Not that this exactly diminishes the suffering. "The future," Levinas writes, "can bring consolation or compensation to a subject who suffers in the present [*dans le présent*], but the very suffering of the present [*du présent*] remains like a cry whose echo will resound forever in the eternity of spaces."[25] As for that gravity itself, it is underlined most forcefully at the heart of *Time and the Other*: "In pain, sorrow, and suffering, we once again find, in a state of purity, the finality that constitutes the tragedy of solitude." Suffering, then, is the impossibility of nothingness, a "being backed up against [*d'être acculé à*] life and being," without refuge or escape.[26] In its pure form, before the subject has sunk all the way into the mute paralysis of horror, we are reduced only to a cry without words,[27] because words imply a purchase on the world that has already fallen away from the afflicted.[28]

The suffering that is coextensive with our subjectivity—we have called it "existential"—is the expression of a vulnerability that is primordial. This is the living root of the hope we've found Levinas tracing to the weight of our attachment to existence. If we are never done with the struggle to escape the grips of a dimension that harbors evil,[29] we also do not cease to reach all the way to salvation from it. Yet hope is not our only mode of relating to our own vulnerability. Evidently enough, until death, whether or not one always hopes for salvation—and thus whether or not the effort of existing is still active—one does continue to live from the material of a world. It will soon be necessary to ask about the plight of those among us who might no longer hope and yet do continue to live, but let us first take note of what Levinas now adds to the understanding of our vulnerability: it is the site of an exposure where, under ordinary conditions, we are opened upon the whole of all else. Of course, what is ordinary collapses in the night of insomnia, in which instead, as Levinas puts it, "the whole opens upon us."[30] Levinas calls what is most ordinary enjoyment (*jouissance*) a living from elements that are not yet implemental in Heidegger's sense of readiness-to-hand. Before tools are put to use, we nourish ourselves without any intimation of our death.[31] Heidegger gives us reason to understand anxiety as the failure of care to secure a world. Levinas suggests that insomnia is the failure of a still deeper impulse to live from the surrounding elements.[32]

We are reminded by this turn of the argument that for Levinas existence has a fullness, a "plenitude" that what Heidegger calls "Being" does not.[33] What Levinas has led us to call "the elements" is nothing more and nothing less than the surface, as it were, of its (existence's) contact with the existent who at once strives to get free of its grasp and yet constantly supports itself there. This is only apparently a contradiction. Enjoyment, as the taking into oneself of what otherwise surrounds and stands over against oneself, is the very means by which one would maintain oneself as oneself within the fullness of existence. Is it necessary to observe that the terms that are mobilized in the service of these claims are not to be taken only in their organic senses? "Enjoyment, living from, elements, nourishment": together, these terms express more than the brute facts about bodies that are moved by hunger and need. To be sure, this is not absent from Levinas's thinking. In *Existence and Existents*, he does not hesitate to ask whether we are willing to think that "I do not only have a body, but am a body."[34] But this is only one facet of his more embracing concern to illuminate a general and pervasive tendency that is both spontaneous and natural. This may be clearer in part 2 of *Totality and Infinity*, where the same themes are developed more rigorously and at greater length. It is not that we first live from the elements and then progress, in turn, to more sophisticated modes such as representation and reflection, but rather that the sophistication is found within and on the constant condition of enjoyment. Representing, for example, occurs as an inner modification and complex form of enjoying, and the representation itself does not cease to be, more fundamentally, elemental.

This is to say that the elements do not appear as themselves, but precisely as nourishment, in the dynamic of living from them.[35] They are in fact closer to us than what would thus appear, and in an important sense are closer to us than appearing as such. This is true even of their own appearing. The elements nourish us anterior to their appearance in enjoyment, let alone use or understanding. We are intimate with them, across the interval that always belongs to intimacy. Enjoyment is not fusion but the first moment of phenomenality.

It is not difficult to see what this implies for our subjectivity. To think that the elements, the bare materiality of existence, are enjoyed— taken up, gathered to oneself—by a subject who is animated by his or her own effort to exist, and to think further that this effort is spontaneous, even natural, and permeates every mode of consciousness, is to make the very meaningfulness of meaning, its occurrence in the life of the subject, the expression of a dynamic that is driven essentially by self-concern. It goes without saying that these thoughts contain the seed of considerable suspicion about the subject's capacity for goodness. We have had occasion to take note of Levinas's conception of existential restlessness. Let us now bring it into contact with what is proposed for enjoyment of the elements: the contentment of possession and satisfaction passes away at the very moment of its achievement. We know this from the more familiar form of nourishment that takes place in a simple meal. As I eat this bread before me, I am at once at ease, perhaps even relieved, in sating my hunger, and yet there is already labor in the consuming and already anticipation that the hunger will return. One thus does not eat without drawing away some of the reserves that the food is to replenish, and beneath the contentment lurks a fear that it is not forever. This may be what Gide has in mind when he invokes "the jealous possessions of happiness,"[36] for this expression alerts us to a tightening of a grip that has already secured what one wants, and thus a propensity in the subject to hold fast to its gains, against any force that might take it away. It will not be long before Levinas will characterize this insistence of the subject on itself—again, spontaneous and natural—as "atheist" in its closure from transcendence, and "violent" in its refusal to cede to the claims of the other person. In *Totality and Infinity*, the two are brought together in a conception of the subject as "separated" from the Other person with whom one is nonetheless in relation before and outside any initiative taken for oneself. Only the face of the Other can open the subject to a Good that serves more than one's own needs. Only the face of the Other can interrupt our natural tendency to serve our own needs first and last, and only the face of the Other promises a way out of violence toward the peace that would consist in responsibility and justice. These few concepts frame everything that Levinas has to say concerning the ethics, which must contend with the fact that neither hope for salvation nor desire for peace and goodness occur in the absence of needs that no living being can long ignore.

Lessons of Suffering

It is not certain that Levinas's position is only the outcome of his particular manner of breaking from Heidegger. There is also his experience as a prisoner of war to consider, and the fact of important continuity between his published texts, both before and after the war, and what is recorded in his wartime notebooks. To be sure, as Levinas informs us, the texts published immediately after the war owe a great deal to studies "written for the most part in captivity," but upon opening them—this became possible only decades later, and after his death—one immediately finds a wealth of material that does not appear in any of his published texts, though one also has little difficulty recognizing convictions, proposals, and entire lines of thought that inform many of them.[37] In the present context, it is especially interesting to note a preoccupation with the simplest conditions of life that is not only an expression of the austerity imposed by the Germans in the *stalag*. In a review of the notebooks, Sarah Hammerschlag draws attention to references to a "falling of the draperies" (*les draperies qui tombent*), and finds the expression to epitomize a general sense that the conventions and adornment of civilization have dropped away.[38] This is congruent with the tendency, especially in *Existence and Existents*, to catch sight of the bare conditions of our existence following the failure of a mode of consciousness that is premised on act, capacity, and comprehension. This line leads past the many notes and short meditations that anticipate *Existence and Existents* (and which, in retrospect, contain only a few surprises), directly to two complete essays[39] and an unexpected engagement with the Catholic apocalyptic writer Léon Bloy that are undoubtedly of great importance. The essays develop a distinctive spirituality from the experience of the Jewish prisoner, and then draw from it some general indications for every human being. The editorial evidence suggests that Levinas began to read Bloy closely just before he would have worked out his spirituality of the Jewish prisoner, and in any case, what seems to hold his particular interest in Bloy does resonate with the stated goal of the essays: Bloy was able to claim that Catholics lived a deeper form of the same existence that others live only superficially; the essays on spirituality clearly make the same argument on behalf of Jews.[40]

It is unsurprising to find Levinas intent on an account of the universal significance of the Jewish way of life or mode of being.[41] Given his situation, it is also unsurprising to find him concentrating on the particular experiences of isolation, deprivation, and suffering. What does give one pause is his attempt to bring these things together in the claim that the experience of the Jewish prisoner opens the way to a recovery of what belongs properly to Jewish spirituality as such—and further, that precisely this constitutes its teaching to all of humankind. The reader of *Existence and Existents* is somewhat prepared for the key association: in captivity one is stripped down to the "fundamental suffering" of our condition,[42] and the Jewish people are a people intimate with suffering. This means that Levinas's experiences in the *stalag* will have enacted a "double reduction," in the phenomenological sense, both to the truth of our subjectivity and to the truth of his Jewishness.[43] Earlier, we meditated on Levinas's claim, in *On Escape*, that we are "held fast" (*rivé*) to being even as we desire to escape it.[44] In the essays on the Jewish captive there is a similar idea: the prisoner and perforce the Jew is "cornered into" (*acculé*) conditions that are generally obscured by the flow of ordinary everyday life, but are presently undeniable, and to say the least, distressing.[45] One might wish to insist that alongside the diverse forms of persecution that an entire people have undergone over the course of many centuries, the extreme degree undergone at the hands of Germans captors represents a case apart, but this very way of conceiving the phenomena is not far from the claim that Levinas actually wishes to defend. The persecution and suffering of captivity differ not in kind but in intensity from what Jews have had to experience already long and too often: in simple terms, isolation for no other reason than evidence of particularity, exile from any sense of home, whether physical, moral, or spiritual, and all of the deprivation that comes with them.

Needless to say, to suppose that the truth of Jewishness is to be found only or especially in the extreme isolation, exile, and deprivation experienced in captivity is to imply that the spirituality that will be drawn from all of this has either not been available in more comfortable circumstances or else that it is forgotten there. It also flirts with valorizing the worst sort of suffering, as if one ought to choose the way down into it as the essential passage to greater elevation.[46] We will return to this shortly, but let it be admitted here that the spirituality that Levinas works out in his reflection on the labor camp is far from cheery. One must face up to the fact that suffering has always been the condition of Jewishness and, it would seem, always will be. If one wants to come to terms with this fact, then there is no better occasion for reflection than when it occurs in extreme form (though one ought to remember, as Levinas certainly does, that the Jews had to face still worse things than what went on in the *stalag*). What do we learn there about Jewishness that is perhaps less evident in its ordinary forms? To begin with, it belongs to the singularity of the Jewish people that the various forms of solitude and of the suffering that accrues to them do not extinguish a thirst for God.[47] Levinas has provided us with an ontological formulation of this thought, manifestly anti-Heideggerian, when in *On Escape* he claims that our being is animated by a desire for the absolute. Between then and now, he has understood a great deal more about the suffering that is involved. Second, as a result of his or her Jewish identity and the persecution that seeks it out, the Jew must know, with a real urgency that non-Jews do not face, that death can truly come at any time (and thus, in the *stalag*, it "hovered over works and over laughter like a familiar shadow").[48] Third, the suffering that is necessarily one's own opens up a gap between each subject that is a defining feature of the relation with God. And this is at the same time a defining feature of the community. All members have in common the burden of their own suffering and a desire that brings them before the divine. Alone and in darkness, the prisoner continues to pray, and in this there is solidarity with all of the others who likewise say their own prayers. Fourth, there is also the possibility of distance from one's own suffering, even if one cannot get free of it. "Between each man and his suffering," writes Levinas, "there was something like an interval that enabled him to take up an attitude toward it before being seized and torn apart."[49] This interval, he immediately states, is the space of meditation and of spirituality. And for the subject who is truly isolated by his or her own suffering, it is a space that is maintained only in dialogue, upon the word of the other person, whereby solitude is nonetheless also relation, and profound self-absorption gives way to the inevitable oscillation of the suffering, between withdrawal into themselves and the expression of meaning.

Let us summarize this in more general terms. Levinas envisions a solitude that is conferred by exclusion, but without extinguishing a desire for God. This solitude includes a sense of the real proximity of one's own death that instills in one a tendency toward preoccupation with one's own concerns, and it is in precisely this condition that one comes before God in prayer and longing. At the same time, the singularity of concern for oneself and prayer before God defines each member of a plurality that cannot be either atomized or totalized because each member has his or her own unique relation with God. This plurality, in short, is a community, and the community, we have just seen, lives and breathes in dialogue. It would not be easy to determine quite how much this vision corresponds with the broader, more recognizable features of Jewish life in general, but it is henceforth impossible to reject the claim out of hand. From close reflection on an extraordinarily particular experience, Levinas has derived the outline of a spirituality that would be proper to the different, more expansive particularity that is Jewishness as such. Remarkably, the central themes of this spirituality also reappear, barely reformulated, at the heart of *Totality and Infinity*, where the effort is plainly toward a universalism in which the Jewish experience—we may add: as distilled in the Jewish captive experience—yields a teaching for all of humankind. We have seen this coming, and will examine it in due course. But before that, there is still the question of one more crucial term that will have to be translated across these three registers, and of what it will mean for how Levinas would have us understand our shared humanity. For the Jew, captive or not, the relation with God, in all of the suffering that it entails, is a matter of *election*.

Deaths of a Certain God

The term "election" is important in Levinas's later work,[50] but it is certainly not absent in his wartime reflections on Jewishness. In "The Israelite Prisoner's Spirituality" ("La spiritualité chez le prisonnier Israélite"), he recalls that the *stalag* contained offenses that drove the Jewish prisoner beyond the bitterness and outrage that arose in response to the exclusions that had been part of everyday life, to a point at which "humiliation took on the biblical flavor of election." In "The Jewish Experience of Being a Prisoner" ("L'expérience juive du prisonnier"), this is understood as the content of a vocation: to discover "in the suffering itself the signs of election."[51] It is not only that his suffering, because it is real, must be a part of his current relation with God, but also, and more importantly, that suffering is always inseparable from his Jewishness, which is also to say his relation with God. This, of all things, he can now see plainly since it has become the one unmistakable fact of his experience. Does this mean that the Jew is called to find God in and through his suffering? That would amount to choosing an identity inscribed in a tradition—Jewishness as historical figure of suffering—such as we have already seen Sartre charge with bad faith.[52] But we have also seen, and at the same juncture, that Levinas has resisted this characterization by rejecting the notion of freedom that it assumes: freedom as contingent, ungrounded, and therefore, whether or not one realizes and admits it, radically self-determining. Levinas has never accepted this notion of freedom except as an inheritance specifically of modern thought, but it is not until he turns specifically to the question of Jewishness that he identifies the keys to a different conception. What modern thought, which on this point includes Sartrean thought, cannot accept is the possibility of an origin for freedom that would be out of reach of its own power to choose for or against it. Such an origin would ground the subjectivity of the subject in passivity, which is not to be confused with the contingency defended by existentialists. Contingent freedom orders itself only by giving itself its own principle. The passivity that would characterize the freedom that Levinas identifies in Jewishness denotes conditions in some higher relation or principle. One does not choose without first having been chosen, and one does not act without first being a creature. It is one of the central tasks of *Totality and Infinity* to free this biblical language of election and creation from recourse to any notion of causality, as if by divine act they are temporally prior to the exercise of freedom and responsibility.[53] Apart from that, when it is only a matter of establishing the particularity of Jewishness in response to the Sartrean attempt to submit Judaism to the same general critique as must be applied to any other way of life, Levinas argues simply that the facticity of Jewishness is unintelligible without the notion of election, which for its part cannot be reduced to a form of modern freedom.[54]

It is one thing to seek God in one's suffering, and another only to come before God as one who suffers. In the former instance, one must believe that God wills the suffering as a privileged mode of revelation. This risks a view that attributes violence to the divine will and, as we have already had occasion to remark, the real possibility of spiritual masochism. In the latter instance, the most that one can say about the divine will is that God only admits of our suffering. This leaves open the door to the idea, thoroughly biblical, that God accompanies those who suffer. As for the question of an origin of the suffering, Levinas has already given us ample reason to think that it belongs only to one dimension of our subjectivity: to exist is to suffer, but the one who exists already surpasses his or her existence in the desire for God. We have already seen this idea more than once. So much is wagered on it, that it is tempting to think that much of Levinas's thinking is organized so as to protect it. A more modest proposal—one that is also close to the texts at hand—is that he considers the desire for God to be indestructible, even if it is also clearly possible to forget it. This, of course, is familiar to the Jewish people, who from the beginning have known profound suffering, the particular company of God, and a lamentable pattern of forgetfulness and falling away. And so, the memory of their experience is also a call to see the truth of their existence: to be Jewish is to suffer and to be with God. Jewish prisoners like Levinas himself would have seen this with particular, terrible lucidity. This is what they have to offer the Jewish people, and it is what the Jewish people have to offer all of humanity. We all suffer in our existence, we are all called to the company of God. When God is revealed to the Jewish people, it becomes possible, in and through their own self-understanding, for every human being to know his or her true condition, and thus catch sight of a relation that transcends the misery of existence. In biblical faith, this is the working of the law. In the philosophy of Levinas, it is accomplished by the face of the other person. There is, then, a particular sense of election that does belong uniquely to the Jewish people, but for Levinas there is also a universal sense that completes his argument for the Jewish nature of all subjectivity. Before we choose to do anything from and for ourselves, even if to turn away from religion altogether, God has already chosen us.

These things having been said, one may still wonder just what distinguishes the God of election, who grants us all of our freedom and admits all of our suffering, from sheer caprice or dreadful indifference. Perhaps this thought does not strike readily against a spirituality that remains confident in the human capacity for taking distance from one's own suffering and for entering into dialogue with others. Yet we know that the Shoah proved capable of destroying this capacity, and every capacity, in some people, and moreover without giving any indication of why it happened specifically to them and not to the others around them. Let us pursue this worry about the God of election in terms of a specific question: What or how much truly separates it from the cruel sense of "fortune" that is invoked by Primo Levi with a view of even darker instances of antisemitism than Levinas has so far addressed?

Levi, we should remember, was a prisoner who suffered under conditions that resemble those that Levinas has described in the *stalag*, though there can be no doubt that they were imposed with much greater severity (when Levinas famously said, on more than one occasion, that his French soldier's uniform saved him from death in Auschwitz, he was frankly recognizing this fact).[55] But the counterpart of Levinas's prisoner is not Levi himself, who after all as a survivor was the exception rather than the rule in Auschwitz. It is rather those whom he reports having been widely called *Musulmänner*, according to a callous play on the etymology of what we have in English as "Muslims": those who surrender. Of them, Levi writes that they have never been able to adjust to the regime of the *Lager* (i.e., the camp), and still less to the brutal anti-morality of survival that takes shape inside its fences. They have been broken by it or succumbed to it, often immediately, so that each day is made up of sheer compliance, and together the days trace a path of steady decline until death from starvation, disease, or murder at the hands of their captors. And this is far from unusual in Auschwitz. To the contrary, the *Musulmänner* "form the backbone of the camp, an anonymous mass, continually renewed and always identical, of non-men who march and labor in silence, the divine spark dead in them, already too empty to really suffer. One hesitates to call them living, one hesitates to call their death 'death,' in the face of which they have no fear, as they are too tired to understand."[56] We have every reason to take these lines literally, and the many others that echo them, from a man who spent many months close to the phenomenon that they describe, and whose prose stays as close as possible to dispassionate analysis. The person of the *"Musulman"* poses important challenges to our understanding. For Levi, as he signals in the original title of the book—*Se questo è un uomo*, "if this is a man"—the primary question is anthropological. What are we to make of the prisoner who has surrendered so completely to a multitude of offenses as to give no further evidence of will or intellect, and for whom even the difference between consent and revolt appears out of reach?[57] The point of contact with Levinas's thinking is easy to identify here: in the *Lager* there is a more profound, or perhaps more *complete* experience of suffering than in the *stalag*. This plainly disqualifies the very possibility of taking it into the spirituality described by Levinas, since in Levi's account there is no longer an active mind to take distance from it. At the same time, however, Levinas does offer us a phenomenological approach to the phenomenon in his descriptions of horror. In horror, let us recall, the subject is emptied of its capacities until reduced only to a mute cry. Let us not pretend that this is more than an instructive resemblance. There is some precision in thinking that life in Auschwitz was not a nightmare, since it was certainly a real occurrence in waking life, but instead was something much closer to horror in the indeterminate rustle of night. And this of course is the most difficult feature of the experience to absorb: we have before us the record of a suffering that is without meaning because the one who undergoes it is no longer able to interpret it.

If Levi leaves unanswered his anthropological question, this is because his real concern is with the sort of thinking that encourages us to think that it can be answered at all. Indeed, if we are troubled by the thought that it cannot be, he has already done much of his work. For the thought we might wish to protect generally involves commitment to an underlying principle of order that he suggests has collapsed under the weight of what has happened in places like Auschwitz. The problem shows up in what he calls "the ambiguous life of the *Lager*," in which there are only "the "drowned" (*i sommersi*, the submerged) and "the saved" (*i salvati*)—there are only those who sink down, most dramatically the *Musulmänner*, and those who hold steady and perhaps even survive.[58] One may seek a reason for this distinction, or one may conclude that it is entirely by chance. As for a reason, Levi is emphatic: the saved were by no means the best human beings. Too often, perhaps in all cases, what enabled a person to survive was either a cunning and ruthlessness worthy of Machiavelli's heroes or a random bit of help that was not always even intentional. Each of these possibilities deserves our attention. In Auschwitz, survival depended on renouncing the virtues cultivated in the ordinary world in favor of others that are ordered entirely to physical survival, without regard for the well-being of other prisoners. Indeed, when in Auschwitz a prisoner exhibits trust, compassion, or generosity, this appears as a sign of dangerous naïvete. In Levi's estimation, the conflict between virtues such as these and the virtues of the camp must shatter our confidence in any moral teleology. It is all too possible for the basic good of survival to be directly at odds with the elevated good identified with human flourishing.

Are we then to think that God, according to the most inscrutable of wills, has had a hand in all of this? As far as Levi can see, an appeal to "divine providence" has also been discredited, since this only begs the further question of *why* some have been given what is needed to survive while others have not.[59] He therefore embraces what must appear to him as the more honest word, "fortune." And whether or not this is the great theme of his book, it does come up at crucial moments. It was his "good fortune to be deported to Auschwitz only in 1944," which is to say so late in the war that he had significantly less time to endure than did many others. It was also his "good fortune" to be chosen among three prisoners assigned to the chemical laboratory in the camp's rubber factory, sparing him much of the severe hardship that fell on nearly everyone else. To escape the camp would be "no small fortune." Fortune always intervened on the side of those who remained alive, supplementing certain skills that they may have developed. Everyone else perished.[60]

This is not the occasion to go into the likely sources for the idea that Levi appeals to here.[61] It will suffice to observe that in his usage, it stands for a refusal of the Christian defense of providence over chance argued by, among others, Thomas Aquinas.[62] Whether or not the "ambiguous life of the *Lager*" prompted in Levi religious reservations about this idea (at any rate, he seems to have been essentially without faith already before he reached the camp), his fundamental difficulty is strictly analytic:[63] from the fact of a sharp distinction between the drowned and the saved, it follows either that there is no God who saves us, or else that there is a God whose willingness to let some be saved and others perish is beyond our comprehension. In the latter case, there is no salient difference between the mystery of the divine will and the workings of what Levi calls "fortune." As far as we can see—and as a matter for how we are to live our lives—whatever comes to pass simply comes to pass.

The conclusions that Levi was prepared to draw from his experience in the *Lager* meet the position taken by Levinas while in the *stalag* on the question of a God who can be expected to ground a moral order and, if necessary, intervene in its service. It is far from certain that Levinas was ever invested in such a God, but for Levi the plausibility of the very idea most surely died at Auschwitz. Strictly speaking, the Shoah has meant the end of any further credence in the God of theodicy, the God who creates the world and whose good and all-powerful will justifies the evil that, to be sure, is a part of it. This strikes an appreciable psychological blow, for what truly has this God uniquely given us if not, finally, the assurance of order and thus security in the course of our unpredictable lives? We should not forget that Nietzsche had seen this long before the Nazis began their terrible persecutions. After all, the death of God that is announced in the *Gay Science* and in *Zarathustra*[64] is also present in the *Genealogy of Morals*, which has no other purpose than to make the entire moral order, including its underlying principle, appear as a prolonged flight from primordial chaos. The call for a "transvaluation of values" that echoes across the ensuing ruins is in the first instance a renewal of the question of what we truly are. Without falling into nihilism, Levi thinks much in this spirit. The death of the God who would ensure order and meaning even in Auschwitz requires us to ask again what it is that makes us human—even if, as we have observed, Levi himself seems without a clear answer.

In his late essay "Useless Suffering," Levinas, too, finds basic agreement with Nietzsche: "Did not the word of Nietzsche on the death of God take on, in the extermination camps the significance of a quasi-empirical fact?"[65] The argument of the essay is important. Recurring to analyses worked out in his wartime notebooks, Levinas draws attention to a suffering that conditions our subjectivity before any question of use, and that is obscured by, among other things, the conception of God alloyed with theodicy.[66] This God will indeed have died in Auschwitz, but in contrast with Levi, Levinas takes the event as an opening to see who or what the living God truly is, and indeed who or what we truly are. And in his view, these things are neither new nor unknowable. As horrific as the event has been, it initiates in contemporary religious thought a gigantic exercise of recollection—of a return from present conditions, through the accumulated effect of multiple distortions, to what has always been the case.[67] In the absence of a precast moral order—created, provided, enforced—each human being is immediately present to the other, and indeed is always already responding to the other, before and outside any assembly on a same plane under a same unifying principle. Levinas's writings on captivity and spirituality have already prepared an understanding of the God that is to survive the end of theodicy: God only accompanies us, and without entering into being, which harbors suffering and violence. God, as God, leaves us to one another, and to the work of peace and goodness. These are among the central themes of *Totality and Infinity*, and of succeeding texts that do not cease to intensify the claims that are registered there.

3

Plurality and Infinity: Ethics as Religion

The Linchpin of Totality and Infinity

True religion, then, takes place in our relation with the other person.[1] Any attempt to situate Levinas's conception of the religious is inseparable from an attempt to situate his conception of the ethical, and indeed it is clear that the latter must set the conditions for the former. One might begin with the positive conception of heteronomy that his position necessarily entails: the separated subject neither provides itself with its own law, nor conducts itself in the absence of any law whatsoever. Levinas's postwar books have already supplied the perspective from which to understand this: he does not deny the *possibility* of living as if one were autonomous, but instead contests the *viability* of that way of life, and indeed its *desirability*. Still, it is giving away nothing at all that is not easily deduced from his basic phenomenological principles to now alert ourselves up front to the fact that this challenge to individual autonomy is meant not only to call the subject back to the truth of its own condition, but also to lay a claim for the rights of the other person for whom one is said to respond in the very movement of one's existence, which is to say already before any pretense to self-rule.

This portion of the argument is well known. What tends to receive less attention—though we have already seen it worked out—is Levinas's suggestion that the pursuit of autonomy involves a conception of personal freedom that turns out to be unsustainable. Without knowing his proposed solution to this problem, one easily discerns a return to critical dissatisfaction with modern conceptions of freedom that has been present since the essay on Hitlerism. In the context of an emerging ethics of radical responsibility for the other person, Levinas's target is the liberal promotion of self-determination and, indeed, the conception of individual rights that it may support. After all, from his perspective, the rights that all individuals must respect must be, in the final analysis, rights that each individual confers on other people out of fidelity to a universal principle. In that case, even if one may know that there are real differences among those others, one nonetheless approaches the differences as if each of them gives voice to the same demand for recognition. This implies a stance from which an exalted commitment to universal justice is never entirely secure from a fall into totalization, since it does not cease to think that the same person who would recognize and serve others first must give himself or herself the criteria by which to judge and act.[2] Such a totalization would certainly fall well short of the virulently suppressive form Levinas has detected in German National Socialism, but in his eyes it is therefore a subtler danger. After defeating the politics of people, blood, and soil, modern liberalism will have settled the matters of justice and responsibility without yet having caught sight of the otherness of the other person. This worry is expressed in the opening pages of *Totality and Infinity*, in the form of a warning that we should not be "duped by morality."[3] Morality, it transpires, lulls us into thinking that when outright violence has been suspended, peace will surely follow. Yet who does not know from personal experience—or failing that, the novels of Dostoevsky, with their depictions of everyday cruelty—that it is possible to wield customs, norms, and even moral regulations in the service of the very abuses that they are meant to curtail? The impulse to violence is cunning. It has no great difficulty infiltrating our moral discourse.

At the same time, the exercise of this discourse also requires a freedom that is in constant need of renewal, from moment to moment and against the weight of every new datum, without the possibility of ever granting itself rest. This vision is enough for us to wonder about the consequences of such a freedom for politics, even as it sets its course by the principle of right. In his wartime texts, Levinas has already registered considerable worry for the fate of individual existents under terms like "insomnia" and "horror." But we should not overlook another sort of worry for social order. An absence of ground need not always lead to unraveling. From exhaustion can come desperation and violence.

For Levinas, the question of responsibility arises prior to any act of recognition. The face of the other person turns toward the subject with a concrete specificity that goes out ahead of any act of recognition that would interpret it, and initiates a response that is already underway before one might grant or withhold rights. If this is true, then the face has a "presence" that is not correlated with a subject and does not depend on the subject's capacity or incapacity to grasp it. On the one hand, even while this reverses the order of initiative by which a discourse on rights would produce peace, it also promises relief to a subject otherwise burdened by the effort of its existing. On the other hand, there is also a command in that same occasion for relief, since the face of the other person brings an end to the assumption, whether tacit or reflective, that the subject is the center and locus of all meaning. Henceforth, and as the price of lasting peace both for itself and for the other person, the subject must somehow come to terms with the fact that it does not and cannot have emprise over all that it encounters. In its effort to do so, we may recognize the primal scene of an ethics that is in important respects close to that of Kant: responsibility originates in the encounter with a command that stands over everything that belongs to personal or particular inclination.[4]

None of this yet explains how the subject who starts out in need of determination by an exterior law actually receives such a law, let alone welcomes it, before making it the condition of its free movement. How, or under what condition, could a subject in whom Levinas sees a natural tendency to comprehend everything in its own terms—taking itself as the center of gravity—in fact prove capable of admitting a law that by definition would arrive from wholly beyond all such terms? It is tempting to appeal directly to Levinas's account of the face of the other person, which in his account is the self-expression of an otherness that exceeds all meaning that the subject may give to it and which therefore, as the emissary of the subject's true condition, stands over the subject even as it struggles to welcome and serve (one easily sees the dynamic: each act of service occurs at the subject's own initiative, and therefore calls for new ethical critique). The many passages that make these claims are undoubtedly and, given what they imply, rightly the best known in all of Levinas's philosophical work.[5] Yet they only beg the question of how one is able to make sense of such an otherness at all, let alone in the specific manner which Levinas understands as ethical. *Other* with respect to what? In what context or against what background sameness? Analytic philosophers would not be wrong to ask for qualifiers to define what is other than me and mine but is nonetheless a meaningful datum of experience,[6] and from the perspective of a more general metaphysics, it can seem that the thesis of an otherness that enters experience from beyond the horizon of a subject's surrounding world is perilously close to the subjectivist illusion of an otherness that is entirely devoid of any intelligible content. Would these difficulties be countered by renewed attention to the subjectivity of the subject? Could it be shown that a single subject is properly responsive both to its world and everything in it, and to an otherness that approaches from wholly beyond them?[7] Only if the relation with the other person is secured already prior to being and appearing, for if not, relations would have to be conducted on the common plane that they define. But in that case, we are either ego and alter ego (Husserl) or, now taking fuller account of the effort of existing, we are rivals. Among rivals, relations are finally a matter of mutual contestation, as one finds claimed in the interpretation of concrete relations worked out in Sartre's

Being and Nothingness.[8] Against any such vision of reversibility, Levinas is
a thinker of radical asymmetry, and he stakes his claim for this on the
idea of a subject who is open to the other person before any question of
closure even according to the natural tendency that makes up enjoyment
of the elements, let alone an active insistence on a privileged position
for oneself. This means, among other things, that the relation with the
other person will have to be considered "an-archic," in the strict sense of
the term: before and without ground, and indeed capable of ordering a
critique of the status of any ground.[9] What comes first is the relation with
the other, and any grounds proposed for it necessarily have the effect
of introducing symmetry, in which Levinas detects nascent conceptual
violence.

These few thoughts impose immense difficulties on Levinas's phenomenological work. The subject who hears a call from beyond all comprehension is a subject who is exposed to the arrival of that call before
any possible closure into the identity that becomes the origin from which
a datum is grasped. One's susceptiveness to the call of the other person
would thus lie deeper than the origin, or as Levinas often prefers it, anterior to the positing of a ground and the setting up of a perspective. One
is always already laid bare; one is passive before any question of activity,
whether this would be altruistic or egoistic.

It is at this most ancient point, "older than the ego," that the ethical
relation—the relation of a free subject exposed to the other person—
exhibits what Levinas is willing to conceive as a religious dimension.
Absolute passivity, the exposure prior to act and identity, is the mark of
being a "creature."[10] As a creature, each human being is exposed to the
other before and outside any possible mediation seized and projected
onto the relation, according to what Levinas variously calls a "plot" (*une
intrigue*), a matrix, and an ordering that subtends every system or set.[11]
This would mean, for instance, that we creatures are a plurality not yet
gathered into any totality even while we are members of a totality that we
have either been forced or seduced into accepting. In turn, it would also
mean that before the otherness of the other person is defined—before
he or she is a citizen, a worker, or a representative of a group—he or she
is already there, closer to me, as subject, than anything grasped in the
acts of discovery or identification. Our relation is "'anterior' to the act
that would effect it."[12]

In *Totality and Infinity*, this vision of human plurality is interpreted
as the inverse figure of Infinity. Our plurality, we are told, is due to the
"creative contraction" of Infinity, by which there is place for separated,
finite being.[13] This expression has an important lineage. In Levinas's own
use, it has a recognizable affinity with elements of Kabbalah and of the

Neoplatonic thinking that partly informs it.[14] But since this suggests a notion of the absolute as at once the principles and yet withdrawn from the order, one also thinks, along a somewhat different line, of Nicholas of Cusa's *aliud non aliud*. Regardless of Levinas's particular place in this tradition, one sees soon enough that he is intent on deriving each of two claims from the other. On the one hand, the fact—if it is established as a *fact*—that the relation of a subject to the other is anterior to the possibility of totality requires the thought of Infinity. This is the deepest stake of Levinas's claim that the otherness of the other is infinite, and that this infinite otherness reveals itself in the face. Short of that, the face of the other person reveals only a lack or limit in the subject's own comprehension, and the relation that it announces is only one between finite beings. On the other hand, the fact—again, if it is established as a *fact*—of Infinity breaks up any claim for totality so that the thought of plurality is required. This, too, is a deep stake of Levinas's claims about the face and otherness. Evidently enough, there is call and response, which is to say that there is relation and not sheer atomism. Is either of these theses strictly prior to the other? They seem rather to presuppose and confirm one another at what is arguably the heart of Levinas's thinking: Infinity is said to reveal itself in human plurality, and the conditions for human plurality are said to lie within the (non-)horizon of Infinity.

Let us try to understand this better. We have already taken note of Levinas's conception of the subject, in need of an exterior law to ground its freedom. The subject is not, for all of that, simply fated to endless striving. Because the other person is always already there with the subject as it strives to establish and secure itself, and because that striving is always, precisely as the self-originating act of the subject, a turning away from the other that nonetheless presupposes the nearness of the other, it is always possible for the other's face to awaken the subject to its own condition and indeed the truth of their relation. If this awakening brings an end to the solitary process of self-assertion—if it offers respite and perhaps even the beginning of a conversation of attitude to care for the other before care for oneself—then the face will have been the approach of an otherness that is unqualified, *and* the subject itself will have been touched in a passivity that is likewise unqualified. This, of course, occurs at the initiative of the other.[15] One thus comes to at least one meaning of Levinas's frequent claim that true peace comes in the face of the stranger: the advent of the other person, as shocking as it may be for the subject, promises the subject a freedom that is no longer consumed with the endless project of self-justification and is no longer, in its harried insecurity, prone to aggression. Atomistic models of the human relation do not take this possibility into account, and agonistic models rule it out entirely. Levinas's use of the word "creature" is plainly a response to those accounts of our humanity. Creatureliness, as the subjectivity of the subject, indicates both a positive relation with the other person and, at the same time, a relation with the transcendence by which that relation is "situated."[16] Put otherwise, the infinity of the Infinite, by admitting the finitude of the subject, effects a separation between the subject and the other person, and according to this separation, everything that the subject is and does both presupposes and responds to the other's nearness. Levinas does not shrink from the immediate implication: to open oneself to the priority of the other person is at the same time to open oneself to the infinity of the Infinite by which the relation is ordered.

There is no immediate need to insist on the importance of this distinction between ethical and religious alterity, since in any case Levinas plainly does recognize that there is one. The other person is not strictly and simply the Infinite, even if, plainly, Levinas interprets his or her face as its revelation, trace, and so forth. What seems less evident is the manner in which the acting responsible subject might also recognize that distinction, *if indeed Levinas considers this to be either necessary or important*. After all, a direct and seemingly unavoidable implication of his close alignment of religion and ethics is the thesis of a consciousness that is open at one and the same time to Infinity and to the face or call of the other person. This thesis of a twofold openness calls for further attention.

Reading Descartes's "Third Meditation"

Levinas's argument that consciousness is always already open to Infinity—though, to be sure, in its movement also already closing from it—is explicitly Cartesian in inspiration. The first five sections of *Totality and Infinity*, entitled "Metaphysics and Transcendence," are concerned to show that ontology is a philosophy of power that promotes totality, by relying on a subject capable of interpreting everything and everyone through concepts such as Spirit (Hegel) and Being (Heidegger). To this is opposed a defense of the ethical relation as prior to any totality, in terms that have already been reviewed here. This effort passes through the argument of Descartes's "Third Meditation":

> This relation of the same [i.e., the subject] with the other, where the transcendence of the relation does not cut the bonds a relation implies, yet where these bonds do not unite the same and the other into a Whole, is in fact fixed in the situation described by Descartes in which the "I think" maintains with the Infinite it can in nowise contain and from which it is separated, a relation called "the idea of Infinity."[17]

In what sense does the *idea* of Infinity constitute a *relation* with Infinity? Levinas places the classical reading of Descartes in the service of his own argument. The *Meditations*, revealing the ego and God as distinct but "mutually founding" moments, present us with "the very meaning of separation."[18] Where Descartes first secures thinking-being in the certitude of its relation to itself, Levinas finds a means to begin his own approach to the intersubjective relation with an account of the inner unicity of the subject. And where Descartes later discovers the ground for thinking-being and its perceptions in its relation with a supremely perfect being (*ens summum perfectum*),[19] Levinas sees proof that the subject's natural inclination to take itself as its own origin and reference—its spontaneous tendency toward closure into itself—already presupposes a deeper opening that must be interpreted as the sign of what he calls "plurality," since each such subject would have its own relation, apart from all other relations, with a principle that is, after all, ungraspable.

Now, the order of progression lain down in Descartes's text is especially important for a proper understanding of what he means by the idea of Infinity. Before reading the Third and Fourth of the *Meditations*, one will have understood from the Second one that the self-certainty drawn from the self-affection discovered in consciousness is still not enough for one to be certain about one's own perceptions, including perceptions of one's very self. This means that until the achievement of those later *Meditations*, or short of it, all perception occurs without the possibility of secure judgment. We might understand the general position this way: as long as the *Meditations on First Philosophy* thus isolate the sphere of perception—of presence and meaning-giving—from the sphere of judgment, we are permitted to speak of ideas only as perceptions of the mind, as opposed to the more familiar understanding of ideas as reflections or expressions of things. It is finally the idea of Infinity that grounds judgment, first by overflowing the idea itself, such that it is impossible to think that, in this one case, the idea is nothing more than a product of the mind; and second by yielding an equation between Infinity as superabundance and Infinity as benevolent God. Yet even here we do not meet with an exception to the preceding, and unsettling, definition of idea so much as its exemplar: in the end, Infinity turns out to be precisely what the well-functioning and properly instructed mind takes it to be—namely, that which exceeds capture in or by any possible idea. The idea of Infinity can serve as the ground for judgment about all other ideas not because it is of an entirely different and distant character, but instead because it is the perfection of what it has in common with them. This must be the essential meaning of the claim that the idea of Infinity is *in us* (according to an expression that is axiomatic for the entire "Third Meditation" and which Levinas, too, sometimes favors). Neither in the world in the manner of finite things that submit to correlation with ideas, nor wholly opposed to the world as if defined by the negation of all finitude and every idea, Infinity has always already entered the mind, which for its part has only to discover it there.[20]

Is it possible for a finite being concerned with the problems of its own existence to discover this exceptional idea entirely through its own efforts? Can we achieve true insight into Infinity without submitting it to the limits that belong inevitably to the finite mind? If the *Meditations on First Philosophy* is, as is commonly thought, first of all a work on the theory of knowledge, and if in its course it generates any sort of argument for the existence of God,[21] then Descartes will have considered this to be achieved. To be sure, the argument claims only to know Infinity as transcending every "measurable and ordered object," but an awareness of that very transcendence would have to include within itself, as another sort of knowing, a sense of immeasurable grandeur.[22] Needless to say, the knowing that corresponds to grandeur must have the character of undergoing, or submission, since what can be seen or measured by an act of the mind necessarily falls short of it. Descartes himself recognizes this, for example in a letter to Mersenne cited at least once by Levinas: "I have never treated Infinity except to submit to it."[23]

One might expect Levinas to accept this sort of conclusion, were it not for the fact that it promotes a distinct affective stance—submission—at the locus of our relation with Infinity, and affectivity, he is convinced, is only a nascent and clouded form of activity. The roots of this argument are recognizably anti-Heideggerian, though the argument itself reaches much farther. Heidegger appeals to affect (*Stimmung*, *Befindlichkeit*) in the course of a defense of the primacy of ontology. Affect is still in solidarity with appearing; what affects us is already crudely possessed by the affection, whether it is anxiety, boredom, or wonder. Levinas's first move against this has been his case for an affect, horror, that diminishes the very subjectivity of the subject until possession of any kind, not least of which is *self*-possession, is on the verge of collapse. His second move, prepared in the texts that finally yield *Totality and Infinity*, is a claim that the subjectivity of the subject is radically passive in its relation with the other person, and that this relation is prior to any form of act. Among the preparatory texts, some provide clarifications that one might wish were also present in the great book. In a number of unpublished notes, Levinas concedes that social order, and specifically shared social values, do require a positive valorization of the affects by which we invest in them. Without these affects, the values in question are only abstract representations, and so there is vital reason to provide a place for—and even cultivate—respect, gratitude, sympathy (*la pitié*), shame (*la pudeur*), gratitude, and a certain kind of love ("life of peace").[24] Of these, the passage on respect is most indicative of his general position: "Respect—perception of the person. What is essential is the mystery that is presupposed by respect." In *Totality and Infinity*, this sharpens into the view that respect attends to an otherness that is radical and self-revelatory.[25] It is true that affects bind us to social values, but for Levinas their relation informs what he sometimes calls justice, in which allowances are made for other others and thus community. In an important sense, his argument for ethics as first philosophy takes the form of establishing an ethical relation that is anterior to any such justice.

Levinas's resistance to an affective relation to Infinity starts out according to much the same reasoning. The affective response has already projected an understanding of the interlocutor, and, let us not forget it, therefore according to an exercise of its own powers. In the special case of Infinity, to which the finite subject would "submit" its full self, this poses a unique danger. To approach what is wholly other without the exterior support is to risk a fall into blind participation or even fusion. Under such conditions, the relation with transcendence has dissolved into a rush of immanence, and the subject has given up the dignity of its own freedom. This critique, as it happens, is applied to any number of phenomena otherwise widely thought to belong rightly to religion. There is, to begin with, the so-called "primitive mentality" described in studies by Lucien Lévy-Bruhl that were known to Levinas, but also prayers of the heart, liturgy, mysticism, and any number of devotional practices in which emotion plays an important role. Here again, a single example will suffice to convey the general perspective. "The ethical relation," Levinas writes, "the face to face, also cuts across every relation one could call mystical, where events other than that of the presentation of the original being come to overwhelm or sublimate the pure sincerity of this presentation, where intoxicating equivocations come to enrich the primordial univocity of expression, where discourse becomes incantation as prayer becomes rite and liturgy, where the interlocutors find themselves playing a role in a drama that has begun outside of them."[26] As for the modern European context, Levinas voices a warning that any attempt to move religion from representations and concepts instead to affects risks a return to the "primitive" condition.[27] Against this, he contends that it is precisely representation, with its lucid presentation of a world of objects present to the subject, that closes us sufficiently into ourselves to be truly separated from the wholly other, whereupon it may reveal itself on its own initiative from beyond our comprehension. In other words, it is above all our trust in representation that accomplishes—settles, as if convincingly, for a free being—a relation in which the finite subject is properly a finite subject and in which we may still conceive an Infinity that preserves its transcendence over every negation and analogy.

This, of course, means that the finite subject is not as such capable of sustaining an adequate relation with Infinity. Absorbed in its own concerns and the relative successes it usually has in pursuing them— spontaneously atheistic, according to the startling definition appearing in *Totality and Infinity*—the finite subject can only await, or be taken by surprise by, the sheer disruption wrought by the face of the other person in order to awaken to the Infinity that positively exceeds it. Yet even then the proper relation with Infinity cannot be direct, since that would reinstate the pretense of comprehension. There can be no arrival of Infinity, no satisfaction of any desire that seeks it. Only the face of the other can ground the movement of a subject who is otherwise itinerant, and focus the desire that motivates it. And this is crucial: the face that calls for help is a face that asks us to put aside our own interests in favor of something higher and better, thus opening a way to what deserves to be called Good. If it is only through our encounter with the human face, putting our freedom in question, that we become aware of our relation with Infinity, a dimension wholly beyond need and comprehension, then it is also only in our response to that face that our desire might be said to move from all that is finite, within reach, toward Infinity. Hence, the close relation between ethics and religion that is so distinctive of Levinas's thinking proves finally to be a matter of thinking *responsibility* for the other person in terms of a *desire* that is literally "meta-physical." The face of the other person is a trace of Infinity—in more familiar terms, it points obliquely to the God who has always already withdrawn from any retrieval into what is present, here and now, to the subject. The desire that would put that person's concerns before one's own is immediately a desire that aims beyond the conditions of our finite existence.

Desire and Excess

Such a desire for "something else entirely," for the "absolutely other," is in fact the first great theme of *Totality and Infinity*. According to Levinas, "the customary analysis of desire" traces it back to a prior loss or fall. This does not explain what he calls the "singular pretension" of a craving for positive excess, a desire that goes beyond wanting only to fill a lack all the way to wanting more than the one who desires could ever hold.[28] Let us note immediately that unless this desire is secured before and outside our relation to the world, its movement must have the character of a flight from the world. Whether or not this complication is fully met by the existential approach to desire taken in an early passage that held our brief attention, in *Totality and Infinity* there is a concerted effort to describe a desire that does move within the world yet cannot be accounted for solely in its terms. On this point, the fact that this desire would find its essential expression in care for the other person—motivated by a desire for the good that exceeds goods that are for me—changes nothing at all. "Metaphysical desire," expressed in a commitment to absolute responsibility, appears *in* the world but is not wholly *of* the world. It is already otherwise than anything that submits to the logic and limits of the world, even as it nonetheless moves in it and through the world.

This claim is evidently fundamental, and so one immediately anticipates that it will open the way to other important determinations. Restricting ourselves to only one of these, we may take note of the pressure that is put on the means to generate a positive account of the natural world, specifically as good in itself. Neither the remarkable solidarity proposed for Infinity and plurality nor the drama of a self-concerned subject awakened by the face of the other person seem to require it. And when Levinas is closest to applying himself to some such sense of the natural world, he defines it as the source of nourishment, first for the life of the subject and then, in the work of goodness, for the needs of the other person. His most concise formulation of this claim is unforgettable: responsibility for the other person commands that I make a gift of the very bread that is in my mouth.[29] Yet for all that, he does not think that the natural world is reducible to material that should be known and then consumed, such as Bacon, with equal claim on our memories, implies in his observation that nature yields its secrets more readily under "vexation" than on its own.[30] For Levinas, we have seen, our relation with what in his lexicon might best pass for nature, the elements, is more intimate than that of the scientist or consumer with raw material. Already before we might understand this relation and take it in, we live from it, and this without any question of choice or achievement. It is essentially this primal nourishment and the primal "bread" which it entails that must be given up to the other person (though this is not at all to say that one is dispensed from making a gift of real bread). The full implications of this are drawn in *Otherwise Than Being, or Beyond Essence*: responsibility for the other person goes all the way to conversion of one's very existence, from being for oneself into being one for the other, as the necessary cost of the goodness of the good.[31]

It is good, then, in this profound sense, that the natural world sustains ethical beings, and even better that it may enter the service of acts of justice and love. But would that same natural world also be good before and apart from this? Might it, too, and in its own way, bespeak the divine? A classical tradition has always thought so, most prominently in order to understand the experience of an entire cosmos emanating from or created in divine love. For a long time, that tradition took it for granted (which does mean that it failed to think about it) that our definition of human nature should be sought within the frame of a wider sense of nature as a whole, and that what is good for human beings is consistent with a more general good for that whole. Levinas's silence on this idea and his tendency to reserve the language of goodness strictly for human activity put him at some distance from that other tradition, which includes of course Aristotle and Aquinas. As for the medievals, they considered the natural world good in itself not only as the work of a Creator God, but also insofar as it is capable of welcoming the revealed Word without immediately muting it. From that perspective, and for reasons that evidently run quite deep, Levinas may appear surprisingly close to the modern perspective from which the natural world is at best "amoral."[32] After all, a considerable portion of modern thought takes it for granted that the world is indifferent to our moral endeavors. Still, this is far from declaring that Levinas is therefore simply a modern thinker. Instead, there is more reason to recognize a modern sympathy in his thinking only where, or to the degree that, his conception of the ethical and religious is defined without foundation in nature or the cosmos. Moreover, if there are difficulties or impoverishments in such a position, they would hardly be unique to Levinas. Environmental philosophers have not ceased to react to many of them, but they have done so according to commitments regarding nature, humanity, and animality that are bound to appear derivative to those who are instead committed to the anarchic priority of the relation with the other person.[33] If perhaps it is not yet clear what it will mean for ethics, and with it religion, for us to have a diminished capacity to think of the natural world as good in its own right, it may at least be said of the philosophy of Levinas that it provides one unflinching answer.

This is not without important consequence for Levinas's own claims about the ethical relation. We should not forget that the notion that the natural world and perhaps natural things might have a goodness properly their own supports the idea that they also have a revelatory function properly their own. One thinks, for example, of Augustine led, throughout the *Confessions*, by his experience of the beauty of the world toward thoughts of the immeasurably greater beauty of its source. In another vein, it may be said that forms or degrees of good cannot be alien from one another, and that experience of natural goodness prompts at least an intimation of the supreme Good.[34] Suspending all of this necessarily strengthens the association of religion and the ethical relation already prepared in Levinas's account of the subject as innately self-centered. In short, after that account has required us to think that the subject does not have access by its own powers to Infinity, so that the relation can be activated only by a revelation that would come from beyond the range of any such powers, the absence of thought that the natural world is good in itself seems to rule out one possible occasion for that kind of revelation. And so, according to Levinas's philosophical works, we may be awakened to Infinity *only* in and through the human face; and our desire for intimacy with Infinity, which in Levinas's Cartesian moments passes for God, *must* be expressed in acts that put the other person before oneself. Everything else is one or another form of idolatry or paganism in religion, and egocentrism in ethics.

All of this returns us to the theme of "metaphysical desire" with a clear and pressing question: Why must the desire for Infinity, religious desire—exclusively, by all appearances—take the form of care for the other person? Let us approach this question in its full context. We already know that (1) the infinity of the infinite ensures that human plurality is defined by separation, and that (2) according to the structure of separation, everything the subject is and does presupposes and in that specific sense *responds to* the maximal nearness of the other. We also know that (3) the face of the other person awakens the subject from a spontaneous tendency to self-centeredness, giving rise to the possibility of a concrete moral response (again, bearing in mind that radical responsibility is antecedent to ordered morality). Finally, we know that (4) the exceptional idea of Infinity, as the opening of consciousness to what no consciousness could ever contain, in fact leaves us susceptible to that awakening by the face of the other person. After all, were there no such anterior condition, the face of the other, if it truly expresses an otherness that is absolute, could only shatter the subject. When on occasion Levinas takes steps to associate responsibility with "anamnesis,"[35] he means not only that the subject is called back to its forgotten truth but also that its soul, as it were, is turned outside in.

We are thus given ample reason to think that Infinity is in fact integral to the human drama: in an important sense, it is *due to* the relation with Infinity, before and outside the cycle of one's relation with the world and oneself, that the face of the other does not merely obstruct or challenge, as Sartre thinks, but puts one's entire being in question. More deeply, and in another register, it is *due to* the relation with Infinity that already before the moment of that encounter, as the condition by which we undergo it, our being is already insecure.[36] That said, Levinas is constantly on his guard against any confusion of this involvement with the active behavior of anthropomorphic gods. *Otherwise Than Being, or*

67

Beyond Essence does admit of the "illeity"—the he-ness—of the constitutive withdrawal of Infinity from any finite grasp, by which each of us is left in separated relation to the other, but not without also insisting that this occurs without "[entering] into a theme like a being" or presenting itself as an "alleged interlocutor."[37] Levinas's long essay entitled "God and Philosophy" is more concise about this relation, in which Infinity is thought to make a difference without an appeal to the anthropomorphism of willing. The engagement of Infinity in the finite, by which each subject is ordered to the other in the relation that Levinas calls "ethical," is generated in the non-indifference of what orders or conditions without causation.[38] It is in agreement with the non-indifference of Infinity to the finite that the plot of our relation is rooted more deeply than in any contiguity, in the responsibility of all creatures.

All of this should dispel any suspicion that Levinas's claim that desire for Infinity, or God, must take the form of response to the other person is therefore straightforwardly a reduction of religion to ethics. A better understanding of this claim would conclude rather that Infinity, positively engaged with the finite, *prepares the way* for the awakening that occurs only when the other person faces us—and that the response to his or her face is at the same time, though not synonymously, a response to Infinity. Put otherwise, Infinity is always already "present" in consciousness, like a hollowing out that goes unrealized until the face of the other causes it to resonate, or a heteronomy to which the subject is awakened by the face and which it can choose against complacency with itself.[39] What, then, will be the religious character of the subject's response to this shock? It will be either a return to the sphere of immanence defined by self-interest, or a movement toward what is unlimited and Good defined by what Levinas calls, in contrast, the "dis-interest" of responsibility to and for the other person—the disinterest of one who no longer approaches the other according to an interest first and foremost in himself or herself, and yet for all of that is not simply uninterested. Here at last is the point at which to correctly understand "metaphysical desire." Evidently, it will be a desire without possession, without satisfaction, and without the fulfillment that they would bring—a "desire without concupiscence,"[40] as Levinas puts it. In the same line, it will also be a desire that aims at what can only be, but at the highest elevation, undesirable in any other sense.[41]

Ethical Metaphysics

Would this exorbitant desire, too, be rooted in the infinity of the infinite, which, after all, is always already present in the subject? We have just found reason to reverse the order of the question: Would Infinity itself somehow prepare the way not only for the shock of the face but also for the awakening of desire for the good—would Infinity somehow stimulate what Levinas calls "metaphysical desire"? The word "stimulate" is admitted here deliberately, since it comes readily to mind but misses Levinas's position. Let us dispense with it. The desire that is stimulated is a desire that is precipitated or even caused by some indication of lack, whether internal or external. In the context of interpreting the subject's relation with Infinity, this would imply some action on the part of the latter, and with that some version of what Levinas wishes to reject in ontotheology: Infinity will have moved to elicit our desire. His own language is cast in part to maintain distance specifically from that. Metaphysical desire arises and moves according to an originary inspiration in the subject:[42] "originary" because the relation with Infinity involves conditions that antedate any that are grounded in lived time, and "inspiration" because the evidence for this relation is found in a movement, or a dynamism, that endows us with a potential that cannot be explained solely in terms of our being in the world.

If we recognize here the deepest penetration of existential analysis, we are prepared for the thought that this entire account begins from the event of interpersonal encounter. A case for metaphysical desire is made beginning from the claim that the face of the other person shocks and astonishes the separated subject.[43] As Levinas's terminology often indicates, this is initially and necessarily painful. The pain in question is existential. One is disrupted in the train of one's effort of existing, and thus also disoriented. Perhaps it would be going too far to say that what has been lost, momentarily, is trust in the world—Levinas gives no reason to think that the subject's world is ever quite stable—but then it is at least the presumption of a direction and momentum that are disrupted. This pain is thus registered as an assault on the egocentrism of a movement that does not call itself into question. The movement itself and with it the world that it ceaselessly projects now appear false, and this must resonate all the way into the profound vulnerability that is, as it were, prepared by the relation with Infinity. It goes without saying that the subject's response to this will consist in one or another attempt to recover. We do not need Levinas to anticipate two general forms that this may take. Some of us, or perhaps all of us some of the time, retreat back into the way of being which has just been exposed, if only we were to see it, as pretentious. This can be relatively innocent, as when one spontaneously recoils. It can also be self-indulgent, as when one neglects to take the matter seriously. And it can be violent, as when one actively rejects any implication of the encounter—sometimes with clear insight into its meaning. Yet we may also move away from that prior way of being, and forward to the positive implications of the face of the other, striving to make what it calls for the focus and ground of our own subjectivity. If with regard to this latter instance, we wish to understand its motivation, we are on the verge of conceiving metaphysical desire. To be open to Infinity prior to any possible recuperation in memory—prior to a recovery into the present—is to be vulnerable in the depths of one's being, so that one is always susceptible to the shock that is the face of the other person. There awakens in this shock a movement that puts aside self-interest and the goods that it would seek in favor of a desire that does not answer to interest and is not contained within the world. This desire is evidently self-emptying, and it issues in acts of responsibility. Such is our creatureliness as ethical and religious subjects.

In order to draw out the close relation of this desire to Infinity, and to register it, we may appeal to what Levinas sometimes refers to it as "infinition." In *Totality and Infinity*, this term is meant to capture the possibility of freedom from the endless negation of "there is" in which the existent maintains itself as itself; in contrast, by the relation with Infinity, revealed in and through the face of the other, the subject is no longer fated to choose itself over and over again, but may now transcend itself in a movement that is eschatological, since it is no longer limited only to its relation with existence.[44] In *Otherwise Than Being*, the term "infinition" refers to the inordinate and inexhaustible character of a responsibility in which each gift of oneself only leads deeper, as the other still in need calls for a renewal and even a redoubling of one's commitment that is the very coming to light of the good. This responsibility that is insatiable is testament to a goodness that exceeds the limits of our every act.[45] Both uses of the term "infinition" are recognizably congruent with Levinas's conception of metaphysical desire. The desire by which the subject puts the other person's interest before its own must appear as a positive disinterest that leads away from all limits imposed by the relation with existence. To thus transcend oneself in responsibility for the other is to work at correcting the "diminution" entailed in what Levinas has called "the creative contraction of Infinity." To care for the other, he concludes, is to contribute to the work of redemption.[46]

Levinas's conception of metaphysical desire supports the idea that our movement toward God, or Infinity, occurs only in responsibility for the other person, even more strongly than does the absence in his philosophy of a means to think that this might occur in our relation to nature or natural things. This still does not reduce ethics to religion, since the other person certainly is not God, but it does seem to ethicize religious desire. We have already seen the implications of these claims for moral reflection in Levinas's own claim that the relation with the other person must be driven by a "desire outside concupiscence." In plain terms, ethics is therefore to be opposed to, and must try to do without, an erotics, in the modern sense of this last term.[47] One should endeavor to love the other person beyond every attachment to him and her, and without the influence or guidance of any prior attachment.[48] Or rather, one must strive for a love that would perfect itself in doing away with all attachments, which is to say doing away with all prior erotic investments, and which would aim at something quite different than a love that simply includes more than what belongs to any attachment. It is not for nothing that *Totality and Infinity* proposes a "Phenomenology of Eros" in which Levinas attempts to admit the experience and nature of sexuality fully into his account of human relations—only to submit them to the ethical relation that must have unqualified priority. For Levinas, the desire that possesses and attaches is a dangerous possibility circulating within the desire that empties and transcends. Yet at its noblest, it nonetheless supports and confirms the movement of genuine transcendence. It is the "fecundity" that he considers proper to sexual desire to bring into existence a new other.[49]

Whatever one makes of this, there is no mistaking the fact that it further secures Levinasian ethics in a distinctive philosophy of religion. Enough has been understood about the relevant features of the position taken in *Totality and Infinity* for it to be clear that both Levinas's assimilation of desire for God to the dis-interested desire to serve the other person and his strong insistence on distinguishing that desire from what occurs according to investment in erotic attachment must be traced to a conception of Infinity that withdraws it from any possible representation or comprehension.[50] All of this suggests the following summary formulation: for Levinas, it is because Infinity is present in consciousness only as the trace of its withdrawal from consciousness, that the desire by which a finite subject moves toward Infinity can only take the form of a dis-interested responsibility for the other person. Or else, if one insists, these two claims support and confirm one another. In them, we recognize a new meditation on the ancient meaning of the words "absolute" and "religion"—that which absolves itself from the relation, and that by which the relation is established nonetheless. For Levinas, this is how to understand ethics.

This does give rise to some reservation, and perhaps some debate. If one hesitates at the severity of Levinas's theses on desire—if, for instance, the notion of a desire without attachment or one ideally unmixed with erotic investment seems to ask too much or to proceed from a mistaken description of the things themselves, and if one therefore wishes to propose a more moderate position on the matter of desire—

then, given what we know about the overall nature of the argument, one should be prepared to also ask whether his philosophy does not accord, if the expression may be tolerated, *too much transcendence* to the other that is called Infinity and sometimes God. Such a question strikes with some brutality when it reaches the metaphysical register, where it calls for a more moderate conception of divine transcendence that somehow would not, for all of that, fall into idolatry. The metaphysical problem puts Levinasian ethics in discussion with Christian theology, which will argue that the appearing of God as Christ is not therefore a submission of divine transcendence to the limitations of finite experience and under-standing. The figure of Christ defies comprehension by always exceeding what it nonetheless gives of itself to us. In this way, it both expresses and preserves the transcendence of God. Is it certain that what infinitely and endlessly surpasses us is greater than what withdraws behind a single and inexhaustible revelation? We will leave the question in suspense until we have found our way into *Otherwise Than Being, or Beyond Essence,* a work in which the particular use of theological terminology is both new in its abundance and quite consistent in its intention.[51]

4

The Ethics of Desire: Levinas and Psychoanalysis

It is commonplace in philosophy, certainly since Hegel, to distinguish between desire and organic need. Without ceasing to have vital needs, the subject in its self-consciousness responds to its own lack of self-sufficiency by laboring to fill it. This is desire. Desire is not need insofar as it is an effect of self-consciousness and moves within self-consciousness; or rather, it is the very movement of self-consciousness. Desire moves us to either cross out or take into ourselves all that is not us, as if toward the perfect satiety of being without limit. Of course, for finite beings there can be no such satiety, as is confirmed by the simple fact that the movement of our being does not end except in death. Until death, according to the condition of our mortality, the objects available to desire fall short of the fullness that it seeks.

Levinas's conception of desire appears to be consistent with this definition, appealing to it already in his account of living from the elements—*until* one sees that he holds open the possibility of a fullness that approaches from beyond our finitude. When he contends, tirelessly, that the face of the other person expresses an otherness that is superabundant and excessive, and when he argues that this is the very approach of the good, he places before us a claim that although we cannot reach what we desire strictly by our own efforts, and indeed cannot even see it coming, this does not rule out a real and positive relation with it. What does this mean? We have already ruled out any identification of the other person strictly and simply with the good. Levinas argues only that one seeks the good in and through caring for one's neighbor, and that desire for the good is what motivates the caring. This way of distinguishing the other person from the good without fully opposing the two leaves room for us to recognize the other person's uniqueness without making it an impediment to desire. The subject desires the good as it approaches in the face of the other person. In its immediacy, their relation is between only the subject and the other. At the same time, but according to a deeper condition, it also involves a goodness that does not fully enter there.

The association of desire with a movement toward perfect satiety, the thought that it is awakened or at any rate galvanized by the presence of an other person, and the attempt to understand moral life as a question of the difference between what we truly want and what we owe one another, do not belong only to the thought of Levinas, and not even within the intellectual milieu in which it takes shape. They have also been developed, though with opposed results, by the Freudians, especially Lacan and his school. Their appearance in ethical metaphysics thus calls for a discussion with psychoanalysis which, by all appearances, Levinas himself saw little reason to undertake.[1]

The "Enticement to Paganism"

Levinas was hardly unaware of psychoanalysis, even if he never goes deeply into it. In his philosophical works there is the occasional explicit mention of Freud, psychoanalysis, and what most will agree are the central concepts of psychoanalytic work: the Oedipus complex, the unconscious, and repression. Levinas's most specific characterizations of psychoanalysis register two kinds of complaints. The first one is hardly surprising. Psychoanalysis poses the question of our humanity in terms of an impossible or inconclusive understanding of one another and thus presents us with the failure of all previous anthropologies, when in fact none of that is necessary for a relation that is defined by immediate and radical responsibility for the other person.[2] The second complaint, which is considerably more interesting, hints at themes still to be explored in the present study. For Levinas, unless we begin from the face of the other capable of grounding the freedom of a subject who in this way puts to rest what is otherwise a ceaseless effort to establish itself, we are without the possibility of genuine language, considered as an authentic "exchange of ideas about the world" and not merely as the field of competing claims about meaning and value. In refusing such a ground—and even suggesting that the very idea of it is fantasy—psychoanalysis seems to willingly embrace the abyss of meaning that opens up when responsibility and language do not commence in the "originality of the face."[3]

Freud calls this "abyss of meaning" the unconscious, imagining it as a reservoir of unbearable wishes kept from any form of consciousness. Levinas's references to the unconscious, or at any rate his uses of that word, are uneven. Leaving aside the small number of occasions in which he clearly has in mind suppression, in the sense only of exclusion or setting aside, there is still an important difference between passages in which "unconscious" is only diminishment of consciousness and others that do accurately present Freud's own meaning. In *Existence and Existents*, the former sense of "unconsciousness" (the very expression is telling) is used in the context of working out an account of the subject's coming into place, which we have had occasion to characterize as a phenomenology of birth. Prior to attention and wakefulness, as their condition, is an establishment of oneself as oneself in the here and now, according to what we have understood as Levinas's conception of the effort of existing.[4] Sleep, which does not go all the way to death or dissolution, is a relaxation of this effort and a reprieve from fatigue. Levinas thus writes of the unconsciousness that belongs to sleep (but which is evidently not that of dreams) that it is "participation in life by non-participation, by the elementary act of resting."[5]

In another passage in the same book, Levinas does come much closer to the Freudian conception. He writes at length:

> Since the discovery of the unconscious—and this contradiction in terms is evidence of a considerable intellectual upheaval—philosophy has been conceiving of the unconscious as another consciousness, failing to recognize the ontological function of the unconscious and its specific relationship with conscious clarity, with sincerity, which separates itself from the obscurity, depth, and ambiguity of the unconscious. The unconscious is interpreted in terms of consciousness, or the reverse. The unconscious appears as a possible, a germ, or as something repressed. In fact, the implicitness referred to in speaking of implicit cognition no longer presents the structure of cognition; the essential event of the world, which is intention and light, no longer means anything here. Consciousness is precisely a sincerity. In taking being-in-the-world as an intention one is above all affirming—and the history of our civilization and our philosophy confirms this—that the world is the field of a consciousness, and the peculiar structure that characterizes consciousness governs and gives meaning to all the infiltrations of the unconscious in the world. It is "before" the world comes about that the unconscious plays its role.[6]

Whether or not Levinas himself thinks that psychoanalysis, and not only philosophy, understands the unconscious as "another consciousness," he wishes to emphasize a sense in which it is cut off from and outside of the field in which consciousness has sway. To a considerable degree, the position that he takes is still in agreement with that of Heidegger in *Being and Time*, where the commitment of phenomenology to light and appearance means that everything antecedent to care and the world that it projects is considered inadmissible or perhaps irrelevant to the analysis of Dasein.[7] It is in a similar vein that Levinas distinguishes the clear, structured, and sincere nature of being in the world from an unconscious that is obscure, ambiguous, and apparently—though there does not seem to be a moral implication in this[8]—insincere. From this perspective, the unconscious appears to circulate without evident continuity with cognition, and before the "coming about" of the world in which, let us not forget, the drama of separation and the approach of the other occur.

The passage also raises the matter of repression, without which what Freudians mean by "the unconscious" is unintelligible. Here, though at the risk of overworking a brief remark, we may agree that Levinas's explicit point is only that the unconscious at most appears *in nuce*, that is, in a condensed and undeveloped or unfolded form. But for Freud, the unconscious never appears except in the form of symptoms, and a symptom is always a complex mix of repressed wish, the contrary wish to repress it, and various residues and collateral material brought to the service of one or the other. Similar reservations may arise in response to Levinas's earlier, related claim that consciousness "separates itself" from the unconscious. One might prefer to say that consciousness is kept free of the unconscious by repression, but then the close reader of Freud will insist that a considerable portion of the repressing is itself unconscious.[9] As it happens, the remark would go a long way toward accounting for the fact that we are genuinely startled when a symptom is brought to our attention: one has been unaware of both the original wish and the opposed one that has kept it out of sight. If the entire complex of repressed and repressing is unconscious, then strictly speaking consciousness is separated from the unconscious due in no small part to work conducted in the unconscious.

Having said all of this, it would be going too far to conclude that Levinas, for his part, attributes to our subjectivity a capacity to turn itself away from the grips of the unconscious, as if consciousness were deployed by the exercise of some power. His claim about consciousness is situated instead at the level of spontaneity, where the sensibility in which we receive the elements reverts into the activity of sensation. And so, it is a matter first of all of the primordial conditions of our subjectivity as such, before any question of its possible feats. When in *Totality and Infinity* Levinas again takes up the theme of the Freudian unconscious, it is still with this in mind.[10] Noting that there is no shortage of claims for an ulterior influence on what we experience as ego or strive to establish as identity, he would have us consider the strange possibility that Paul Valéry proposes with the character Monsieur Teste, in his novel by that name (Anglophone readers may think more readily of Melville's Bartleby). Teste wants to be nothing other than himself, in all of his inner complexity, and thus from a perspective capable of recognizing and accepting it without simplification or suppression. Or better, the will to be only what he is has the effect of drawing together all of what he is into a dynamic unity. In this way, the "absolute I" of Teste—its possibility as an idea and perhaps as an experience—warns against the thought, defended in different ways from Socrates to Freud, that since we are made up of parts or functions that are irreducible to one another, our subjectivity is without the solidity that Levinas, for his part, finds at the heart of what he calls "separation." The absolute "I" would represent only a final, willed agreement with a possibility that is operative already in the spontaneous movement of the existent. Whatever our inner conflicts, we draw ourselves together in the unity of our effort to be.

This much informs Levinas's rare negation of the word "consciousness" in order to define some of his own claims. "Proximity, obsession, and subjectivity as we have expressed them are not reducible to phenomena of consciousness. But their non-consciousness [non-conscience], instead of giving evidence of a pre-conscious stage or a repression which would oppress them, is one with their exception from totality, that is, their refusal of manifestation."[11] In *Otherwise Than Being, or Beyond Essence*, "proximity" and "obsession" designate the immeasurable nearness of the other person who is already there before one catches sight of him or her, and the sense in which this grounds a claim that returns to place new demands on everything that one may say or do in response. Consciousness, in which the data of experience come to light and receive meaning for a subject, necessarily operates after the fact of proximity and obsession. However, it does not therefore repress those data, in the Freudian sense of expelling them, so much as it simply turns from them, until we are called back to them (the face, we have already noted, enacts recollection, to conditions only temporarily forgotten). As for what returns, or perhaps resurfaces, there can be no doubt that it does so without submitting to the distortions that Freudians recognize in the symptoms by which an unbearable wish is both present and not-present. Separation is not a symptom, and the face of the other person is not a psychoanalysis. The face that is immediate is a face without conflict or distortion.

Let us recognize what these terminological equivocations represent in the argument. When Levinas is closest to an agreeable representation of the Freudian conceptions of the unconscious and repression, he takes care to suggest that the psychological realities that they express are a matter of indifference for phenomenological accounts of subjectivity and responsibility. When he is willing to use a word like "non-consciousness" in the service of defining the concepts that do capture the necessary field for phenomenological work, he has in mind a sense in which they only antedate and transcend the movement of consciousness. Concepts like "proximity" and "obsession" belong to an understanding of the subject as related to the other person before and beyond consciousness, which is also to say, before and beyond the appearing that is always appearing *to* the subject. These claims run quite deep. We have only to recall that for Levinas, appearing is always submission to the gaze of a subject who is by nature inclined to situate any single thing it sees in relation to all else that it sees, and to grasp them as a sum, in order to then understand that it is one and the same thing to claim that what is "non-conscious" refuses manifestation and to claim that what is "non-conscious" refuses totalization. It is in a positive sense that the structures of plurality are "non-conscious."

From this perspective, the Freudian concept of repression must appear to Levinas only to designate an exclusion internal to the overall life of the subject, as if it were essentially a complex feature of one's relation with oneself. One might then expect that it is convergent with what he understands as totalization. We should not accept this claim without asking what the repression serves. A wish to avoid the unbearable, yes, but then *by what measure or principle* would this or that impulse receive that judgment? The question always had considerable force for Freud himself, because it was clear to him from the beginning of his work with the mentally ill that what is repressed sometimes turns out to seem, at least when considered in the circumstances, entirely unremarkable and even commonplace. Under these circumstances, there is no avoiding the hypothesis that "unbearable" in fact means "unacceptable," and according to some rule or law that the subject has integrated—and indeed, clearly on his or her own terms. One wants not to have wanted this or felt that. Accepting that one nonetheless did so would amount to being a somewhat different person than one would like. Certain wishes, should they ever appear, would be evidence of a failure to satisfy this law, and of an identity that one is eager to overcome or perhaps deny. Hence there is repression, and it has an immediate moral significance.

This, *grosso modo*, is the way to what some of Freud's texts call "the Oedipus complex."[12] Without going further into its precise status within the theoretical articulation of Freudian thought,[13] we may immediately note, by way of serious concession to Levinas, that in Freud's Oedipus complex we find the suggestion of a law that would be universal in its occurrence. To be sure, when Freud applied himself to the Oedipus complex, it was soon enough apparent to him that what he had worked out for male experience would have to be significantly adjusted for a plausible account of female experience, but this led him only to postulate a "negative Oedipus complex" and a "feminine Oedipus attitude."[14] And by a similar insistence, the history of psychoanalytic thought is replete with attempts to confirm the presence of some corresponding instance in cultures that are not even patrilineal. What Freud encountered in a patrilineal culture imbued with patriarchal norms and values, psychoanalysis has had to think is in fact only one instance of a general symbolic function.

This does not mean that the idea of a complex—a set of relations, in this case centered on the imposition of a law—leaves no room to recognize the particularity of each subject's relation to it. On the contrary, psychoanalytic therapy takes aim at precisely this when it poses the question of desire, which is always a question of the patient's *own* desire, and in turn of his or her *own* relation to the law that is felt to rule over it. And yet, everything does proceed in a manner that necessarily considers the particular nature of the patient's desire—its definition, or specific character—to be shaped by its relation to some experience of lack and of law. In Freud's eyes, none of us is without a relation to the law to which we feel answerable, and none of us is free of at least some difficulty accommodating the desire that is at odds with it. This is the source of a patient's complaint, and the focal point of therapeutic work. That work necessarily attempts to loosen repressed conflict. It does so in the form of negotiating the effects of a law that was imposed from the outside, though the patient does not and could not know this in any other way than through the particular manner in which he or she has happened to understand it and take it in.

This is enough for Levinas. From his perspective, recourse to a single and recurrent principle that would be inscribed in each member of a group or community, however differently in each case, is in fact tantamount to totalization. However varied in their psychical makeups and in their complaints, all of Freud's patients, and more generally every human being as seen with Freudian eyes, would in the final account be distinct expressions of the same defining principles. Perhaps more seriously, to the degree that psychoanalytic work suggests anything about moral life—and we will have to return to this[15]—it will proceed from original reference to one's own desire and, as we have just seen, one's own relation to the law. This certainly does not lead straightaway to moral determinism, but it does imply that one's freedom will always be limited to what that law and that desire will permit. More concisely, it implies that the exercise of freedom is first and always defined from within. For his part, Levinas cannot be content to leave the matter there. True freedom, he contends, is born in and through the face of the other, by which one is no longer bound to an existential destiny (genetic, historical) but is now given an ethical vocation. But this requires a law that arrives from beyond our existence, and beyond the sameness of the same where there would be only the inner differentiation of an immanence that closes itself from transcendence.

As for Levinas's assessment of the religious significance of Freudian psychoanalysis, he has said very little, though we can be sure that from his perspective, any complications for plurality will necessarily imply others for infinity. To this it should be added that he has on occasion hinted that there is a particular reason to be wary of the manner in which psychoanalysis interrupts our relation to both of them at once. Freudian theory exercises considerable charm, and even a fascination on those who become familiar with it, and can give the impression of explaining all of life's peril and promise in terms of things as fundamentally subjective as pleasure, reality, wish, and conflict. As Levinas sees it, whatever its promise in the domain of mental health—and on this, he seems to have been largely silent—as a philosophy, it is therefore an "enticement to paganism."[16]

The Therapeutic Relation

If we suspend the discussion with psychoanalysis on this final word from Levinas, we fail to learn from its essential challenge. This challenge is met most directly in an approach to subjectivity that asks with unmatched persistence about the inner motive by which we accept and live by a particular conception of what is desirable and good. Of course, we can be sure that Levinas will regard the entire question of motive with considerable suspicion, since it seems to frame the definitions at stake within the limits of a self-interested and solitary subject. His objection would of course be made in the service of upholding the possibility of a desire that is "metaphysical" and "dis-interested," and with it a supreme good that would exceed the mere satisfaction of mere interest. And yet, as sharp as this difference seems to be, more can be said about it, since the phenomenon of a desire that runs contrary to interest and the notion of a good that transcends its reach are not alien to psychoanalysis any more than is a distinction between the otherness of the other person who faces me here and now and the otherness of another other who does not.[17] The Freudian understanding of these various matters is most accessible in the therapy itself, which in any case is also the proper ground and source for an adequate understanding of his concepts. Let us therefore review the relevant features of the analytic setting, before engaging Levinas.

In its classical form, Freudian psychotherapy engages the analysand's desire immediately. When the would-be analysand asks for the help that is to be gotten in therapy, this is already an expression of lack and of a wish to somehow address it. It is therefore also the beginning of a trust in the expertise and authority of the analyst that will be necessary in order to undertake the work to be done. Yet the specific nature of desire is generally not stated, at least not in what later proves to be its authentic meaning, because for a long time the analysand himself or herself sees it only poorly or even not at all. This, of course, stands to reason, since the effort to get at one's conflicts must proceed from within the field that they dominate. At the same time, the specific meaning of the authority of the analyst also emerges only slowly because, again and for the same reason, the analysand does not know what it is. Lacan captures the matter well when he refers to the analyst as the "*sujet-supposé-savoir*": the therapist is a subject assumed by the analysand to know something important—the key or necessary plan for the satisfaction of his or her desire for health and happiness—but in the course of the therapy there prove to be any number of versions of what this knowledge might be (and in fact, the process of shedding them in turn makes up one thread that runs through the therapy).[18] This supposition belongs to what psychoanalysts call "transference." Without it, the therapy cannot proceed. The patient transfers onto the analyst an identity and an understanding that he or she—the patient—needs to trust, or perhaps lean on, in order to conduct the arduous and often frightening work of uncovering wishes that are, to repeat an earlier term, unbearable. To be clear, both the transference and the desire itself are unconscious. It is the remarkable achievement of Freud to have developed a therapeutic setting in which a patient's relationship with his or her therapist takes a form that makes it possible to engage the repression that stands in the way of recognizing and perhaps loosening a conflict that has made life unmanageable.

It is needless to say that this is no easy process. Most evidently, there is a great deal of confusion and self-delusion to work through. There is also the fact that it soon enough becomes clear that at least some analysands are content to settle into therapy even as their interest in the work itself appears to decline after an initial problem is dissolved. Freud recognizes these complications early on, pausing in an important case history to warn against placing much credence in the analysand's specific formulation of his or her complaint.[19] On one hand, this is simply a gesture toward the reality of the unconscious: the formulation is almost certainly distorted. On the other hand, it also anticipates the more serious and deeper-reaching phenomenon of actual resistance to a positive conclusion of the analysis—and indeed, precisely as the way to healing and happiness comes into view. If lethargy may be suspected of serving repression by suspending a serious engagement with it, then actual resistance to healing seems to work against life itself, at least in Freud's sense of life as the free pursuit of gratification.[20] With these two sorts of complication in view, one must ask about the status of what the analysand actually says about his or her suffering and desire in the therapeutic setting itself. In short, if what the analysand says cannot be accepted as necessarily accurate, then it is not clear that he or she will be able to do the work of speaking, reflecting, examining, and so forth. And in turn, it is not clear that his or her desire will direct the process in a helpful direction. This leaves only the speech and comportment of the analyst to somehow focus the work, and only the analyst's desire to ground it.

Such a conclusion opens the question of the ethics of therapy, and underlines the fact that for the analyst, the analysand is fundamentally another person in need. On this point, however, any resemblance with Levinas's account of the ethical relation is only superficial, for it belongs to the responsibility of the analyst that this other person, the analysand, *not* be given everything. The reason for this is not difficult to come by: the analyst necessarily finds himself or herself in a role that has already been coded by the analysand's transference, so that there is every reason to think that what he or she says may be absorbed into an impression of the relation that is, after all, generated by the analysand's neurotic expectations. One knows the scenario: "my analyst smiles a lot, she finds me endearing," or "when he asked me to repeat that thought, he sounded irritated, I am off track." The Freudian response, radicalized by Lacan, is to remain vigilant about what might easily be drawn into this scenario, and to track the manner in which what has been offered is taken up. This is not only a matter of managing counter-transference, in which the analyst's desire and feelings inform a projected understanding of the analysand. In the same stroke, the analyst endeavors to leave the analysand with his or her own desire and, of course, step back from the long reach of the transference so that it, too, may come into view. One understands, then, that some theorists of these matters counsel saying as little as possible, and indeed moving and acting as little as possible, so that the reach of the desire and transference are left without purchase on the analyst in the room. The implication for the ethics of therapy is clear enough: the analyst is committed to helping the patient to deeper self-knowledge and the enhanced capacity for self-responsibility that would come from an integrated sense of his or her desire and its vicissitudes.[21]

This does not at all mean that psychoanalytic therapy leaves the analysand entirely alone. To be sure, it is not for nothing that in the classical arrangement, the face of the analyst is out of sight while the analysand endeavors to speak. Yet against this, it should be taken seriously that many people cannot bear this for long, so that a great many sessions are instead conducted face to face. Whatever else one makes of this, it reminds us that to a considerable degree, and for a considerable time, the vulnerable analysand needs to rest on the transference. In even the most ambitious case, the analyst's painstaking efforts to withdraw from every support for the transference meet their limit at his or her continued presence in the therapeutic relation. This is both stabilizing and instructive. The relation will go on and, importantly, the analyst plainly desires it.[22] But then this is a desire that precedes and transcends whatever is imposed on it by the transference. Not that this itself would be (or should be) openly expressed; the desire of the analyst appears whenever and to the extent that the transference fails. We may make the same point from the side of counter-transference: there is an important distinction between the analyst's personal preferences regarding the direction of the therapy, and the desire that would support only the relation itself. When the analyst suspends personal preference, the analysand is held in a relation where his or her own desire circulates without signs from the analyst that might be taken to direct it in some way. This is reinforced by the analyst's silence; without words to attract transference, the analysand has only his or her own language to rely on.

It should not escape notice that as the transference dissolves, the analysand begins to recognize the difference between the analyst in the identity that had been projected entirely from his or her desire (e.g., as wise counselor, expert healer, sexual partner) and the analyst as a real and unique human being whose personal desire is in fact unknown. The therapeutic import of this distinction is clear enough: the analysand now sees that the understanding of the analyst that has hitherto prevailed is in fact a fantasy—to be sure, one that has been generated from within the original pathology, and yet one that has also been productive. For after all, it was the fantasied understanding of the analyst that yielded a motivation powerful enough to overcome the anxiety that arises as one approaches conflict and vulnerability in the depths of oneself. To take up only a single possibility, one has felt compelled to obey the analyst as master, who expects certain things and knows what is right and good. But then the attempts to please this master necessarily took the form of trying hard to face up to who one truly is, until eventually it began to dawn on one that this includes the inclinations that have produced the transference in the first place. In this way, the pathology has been turned to the service of healing, and the operative fantasy has finally undone itself.[23]

The last thing to be said about these matters is that psychoanalysis does not promise to purge or erase entirely the conditions that are present in acute form at the core of pathology (in this sense, the familiar expression "talking *cure*" is a misnomer). The obsessional neurotic does not cease to be obsessive in every way, but only reaches a level of mental equilibrium at which life is pleasing and manageable. This can be grounded in either of two ways. One may appeal to the developmental psychology

that includes Freud's "Oedipus complex" as evidence that there is no re-
versing or getting back behind the formation of the subject that occurs
in the encounter with a law that sets the coordinates for desire. In that
case, development would be a destiny. As soon as the subject is formed
around guilt and resentment, this will be its nature ever afterward, with
only the question of intensity still to be decided. But one may also appeal
to the experience of therapy, which exploits a distinction, present in every
moment of the work, between wishes that seek gratification here and now
and a desire that proves capable of suspending and even opposing all
of them at once (everything presently for oneself is given up to please
the analyst). We have just observed that the therapy turns the pathology
against itself. We might just as well have said that the therapy converts a
desire which, in its pathological variant, one has every reason to associate
with death and destruction, into the vital form of our relation with what
instead resembles a supreme good. The termination of analysis does not
abolish the difference between the goods that we want for our gratification and the good that we desire beyond them. Nor does it do away with
any further sense that some things are more desirable than others, and
indeed that still others are prohibited. These things still speak in us. But
with richer insight there comes some distance from the claims that are
voiced, and thus some freedom to choose for or against them. Lacan has
this in mind when, concluding his exploration of what psychoanalysis
might contribute to an ethics, he says that in the end the most important
question for the analysand, and the lasting one for us all, is "have you
acted in conformity with your desire?"[24]

The Ethical Relation

The therapeutic relation defined by Freud is evidently not the ethical
relation defined by Levinas, and indeed it cannot be mistaken for any
other relation one might find in ordinary life. Yet what happens there is
real, and thus has a claim on any attempt to give an account of the human
experience as such. In the present case, it is a matter of the subject's relation with the other person, and in a narrower optic the subjectivity of
that subject itself. Freud's understanding of our subjectivity is drawn from
reflection first of all on those subjects whom he meets as analysands. This
does not mean that his claims may be restricted to something as simple as
an anthropology of the mentally ill, since after all, those of us who may
claim a healthier condition do share with the ill a common humanity,
and in any case we must recognize in their afflictions the signs of certain

possibilities that no one can be sure of avoiding. As for Freud himself, his clinical experience enables him to make a powerful case for the claim that differences between the more profound instances of each mental pathology and what we might agree is mental health are a matter of degrees, and that all possibilities appear along an unbroken spectrum rather than, for example, a set or series of distinct types.[25] What transpires in the analytic setting says something about all of us.

We learn most from Freud about our subjectivity if we study the experience of the analysand rather than that of the analyst. After all, little lies in the way of understanding the analysand as another person calling for help, but a great deal stands in the way of understanding the analyst as an ethical subject in Levinas's sense. As we have observed, in the psychoanalytic therapeutic relation, it is quite often the case that the most responsible thing the analyst can do is to give the analysand almost nothing. This leaves the subject alone with a decisive series of questions. What do you want? In what sense would it be good? And what would it mean to choose against it?

We get closer to the theme of ethics if we take seriously what at first appears as only a banality: the aim of the therapy and the constant goal of the analyst is that the subject achieve happiness and well-being. On this basic point, Freud's thinking can appear quite classical, but his conception of happiness cannot be eudaimonistic for the simple reason that his conception of our subject is that it is irreducibly conflicted. What the therapy reveals, the theoretical texts affirm: a human being is irreducibly and unendingly conflicted. And yet human beings also exhibit a powerful desire to overcome this. How far is that desire from the one that Levinas calls "metaphysical"? As it happens, there is at most a family resemblance between the two, resting mainly on the etymology of Levinas's term *"metaphysica"*: beyond physical or natural things, or as phenomenology would have it, beyond things that are present and available to us in the world. Of the psychoanalytic variant, we know only that there is said to be in us a desire that would set aside our various investments in the goods available for gratification in order to reach the higher good that is achieved, in the therapy, by satisfying the master analyst. It is only a very short step from there—and many psychoanalysts take it—to the idea that in ordinary life that same good is sought in the more familiar goal of perfect conformity with an austere moral or spiritual ideal. This returns us, for a moment, to the significance of Lacan's interest in raising the question of conformity with one's desire. We can now grasp this as a matter of relations with others. In the therapy, the desire that initially defines the relation is directed by the transferential identity of the analyst, until the transference dissolves and the real identity of the analyst comes into view. This initial desire is essentially depersonalizing, since it insists that the analyst is strictly and only this one whose will must be satisfied as the price for perfect happiness. In ordinary life, we may see something very much like this in the behavior of those among us whose morality follows rules that point necessarily over and beyond the particularity of concrete relations with real human beings who have their own needs and desires. And we recognize the difference between this and the gentler morality that we are inclined to accept as authentic, which detects genuine humanity in those who truly see and enjoy other people.

Levinas, of course, sees these matters very differently. What galvanizes metaphysical desire is not at all a fantasy expressed in the transference, but the real face of the other person, here and now, "wholly by relation to himself"[26] and thus naked prior to any metaphorical sense of nakedness. Of course, Levinas too sees in the movement of desire a suspension of self-interest, but in the terms of his ethics this necessarily takes the form of making goods for me into goods for the other person. Such a kenotic responsibility has no analogue in the psychoanalytic account. For Freud, while it certainly is possible that the pursuit of gratification may give way to a desire that opposes it, or at any rate suspends it, there is no reason to think that this would be strictly for the sake of the other person. This does not mean that the Freudian position cannot recognize the possibility of what we might recognize generically as a moral act, but only that it interprets such an act entirely within the horizon of the life of the subject. Let us recall Levinas's image of a subject who makes a gift of bread from his own mouth,[27] and of his argument that this is motivated by a desire that moves directly toward the other person. The findings of psychoanalysis suggest that this is really the expression of a desire to satisfy an inner compulsion, and that this compulsion emanates from a moral law that is already inscribed in our subjectivity.

The key to what would assuredly be Levinas's objection to all of this plainly lies in his insistence that the law arrives from outside and beyond us, in the face of the other person. The face, in short, would dispossess us not only of self-interest, all the way down to the brute inclination that would belong to living from the elements, but also—and even—the inscribed formulations of law that psychoanalysis has identified. Like Kant before him, Levinas thinks that our response to a genuine command against self-interest opens us immediately to unqualified obedience (though neither of them is under any illusion that we necessarily keep to this). According to the rudiments of Kant's practical philosophy, this occurs in respect for the moral law itself, which introduces the possibility of an act unlimited by conditions that are personal and thus particular. The moral law is thus a universal law. It is one and the same thing to be raised up by the law to freedom from self-interest, and to apply that law universally in one's affairs with others. Levinas's relationship with Kant is complex and sometimes ambivalent.[28] At this juncture, their agreement that acts committed at the brute initiative of the subject cannot be fully moral is less interesting than Levinas's reservations about Kant's move to what he might be inclined to characterize as abstract universality. For Levinas, both the call and response that belong to ethics are essentially concrete. The call is voiced by the particular other who faces the subject here and now, and the truly dis-interested response goes directly to him or her. Moreover, this response occurs as speech, which is the essence of a reason that cannot harden into a system because it must always be renewed in view of a new call for help.[29] It would be difficult to convince Kant that the exercise of reason is self-interested, but there is no denying that it operates between the subject and the other person, and in that sense violates the immediacy that for Levinas belongs to the face-to-face relation.[30]

This same insistence on the exteriority of the law and on the immediacy of the relation that it brings to light also puts Levinas at some distance from the claims of psychoanalysis. At this point, the pressing question is no longer whether we can agree with him that the psychoanalytic claims concerning desire, law, and relations with others are only features of an inner life that he characterizes as "the Same," but instead whether it is possible to uphold the claim for an exteriority that would be at one and the same time singular in its presence (this person, here and now) and yet transcendent in its meaning (absolutely other, etc.). Evidently enough, this question awaits any serious reading of Levinas. Approaching it at a great distance, Derrida spends considerable time showing that the ethical relation that subtends Levinas's claim would have to lie outside of being, language, and history.[31] This is well in line with what we have just learned from a brief confrontation of Levinas with Kant: there can be no mediation of the ethical relation, not even by a form of reason that will have suspended self-interest.[32] The encounter with psychoanalysis requires us to ask about the claims for exteriority and immediacy with regard to desire itself—or, in full, with regard to the movement of responsibility that would be animated by the desire that Levinas calls "metaphysical." We have seen this question coming, in the course of reviewing some implications of Levinas's submission of sexual relations to the ethical relation.[33] When it is a matter of sexuality, there is certainly room in his conception to think that the desire one feels for the beloved and the pleasure that one may take from the relation are specified by context, predisposition, and his or her particular features and attributes. But this can only mean that it is therefore a departure or perhaps a detour from what Levinas is bound to insist is the more elevated with the other person *as other.* Sexual desire is not metaphysical desire, which we now see plainly cannot be determined by any investment in the concrete specificity of the face of the other person. So let us ask about this desire, as it moves the subject to kenotic responsibility. By what condition would the subject give itself up to the other person without having first invested him or her with some sense of the supreme goodness and desirability that this would imply?

This question leads directly to some of Levinas's basic principles. When he claims that the face of the other shocks and astonishes, the emphasis is on a dimension that cannot be predetermined, forestalled, or anticipated.[34] But then, whatever change this would inspire cannot be attributed to an approach from afar, as if from another land or via an original resemblance, because in that case preparations would always be possible and perhaps even inevitable as the other comes gradually into view. This suggests that we proceed with great care about everything that is entailed in Levinas's memorable claim that the other person has the face of "the poor, the stranger, the widow, and the orphan."[35] It is not that they arrive from elsewhere, but rather that their faces awaken us to the fact that they are already here. Such a claim has powerful resonance in the ethics and politics of liberation,[36] but for Levinas its significance is primarily phenomenological. In his reasoning, it belongs to what we might call, provisionally, "the fact of plurality" that we are in relation anterior to the establishment of lived space and time that belongs to the separation of the subject.[37] What is primary in space and time has already covered over what is primary in the order of goodness and value. This means that the relation with the other person is presupposed by the very movement of our being, or what Levinas's early works call the effort of existing, but also that the relation is forgotten by that movement, since this is always driven by one's own initiative. This would be the deepest meaning of Levinas's use of the biblical trope "widow, orphan, and stranger": I, as subject, am centered on my own concerns, and with some success, naturally but blindly, until this other person has appeared. The face of the other is his or her entry into a world projected by the subject, and so its arrival is immediately submission to the power of that projecting. So likewise is the world that the face breaks into, a world in which things are defined by the use that the subject makes of them, or in which the elements are defined by the manner in which the subject lives from them. The other person has none of these. This vulnerability does not contradict real, material deprivation, but, at least in Levinas's reasoning, it is more profound. And this distinction matters a great deal, for were we to identify need and vulnerability only with material conditions, there would be considerable reason to doubt that every human face truly awakens us to responsibility.

From the fact of plurality and the self-interested movement of our being, it follows that the other person is the—forgotten, rejected—"first one on the scene [*le premier venu*],"[38] and is there before the subject could have even begun to suspect it, and is indeed presupposed by everything the subject is, does, or says. For its part, the subject is always already responding to the other, even while entirely unaware of this and even while perhaps denying it. Because the other person is first on the scene, and because this priority maintains the other in exteriority over against any interiority, the subjectivity of the subject most fundamentally is its responsibility. Being, in its dynamism, is a usurpation that both suppresses the otherness of the other and leaves it intact. Insofar as one *is*, one is in the place of the other, according to what Levinas calls, throughout *Otherwise Than Being*, "substitution"—a substitution that is in the first instance violent, but in the second, may be converted into ethical responsibility. This is already enough to see how Levinas's concept of exteriority, and the theories of subjectivity and relation that it informs, ground his claim that desire, in its metaphysical form, goes toward the other person without subordinating him or her to any function of the subject. The desire that goes toward the other person, animating responsibility, is a desire that seeks the good which is not limited by finite personal interests, and indeed urges against one's natural commitment to them.

There is no longer anything standing in the way of posing the question, psychoanalytic par excellence, of the desirability of this good, or if one prefers, of the conditions in the life of the subject by which one would be moved toward it. This cannot be reduced to a matter of acting in agreement with our being, since Levinas has never appealed to the theory of natural law and flourishing that this would require,[39] and in any case, remaining strictly within the terms of his own argument, it would be difficult to make sense of the idea that one is motivated to "turn oneself inside out" for the other[40] strictly out of fidelity to oneself. The face of the other person brings the subject to a crossroads where it is necessary to choose between an insistence on oneself and an openness to the other, between violence and peace, and thus where responsibility would lead away from anything kept first or apart for oneself. What would it be in the face which keeps its exteriority even while it breaks into our interiority, that calls us to turn back against the very current of our being—a current that seeks the comforts of home, the pleasure of things within one's own grasp, and the security of a perspective? And how do we know this, or recognize it, precisely as *desirable*?

Trauma and the Good

It will be necessary to suspend any thought of associating desire with lack. Levinas, for his part, associates lack with existence, or rather the insufficiency of existence that is felt already in the movement of existing. Considered as a whole, existence, or being, does not ground or support us in our freedom. We first caught sight of this when following Levinas's attempt to understand the existential condition of violence, and already at that time we called attention to his claim that against the weight of existence the subject has a "savor for the absolute." These are the keys to his lengthy analyses of the effort of existing, which one might justifiably consider as a detailed extrapolation of them. The subject as existent is left alone with its finitude, which is at once the principle of its movement and the occasion for it to suffer. Yet the subject is more than an existent, or in the terms of late texts, is "otherwise" than any subjection or containment by its existence. This theme becomes prominent in Levinas's meditations on the relation with Infinity, and of course in his claim for radical responsibility.

The Good that is introduced in the face of the other, disrupting being from beyond being, must therefore be thought in terms of abundance, surplus, and excess, understood in each case as the positive transcendence of any limitation.[41] Levinas's use of these words advises us that the Good beyond being is not merely the other of being, and if being is the domain of insufficiency, then the Good does not in any way belong to being. It breaks into being without having been either excluded by being or opposed to being except on terms that have been defined entirely within being. This is the full sense of a remark made, perhaps too quickly, in *Totality and Infinity*: "The Good is Good *in itself* and not by relation to the need to which it is wanting; it is a luxury with respect to needs. It is precisely in this that it is beyond being."[42] Evidently enough, such a Good cannot lie behind the face that reveals it, as if the face hinted at it or revealed it only poorly, since in that case being or one of its avatars will have interceded to set limits on the Good. For Levinas, the face of the other is the overflowing of the Good into being. It belongs to the subjectivity of the subject that it struggles impossibly against its limitation in being, and it belongs to the goodness of the Good that it transcends the entire drama of limitation. There is another way to put this: the effort of existing is the very dynamism of what phenomenologists call "horizons," but the Good that is revealed in the face of the other breaks up this dynamic without submitting to any horizon. Or else, if we may risk this formulation, it comes with its own horizon.[43]

None of this is to say that the Good is strictly compelling of any particular choice or act by the subject. The deepest roots of Levinas's conception of freedom actually celebrate our capacity to choose not only for order but also against it.[44] But there is no mistaking the claim—indeed, it is central to his entire argument—that the face of the other crosses any distance and cuts through every layer or surface that belong to the life of the subject in its world. Without annihilating our freedom, the goodness of the Good thus surrounds it and even envelops it. All that remains, though it is everything, is the question of whether one will move wholly toward it or else, by definition, fail to do so. *Otherwise Than Being* comes back to this situation time and again. The goodness of the Good has already chosen us in the constitution of a subject that can choose against its own interests and instead choose the responsibility commanded by the face of the other.[45] Its choice is thus prior to the difference between our own free decision for peace or else for violence, and yet the choice orders us to itself with a violence of its own that Levinas is willing to call "good."[46] It is better to choose for responsibility and peace, and better to seek the Good—not according to our natures (again, a notion that is foreign to Levinas) but according to the undeniable authority of the face, which addresses us with "the Mastery of the Master" who speaks from on high.[47] It is still the case, as Levinas does not deny, that one may truly choose against responsibility and goodness, but this would be an act that continues to insist on the power of individual being which Levinas has already argued is in fact contradictory. It is the exercise of this nonfreedom that is violent, and only the advent of the Good in the face of the other would enable us to avoid this.[48]

These few passages call for some adjustment of any thought that the face such as Levinas defines it would visit undue violence on the subject. If this is said about the event itself (shock, outrage, etc.) or the weight or responsibility that it commands (infinite and therefore, as we have seen, all the way to assuming the very responsibility of the other), Levinas himself could hardly be expected to dismiss the suggestion out of hand. But what plainly grounds these claims, and in that sense justifies the concepts expressing them, is his definition of the Good. By identifying the Good with Infinity and sharply distinguishing its transcendence from any appearance or incarnation that would make them available to the subject, Levinas makes it inevitable that there can be no space for independent consideration, integration, or movement that does not proceed directly toward the Good or else refuse it entirely. In everyday language, one is tempted to object that such a Good "gets too close," and indeed Levinas himself has already said that the face which opens us to it is closer than any measurable interval. One might well wonder, then, whether this does not threaten to suffocate the subject, who is pressed back by the face of the other and the goodness of the Good to the least condition of its own freedom. Some of the most discrete moments in *Otherwise Than Being* seem to recognize this possibility in the course of describing the manner in which the face awakens in the subject an assignation prior to consciousness and knowing. The call for help is also the awakening of the nearness of the other person ("already here," "first one on the scene"), and is the realization of what Levinas calls "obsession": the other person has always already intruded, interrupted, and opposed the effort to close in upon oneself. Of this obsession, we can be sure that this is what prevents the subject from deafness to the call of the Good, and from indifference to it. To be obsessed by the other is to undergo, ceaselessly, a pull against the effort of existing, and a pull toward goodness. There is in this, Levinas says, a kind of "shuddering" (*un frémissement*) as our direction is reversed and difference becomes non-indifference—perhaps all at once, if we accept the premises of the argument, and yet not without effects on the body and on breathing that would be the signs of an adjustment and a recommitment of oneself.[49] This image deserves close attention, since it does not comfortably belong to either self-interest or responsibility. The shuddering of a subject who is obsessed and commanded, and for whom there is only the goodness that must be bought in sacrifice or else a refusal of what is best, can only signal the agony of a choice that has already been made for us, even if there is still the appearance that we are still free. This is not at all unlike the situation that certain psychoanalysts describe of a child whose mother gives too much, always in the name of love[50]—or in terms closer to the work at hand, an analysand whose analyst says and does too much, all the while giving the impression that this is for the best. Where might the refusal of all of this begin? Perhaps one shudders in primal defense.

At stake here, between two very different forms of thought, is the status of an internal limit for impulses which of themselves would accept no such thing. The psychoanalyst Bruce Fink, following Lacan, calls the acceptance of these impulses "subjectification."[51] Psychoanalysis considers this necessary and all but inevitable, and the therapy addresses the resulting conflicts. In the fullest sense of our subjectivity, one will have accepted a limit for desire and found a way to live well, even happily, without access to the absolute good that would exceed pleasure and use. On this point, Levinasian ethics could not be farther from Freudian psychoanalysis. For Levinas, the subjectivity of the subject, again in the fullest sense, is formed precisely in transcending any such internal limit. The responsibility for the other person that concretizes metaphysical desire attempts neither to close up an ulterior lack by pursuing sheer indulgence, nor to find a manageable relation with lack through surrender to a limit.

Metaphysical desire refuses lack altogether, or if one prefers, refuses the domain in which it would be a necessary condition. This desire constitutes an escape from the shackles of existence without ending in death, and informs a way of existing that cannot be totalized any more than can the other person whom it serves. In moving toward the other and the Good, the subject rejects its own initial position in being.[52]

There is another way to raise the question of a necessary limit for access to the Good. The thoughts of shock, overwhelming, and departure from position may cause one to wonder how the subject survives everything that Levinas envisions. This concern should not lead us to forget that he does take care to specify that the subject is not wholly unprepared for the call to responsibility and goodness, even if its attachment to being prevents it from seeing it coming. We have already observed how, in *Totality and Infinity*, the paradoxical idea of Infinity, of more in less, hollows out the subject, holding open a moment of heteronomy prior to the natural movement toward autonomy that forgets it. We have also found reason to associate Infinity with the Good. Together, these two theses may seem to support the idea that the subject already has a presentiment of what is still to come, as if Infinity, by withdrawing from any possible comprehension, left a hint of itself as goodness still to come. Medieval theologies of creation have been able to take such a view, holding that since our creatureliness cannot be alien from the Creator, it will be possible to detect in our striving for happiness a foretaste of its perfect state, even if by our sinfulness we do not easily recognize it in ourselves. It is difficult to know whether such an idea can be extracted from the metaphysics and teleology that the medievals drew upon,[53] but even if so, there remains the fact that in some sense the divine will, or perhaps divine love, would be present in human existence such as is ruled out by Levinas's conception of Infinity. Infinity, let us recall, is *not* present, and does not intervene either in our natures or in our history. The fact that the face of the other is the advent of the Good does not signal any sort of act from on high, but only our originary relation to one another, according to the withdrawal of Infinity from being and knowing. This leaves us with the simple thought, by now familiar, that the face of the other person awakens the subject to a relation to the Good that it did not know it had, and it is this sense of the Good, rising from a forgotten depth to permeate immediate experience, that makes the face the object of desire rather than, for example, terror.

This is recognizably a theory of trauma, a word that we have deliberately withheld until this moment when it has become unavoidable. To characterize the face as a trauma, as Levinas on occasion does, is to say somewhat more than what one says when one invokes surprise, shock, outrage, or offense. These latter terms can mean nothing more than a violent blow that either throws one back on oneself or forces some basic adjustments. It hardly needs saying that this does not yet touch on what for Levinas is essential. A trauma, for Levinas no less than for Freud, occurs in two times. There is a present event or encounter, and a prior condition. The prior condition remains latent, however, until the present event awakens it. And this condition supplies the meaning of the present event, which for its part confirms that meaning in a simple realization. In Levinas's conception, the face of the other touches the anarchic wound to the narcissism of the subject that is the site of its relation with the other (heteronomy prior to the movement of its being), and from this wound there arises a responsibility and desire that go first toward that other. This meaning is confirmed in the subject's love of justice and the Good.

The temporality of the trauma is striking. In lived time, the meaning of the original wound is unknown and without a determining claim on our will until the face of the other strikes. In retrospect, we can of course say that it always *will have* meant being responsible for the other, but this only underlines the fact that what is first the case is realized only afterward, and indeed in the fullest sense has meaning only afterward. Conversely, the face of the other is realized as ethical only insofar as—or *when*—it touches the earlier "wound" by which we are already open to the other person.[54]

It is important to remember that the older time of the ethical trauma is a pre-original condition and not, as it is for Freud, the impression of a psychological event: "The one affected by the other is an anarchic trauma, or an inspiration of the one by the other, and not a causality striking mechanically."[55] This goes hand in hand with Levinas's contention that the relation with the other person and with Infinity is not determined by any erotic investment in their meanings, and that desire for the Good transcends any personal satisfaction allegedly to be gotten from it. This is not the occasion to go deeply into the Freudian theory of trauma, but its contrast with that of Levinas on a central feature can be instructive.[56] Freud leads us to understand trauma as entirely a matter of inner conflict between wishes for pleasure and a contrary wish precisely not to have any such wishes. What is traumatic is the fact of an experience or a thought that one wishes not to have had. In his famous "Case of Emma," sketched in the unfinished "Project for a Scientific Psychology,"[57] it is not a girl's memory of assault by shopkeepers that contributes to a later trauma, but instead her memory, clearly repressed, of having gone back to the scene later, according to what Freud surmises was sexual curiosity and perhaps an intimation of pleasure. What Emma finds unbearable is any evidence of an investment in the curiosity or the pleasure, *which her moral sense tells her is wholly unacceptable.* One thus sees that the conflict has everything to do with her conception of the good and of the law that would define access to it. These things speak in her, against the pursuit of pleasures that might well seem normal, if also, though it would be inevitable in a young girl, misguided. One also sees that the opposition of law and good, on the one hand, to pleasure, on the other, is dynamic and, again, internal. It is according to some investment of Emma herself in the moral law that she is blocked from pursuit of anything that would seriously violate it. Emma has not yet achieved sufficient distance from the demands of the Good that is promised by the law for there to form what we earlier understood as an internal limit by which life is bearable, and the distance necessary for personal variation and free choice is possible. The root of her problem is clear enough: it is she herself, surely without knowing or willing it, who has accepted and integrated the conceptions of moral law and good that are so severe about any inclination to pleasure.

Levinas's notion of "anarchic trauma" stands directly against the idea that what transpires when the other person faces the subject would express an ulterior interpretation and personal integration of either law or the Good, just as his notion of "exteriority" stands directly against the idea that the meaning of the face is in any way formed according to a disposition of the subject. These few claims supply nearly all of his philosophical reason for considering psychoanalysis at best a matter of indifference for ethics, and at its worst an abasement. The entire drama, including its outcome in a confrontation with the real demands of one's wishes and the desire that strikes against them, is enacted without ever opening itself to the anarchy and exteriority that frame the ethical relation. It may be, in the final analysis, that to contend against Levinas that his conceptions of the other person, desire, and the Good belong to only one possible ordering of a deeper conflict among impulses, or to point out that the demands that they place on the subject have the appearance of an aggression that Freudians would identify with a drive that opposes life itself, would be to argue *petitio principii*. Even if this is so, it is worth raising the argument at least long enough to bring into relief the specific consequences of Levinas's move entirely away from its initial premise. The first such consequence appears in his claim that the ethical relation, which is the true relation, is prior to any attachment governed by any form of self-interest or gratification. The second consequence, subtending this first one, is registered in his understanding of God. To the anarchic trauma that is not in any way "caused" corresponds the God who, as Infinity, does not intervene. Such a God has not brought anything into being and does not draw anything toward itself, but only leaves us to one another—and according to an identity that transcends even the most primordial interpretation we may make of it. In chapter 3 of this study, we have seen at length that in *Totality and Infinity* our plurality is the inverse figure of God's infinity, and that Levinas proposes to understand this in the quasi-mythical terms of a "contraction" of Infinity by which each subject is both closed to and open. This condition, "separation," makes up our relation with the other person and with the other others whose faces appear in this one here and now. But the contraction by which Infinity permits such a plurality constitutes a withdrawal from comprehension rather than availability to it. In the face of the other person that calls us to responsibility and goodness, God thus speaks to us without us counting on God.[58] This alone would be deserving of that exalted name: it is that by which we are ordered to one another without indifference to one another, in the "trace" of a transcendence that could never be either present or absent.[59]

"God," then, is a name for an entire way of life that specifies the meaning and value of everything that one may think or do, including the very act of grounding oneself in that order. By God, one is first and above all one's responsibility for the other person, before knowing how or why. By God, one is already "under assignation" to the other person, before any beginning and without any question of choice in the matter. Subjectivity is strictly and only its metaphysical relation with the other person. God alone has seen to that, but again: without causation by God and without reliance on either the freedom or any disposition of the subject. If the name "God" were to imply either of these, then Levinas has disavowed it. Or rather, it is disavowed by the essential principles of his argument. "God" does not name an interlocutor we would know in some experience or history. In fact, Levinas's word "God" is a name for the impossibility of any such God, and the expulsion of any purchase on the name of God from the ordinary circulation of understanding and language. In this sense, which is to say both in terms quite close to psychoanalysis and according to Levinas himself, the religion of ethical metaphysics is a "psychosis."[60]

Speech and Transcendence: Language as Ethical Relation

"The name has a name," Levinas has written, because "the name is revealed as hidden."[1] That sentence appears in a Talmudic commentary that takes some distance from theological language about God. This is also an important feature of Levinas's own philosophical work. Whether one contends that the idea of Infinity is consistent with the relation with the other person in which responsibility is also desire for the Good (metaphysics), or that analysis of what transpires between the subject and the other person leads back to the thought of Infinity (phenomenology), reflection on what he calls "the ethical" proves to be inseparable from reflection on the word "God." Levinas conceives of God according to the provisions laid down by an ethics that succeeds ontology as first philosophy and refuses any reduction to anthropology. The God who would be discovered in the elaboration of this ethics would be a God who does not appear within the horizon of our relation with being and who is not in any way inscribed in the recesses of the subject's own inner life. Were we to think that we have found a name that reaches God in the darkness beyond being and consciousness or which has perhaps drawn God forth from there, we will have conceded, against the whole of Levinas's teaching, that the passage to names must proceed through being and consciousness, if only to arrive on the other side of them. Against this, it belongs to his case for the primacy of the ethical to insist that every act by a subject is already a response to the other person and that one is awakened to this fact precisely by his or her face. Only in this way, only when speech knows itself to be prompted by the face of the other, would the name of God be said properly. But then this would not be a name that illumines, and the one who speaks it would not pretend to thereby enter into the presence of the one who is named. These would be the conditions of highest fidelity and obedience.

Being as Language

Levinas's theory of language is prepared by his reception of what Heidegger calls the ontological difference between being and beings. In his early essay "Martin Heidegger and Ontology," fundamental ontology is celebrated for awakening us to the "verbal" sense of being and for teaching us to think of it in terms of time. Before any alleged "essence of man," we are our way of being, which most fundamentally is temporalizing. However, according to Levinas, this is only of preliminary interest for ontology, since it "goes toward the meaning of *being in general*. But in order for being in general to be accessible, it is first necessary that it disclose itself." How does this come to pass? In the very being of the being, *us*, in whom, according to our way of being, being is revealed. Our being-there is the event of this disclosure, the very working of truth.[2]

There is little to challenge in this reading of Heidegger and of the basic account of our existing that it supports. And it remains intact in Levinas's subsequent works, even as his own existential ontology decenters it, and the ethics of radical responsibility submits it to censure. In *Existence and Existents*, we know, to exist is to suffer, and this is only aggravated by our natural persistence at trying to master the situation. In *Totality and Infinity*, the face of the other person teaches us that all of this is pretense and offers us salvation in the form of absolute responsibility. In our understanding of these developments, we may be tempted to overlook the role that language plays not only in the Heideggerian theses that Levinas takes himself only to repeat, but also in Levinas's own movement away from Heidegger. In fundamental ontology, the topic of language must be identified where Levinas draws attention to the manifestation of being by which alone it is possible even to pose the question of its meaning. We do not fully appreciate the implication of this thought unless we hold in view the distinctiveness of being with respect to beings. Didier Franck captures this with admirable precision when he observes that "the verb *being* is not a verb like the others because it neither designates any action nor names anything. It is the verb of verbs,"[3] the one in which and by which all of the others are realized. Which is to say, now strictly in terms of Heidegger's analysis of Dasein, not only that all speaking occurs within the horizon of conditions that are given in our thrownness as being toward death, but also that our comportment, as care for our own existence and concern with what is at hand, is itself language. In this profound sense, our being is language itself.

In *Totality and Infinity*, this position is inscribed in the separation of the subject from the other person. Truth, for Levinas, is still a function of interiority, in the opening of the subject to illumination by being, but this occurs on the prior condition of a plurality in which the relation of the interlocutors is established outside any comprehension by the subject. For one to express the truth is already for one to speak to the other, who for his or her part already slips away from the expression. The relation of truth thus "rests on language: a relation in which the terms *absolve* themselves from the relation."[4] Such a conception of the relation is evidently meant to ground the possibility that the other person reveals himself or herself without submitting to the conditions of disclosure or comprehension. The face of the other person is expression "*kath'hauto*"— "in and from itself," as distinct from relative to anything else (*pros ti*).[5] "Manifestation *kath'hauto* consists in a being saying itself to us [*se dire à nous*] independently of every position we would have taken in its regard, *expressing itself*."[6]

Levinas's thinking sometimes includes an interesting play of manifestation as presence and manifestation as speech. Evidently enough, what Husserl or Heidegger have accustomed us to conceiving in terms of objectness or thingness is understood by Levinas primarily in terms of reference or orientation to the subject, who in turn is already in relation with the other person. In *Being and Time*, the givenness of a tool is defined by its readiness to serve Dasein's care for its own existence, and indeed when or to the degree that it is not ready in that way it is no longer a tool. Here, the primary manifestation of tool is tacit, becoming known only through the different sort of manifestation that is its conspicuous refusal to work, or serve. In neither case is the centrality of the subject's motivation in question. This principle is not always absent from the postwar books, where Levinas engages Heideggerian ontology at greatest length. In *Existence and Existents*, subjectivity is thought to be capable of "reaching the other" (*atteindre l'autrui*), and in *Time and the Other* of "positing" her otherness (*en posant l'altérité d'autrui*).[7] In order to go further along this line, and in that way truly break from the strictures of fundamental ontology, Levinas must defend the possibility of an otherness that does not only stand over against the subject, awaiting its respectful approach, but instead comes with its own horizon, striking from beyond comprehension. The face, he therefore says, is "revelation: a coinciding of the expressed with him who expresses"[8]—without lack, therefore, and without remainder.

The characterization of revelation as speech is familiar in religious thought. We have the monotheisms to remind us that the invisible and incomprehensible God may make itself known with words without falling into the grasp of those who hear. The one who hears knows that he or she has been addressed, and thus also that the God who has spoken is not excluded from the domain of human meaning, but just as assuredly that person knows that God transcends any understanding that we may constitute on the basis of our hearing of those divine words. Levinas takes great care to distinguish the other person from God, but he does treat the face of the other in much this way. As distinct from "manifestation," which still in part submits the manifested to the experience and understanding of the one who receives it, "revelation" preserves the transcendence of the revealed.[9] Concepts like "surprise," "astonishment," and "trauma" specify Levinas's manner of making this claim: the face of the other person is a word spoken suddenly, and from wholly beyond the words gathered to the subject, and "what" it reveals—the otherness of the other—is already gone from the moment in which one hears it.[10]

Unless the face of the other person is nonetheless also a surface of the human body that includes eyes, nose, and mouth, Levinas's claim will appear abstract and perhaps contrived. He certainly knows this. In the same passages that take up face as speech, and in that sense as revelation, the face is also understood as form and thus as manifestation. Properly speaking, the face is a distinctive manifestation: unlike the manifestation of nourishment, things, or tools, the face is "already discourse," having a presence that is unique insofar as it does not submit to the consciousness of the subject but instead—and this is consistent with "trauma"—"dominates."[11] Yet things are necessarily more complex than this. We do not need Levinas to tell us that a form in the usual sense—let us say, the face as *countenance*—already submits the otherness that it expresses to the comprehending gaze of the subject. Perhaps this requires some ambiguity in the word "form," or else it requires a subtle distinction within it. The form that is "already discourse" is pure presence, dominating consciousness all the way down to sensation by refusing the specifications that it would impose. But form already in this sense, of itself, congeals into the plasticity of a surface that can be grasped and, indeed, interpreted from a perspective. Levinas would have us understand this event from both sides. The other person submits his or her face to the gaze of the subject already upon arriving in the present, and yet in so doing also transcends the image in which the gaze would arrest it. Conversely, the subject achieves its understanding of the other person only on the basis of seeing his or her face (as countenance), and yet this seeing is already the seed of exclusion and suppression.

Appearance, which must include the face as countenance, is ambivalent, and insofar as it adheres to being, it surrenders what appears to the gaze of the subject. Levinas considers this ambivalence to be surmounted in "expression . . . the primordial event of signification" that must be received as teaching over against any tendency to grasp and possess.[12] As distinct from the comprehension of things, in which distinct instances are seized in their identity, a teaching arrives in signs made by an interlocutor who is strictly the other term of a relation. This occurs primarily in the face of the other person, which thus would be pure expression. And if the other person is, as we have already found Levinas to propose, "the first one on the scene," then his or her face brings with it the signification of things not according to identities that become known to the subject, but in their reference to a freedom and a suffering that is not one's own. This, moreover, would be the primary nature of all things, if indeed the subject is the first one on the scene. Yet we are constitutionally unable to recognize this on our own. Levinas conceives of violence most often as a direct affront to the other person in his or her need, but he gives us reason to think that there is already violence in the spontaneous enjoyment of elements that have already been claimed by the other person.

It is not difficult to follow this thought into the heart of some basic claims: the face has already had its effect before understanding is mobilized, so that even the "yes" of assent is already a linguistic act committed by the subject. Prior to this "yes" is only the "here I am" of subjectivity singled out as this one who must now choose for or against its responsibility.[13] We already know that for Levinas, the fact that the subject is not indifferent to the other person even at this level bears witness to the Infinity by which each of us is ordered to the other.[14] We also know that he considers the fact that the subject retains its freedom to confirm for us that the relation is ethical. Indeed, for the other to face the subject is immediately for him or her to draw the subject into a relation where power is simultaneously afoot and under critique—it is simultaneously ready to kill and prohibited from doing so.[15] To all of this we can now add that these relations occur in language, or rather, that they are established before and outside of language and mobilize language in a manner that cannot be reduced to a function of the subject. Heidegger would have us think that being is language. For Levinas, being and thus language must be understood in terms of the relation to the other.

The Ethical Relation as Language

It should not escape our notice that Levinas's position courts serious difficulty on an essential point. Let us try to be precise about its location. The apparent strength of his position lies in its manner of highlighting the depth of one's responsibility for others. Whether or not one is entirely convinced by Levinas's most immoderate propositions, one is likely to agree that there is something basically correct in the claim that responsibility is a matter of one's entire subjectivity. If I am responsible, it is me entirely, and not some part of me. However, this embracing responsibility is not necessarily the same thing as a responsibility that is unqualified. One can be entirely the person who is responsible for the other but only to a limited degree, as when one assumes the role of solitary caregiver for a friend or family member without relinquishing other important concerns. Needless to say, Levinas's conception of responsibility does not align with this latter instance. This has an important implication for his philosophy of language. His principle of radical responsibility means that the expression of meaning is immediately to and for the other person. Evidently, this would be the case regardless of quite *which* meaning is expressed.

It is important to understand this claim in the context of what Levinas has established elsewhere concerning the effect that the presence of the other person already has on our relation to the elements. One finds oneself in language—one expresses meaning at all—only because the other person has already interrupted the self-evidence of one's own claim on the elements by drawing them first toward himself or herself. To say that one lives from the elements is to recognize a profound intimacy with them, but intimacy is not fusion, and indeed we don't need Levinas to realize that even nourishment is restless. The non-accommodation of the elements to one's tendency to enjoyment is the fundamental condition of language: it is because the other person is "the first one on the scene," and because he or she already lives from the elements, that things stand apart from us, demand an interpretation, and thus are intended as a "this" or a "that."[16] Such would be the condition of language as predication. Of course, one sees immediately that this continues to depend on the power of a subject, which is to say on the being of a being capable of speech, even if this same power, like being itself, is already exposed to the claim of the neighbor who is in need. Derrida alerts us to the strange tension that this implies between language in its only possible occurrence and language in what Levinas must nonetheless understand as its ideal form. "Nonviolent language," language which would truly respect the priority of the other person, "would be language that would do without the verb *to be*, that is, without predication. Predication is the first violence."[17] Derrida also makes plain, and in considerable detail, what is at stake here. Unless the ideal form is possible, it must be conceded that violence is our irreducible condition, in which case the transcendental critique proposed by Levinas is incoherent. We would instead have license to speak of peace only according to an economy of violence.[18]

In order to escape this conclusion, it is not enough for Levinas to argue, as we have seen him do, that the face shocks and surprises without becoming inscribed in being and language. To be sure, an entire range of experiences, from bumping one's head in the dark all the way to what is worked out as ethical trauma, fit this very description. But no one, including Levinas himself, would doubt that the subject moves immediately and even, if necessary, "*violently*," to interpret them. As he sees it, the real problem lies not with the act itself, but instead with our alleged right to hold fast to its result. For Levinas, the moment of response is thus irreducibly ambivalent. One cannot *but* express the meaning of what one undergoes, and one cannot *but* do violence to its original conditions. Does this mean that the truly ethical response must be one that eschews language altogether? This can hardly be the case, yet one cannot help but wonder whether the pressure that Levinas puts on ordinary predication might actually work against the possibility of real service to the other person, in which one first takes possession of things, if only one's own words, in order to have anything to offer him or her. In what is surely a hyperbolic moment, Derrida suggests that precisely this is ruled out—and not merely placed under great pressure—by the ideal conditions for peace (and thus responsibility).[19] Prescinding from this, we might instead concentrate on what this line of resistance highlights in ordinary syntax. In stressing the mutual exclusion of the sameness of the same and the otherness of the other, Levinas comes perilously close to the charge that the expression of a specific meaning is by definition necessarily violent. Even accepting the proposition that the face of the other, as call and command, places the very movement of being under ethical constraint, it is difficult to understand how the subject would alter the conditions of expression without nonetheless continuing to express, or for that matter how a content might ever be conveyed in any manner—offered, surrendered, given—which does not impose a tacit meaning. And if this is in fact the case, then one must insist, seemingly against Levinas, that if the subject is to be of service at all, it must adhere at least minimally to the conditions of being and language while proposing to truly open itself to the other person and indeed, as the argument contends, simultaneously to God.

This difficulty is appreciable, since it is easily traced to some of Levinas's founding themes. What Derrida highlights in the implicit thesis of ideal language echoes a much deeper, and as it happens, older claim to a prophetic vision of the peace that would be prior to any violence. Levinas nowhere suggests that such a peace is fully realizable among human beings, but his embracing critique of being as violent depends constantly on the idea that peace does come first. When it is a matter of ethics, Levinas argues time and again that the originary relation is a peaceful relation even if our initial movement is already violent. When it is a matter of the religion that is concretized in ethics, he suggests that before the violence of being there were the altars at which we once hoped to reach the good, only to eventually learn that the Good destroys the altars at which even humble worship would draw it down into being.[20] The death of God unveils the true form of things established before and outside being. Without this, unless it is true, it would instead be the violence that comes first, in which case, as Derrida has suggested, the pursuit of peace can achieve only an economy of violence. This is enough for us to understand Levinas's recurrent interest in the Platonic notion of a good that is *epekeina tes ousias*, or "beyond being," which accompanies his interpretation of being as essentially effort and thus as violence. It is also enough for us to understand that Derrida could not be more serious when he asks whether this "beyond" is in fact only the beyond specifically *of* being, as he seems to do when he suggests that any tendency to reduce being to the effort of existing necessarily bleaches it of any goodness.[21] If the good is to being as peace is to violence, then the good is precisely the other of being. In that case, the good would necessarily be limited, and we for our part could not approach it in any other way than according to the free exercise of our own being, which therefore cannot be strictly opposed to authentic peace and goodness.[22]

One is certainly entitled to wonder whether any of this has truly escaped Levinas's attention, and not only because he has learned from his study of Descartes that Infinity is not merely the non-finite.[23] We may now add to this that his philosophy of language can be interpreted above all as an attempt to show how it is that a good which does not enter being is not therefore alien or opposed to us. For all of that, some of its basic principles do appear exposed to the sorts of questions raised by Derrida. In *Totality and Infinity*, the face that is the first word is understood to be the very nearness of the good, and it is thought that when one speaks in sincere commitment to the other person, one assuredly participates in its further diffusion. But it has not always been as evident as one would like that such words are not still aspects or functions of being, as if their very intelligibility confirms a pre-ethical moment of comprehension and thus possession by the subject. In order to argue that this is not in fact the case, it will have to be shown that the subject is already in language, as discourse, which we know for Levinas means signifying to and for the other person, even in the effort that makes up its attachment to being. Now, it is not certain that he has taken quite this view in *Totality and Infinity*, where a concern to establish ethics as first philosophy sometimes leads to claims that the ethical relation, which is to say "discourse," is fully prior to the self-relation, which is to say "being."[24] His subsequent texts develop a somewhat different position, though still in defense of a good that intervenes without becoming present. Two of these texts appear crucial for the matter at hand. Applying himself to the most rudimentary conditions of our existence, Levinas observes that when according to our natural tendency, we attempt to grasp the data we encounter in a single image or under a single concept, there is detectable resistance that they must overcome. A great deal of the time, he is intent on interpreting the effort of mastery as the original movement of what becomes power and suppression. But this does not prevent him from also interpreting the resistance itself as the expression of a prior interruption of what would otherwise be a comfortable assimilation of data into the perspective of a subject. This thought is not entirely new to us. When exploring the sense in which the elements resist our spontaneous effort to enjoy them for ourselves, it appears that this is due to the prior claim on them made by an other person who has not yet become present to us. In "Phenomenon and Enigma," this is straightforwardly a question of appearing. In that essay, Levinas invokes the "enigma" by which something shows itself without showing itself, which is to say only in effects without a visible cause.[25] Ultimately, the enigmatic refers to the anarchic relation of the subject to the other, separated without indifference, and to the Infinity by which finite beings are ordered in this way.[26] The enigmatic cannot be brought by any means into the light where it would take its place among the appearance that it has disrupted, though this is by and large what phenomenology has often tried to do. By refusing any such effort, the enigmatic calls us away from a proclivity for thematization and mastery into discourse, in which meaning is conditioned by call and response.

This notion of enigma has important implications for how we may henceforth understand the face as of the other person. If the enigmatic defines a disturbance in appearing by which Infinity is manifest without manifesting itself, the face is the very approach of what disturbs. But the face no more submits to being and appearing than does the enigmatic—it no more manifests, makes present, the otherness of the other person than the enigmatic does the Infinity of the Infinite. This positive refusal, which is not flight but interruption, Levinas calls "the trace of the other." In the essay by that name, we are led to think of the face as etching or burning itself into the order of the subject's world by disrupting it without belonging to it. To say that the face is a trace of the other is to say that the other has always already absconded from presence and the absence that is only the counterpart of presence. In this way, the world and everything in it appear as signs and aggregations of signs made to the other person to whom the subject is bound from before and beyond any presence— according to an ordering which would be, as we have just observed, enigmatic. This says a little more than was possible when it was only a matter of understanding how the face both is and is not form.[27] From the latter, it was possible to understand that an excess of givenness over its own appearing brings into view the fact that seeing is already a mode of responding, even if it contains within itself the possibility of forgetting this. We may now add that this comes to pass according to conditions lain down outside of the effects in which they appear. Which means that the face, as trace, or as a call that does not make manifest the one who calls, is not merely one word among others but, in its refusal to belong to the subject or in its world, is the first among them, as the very institution of language as discourse. And yet herein, too, lies an essential equivocation, for the proper ethical meaning of the face is certain to be lost already upon being heard and understood. There is equivocation, then, both of the trace that commands responsibility and at the same time surrenders to possession, and of the subject for whom the hearing of the command both binds and severs the relation.[28] It could not be otherwise without violating the terms of the argument. Let us not forget that it is by the Infinity of the Infinite that the subject is ordered to the other, separated and yet disturbed in a manner that produces discourse—but discourse, then, in which the word of the other person, for all the goodness and truth that it bears, is spoken to a subject who, separated and finite, cannot but interpret it in a context. To hear, we have noted, is already to grasp, even if in the final analysis the word that one hears always has the character of signification to an interlocutor.

This twofold equivocation is plainly unresolvable. In fact, in Levinas's conception, language turns around it, or as he sometimes says, oscillates between its two poles. The expression of meaning is fundamentally discursive, occurring in the speech of a subject that is necessarily in response to the face of the other person. Whatever the specific content of the speech in which this is registered, its deepest sense consists in what Levinas calls "saying" (le Dire). Conversely, this saying is never without such specific content—it could never occur, unless as strictly unintelligible, without submitting to the limits of a grammar and some minimal adequation with an articulated world. Saying, then, is already what Levinas conceives as "said" (le Dit). These are the conditions of consciousness itself, according to the extraordinary obsession by the other that belongs to ethical metaphysics. To intuit meaning is, in Levinas's technical sense, to say it. One speaks the entire world to the other person, whether or not one always has this in mind. The saying is not a creating and does not simply envelop its contents—speech is not an idealism—but necessarily takes up what has been said. Will saying only repeat it, augment it, call it into question, or perhaps even offer it to the other person? This is a question for ethics, and for the attempt to recapitulate everything that

Levinas has said about responsibility, justice, and service in the terms of his conception of language. We will forego that general effort, which in any case would not be difficult to pursue, in order to instead seek a better understanding of what these developments imply for Levinas's abiding theme of ethical transcendence.

Language as Metaphor

The phenomenological definition of transcendence draws attention to the fact that the subject, in its temporality, is always already beyond or, as it were, out ahead of each present experience. With regard to language, this would be the condition by which speech does not merely discover a datum and then report it, but produces something new. The ethical definition of transcendence developed by Levinas characterizes what we might generically designate a dimension of excess or superabundance. He reserves this latter sense of transcendence for the otherness of the other person and, according to a complex association with it, Infinity. At the heart of this philosophy is an attempt to show that the subject's relation with another person and with Infinity accounts for the possibility of the former, phenomenological sense of transcendence. The subject is restless, its temporality is futural, it goes out ahead of itself, because the other person, to whom it is ordered by the Infinity of the Infinite, interrupts every pretense to autonomy. The richness of speech, in which the urgency of life informs a unique perspective on the world, would therefore be assured by the anarchic conditions of ethical subjectivity. "God" is a name for the authority that these conditions have over us. What would it mean for us to say this word that seems to secure the meaning of all the others? We will return to this question at some length.

If the problem of language is underdeveloped in *Totality and Infinity*, this must be due in no small measure to the fact that that work is still preoccupied with the need to liberate the ethical relation from the dominance of appearance, visibility, and in the end, light. To be sure, it is argued in brief there that "discourse is not simply a modification of intuition (or of thought), but an original relation with exterior being."[29] But this formulation is itself evidence of an orientation that is still in the process of being overcome. After *Totality and Infinity*, Levinas refers to "exteriority" less and less, and the conception of language recorded there, though only in nascent form, becomes more prominent. One also finds in the same work, near its end, the conclusion that "discourse is discourse with God and not with equals," but then again comes a reference to being: "Metaphysics is the essence of this language with God; it leads above being [*au-dessus de l'être*]."[30] Nearly everywhere else, the word "God" belongs to Descartes or else to a theology that is indicted for submitting it to being.

We do find the relation of self-transcendence to ethical transcendence addressed as a matter of language, and with important attention paid to the word "God," in some texts from the same period that have since been published in volumes 1 and 2 of Levinas's *Oeuvres complètes*. In the most interesting of these, his topic is metaphor,[31] which for him represents language in a form still capable of fidelity to the ambiguity and polyvalence that belong properly to the lived world.[32] It would thus be metaphor that attends properly to the profusion of meaning evident in speech, and in the advancement of understanding among subjects. These things, let us immediately note, are threatened by the thinking that seeks what objects have in common at the cost of marginalizing what distinguishes them. Such a thinking appeals decisively to concepts, which are said to transcend particulars and are prized for their capacity to assemble them and unify them as if from above or below. According to Levinas, to apply a concept is inevitably to seek a transparency that is untroubled by singular differences. Univocity, in short, necessarily entails impoverishment. This, he adds, is typical of philosophy as such so long as it understands its central task to lie in the pursuit of universal principles. Socrates's willingness to place any poets in his ideal city under strict control would be instructive in this regard. Poets make ample and explicit use of metaphor, in which resemblances are forged without aiming at perfect identity, so that new meaning is produced.

Levinas considers this to be more than a difference between genres or styles. And he is unwilling to think that poetry and metaphor are only exceptions or interruptions of the prevailing deployment of language grasped by philosophy, as if a general orientation to ideal meaning must occasionally make room for—or, under certain conditions, find reason to repel—figurative meaning. Yet this does not speak favorably of philosophy, since any inclination toward privileging the univocity expected of concepts over the figurative resource of metaphor is already a threat to a proper understanding of how it is that we can express meaning at all. Most generally, the appeal to metaphor is a defense of the original possibility of language against an intellectualism that would suppress it. But it is also recognizably a revolt against the metaphysics which, founded on an exclusion of metaphor, serves what Derrida will later call, in the course of stating remarkably similar concerns, the "telos of language" toward ideality.[33]

Considered as metaphor, language would not merely translate

conditions between objects or situations. Rather, it detaches itself from the immediate givens of experience in order to free significations incarnated there, bringing some that have been associated with one object or situation into contact with those of another.[34] We can be sure that there are gradients of metaphoricity. A forest in a windstorm appears as a turbulent sea, a lecture hall feels like an empty tomb, my desk is a table, and I see what you mean. None of this would be possible if each single word or proposition were fixed exclusively to single objects or situations. Yet it seems difficult to suppose that when our intention is fixed on the meaning of a particular object or situation, *any word or proposition* will do equally well. Since it is therefore clearly wrong to think that in speech, as metaphorization, it is a matter of indifference which word may be joined to another, we are obliged to understand that an object or situation admits of multiple meanings, and that speech always involves some restrictive choice from among the field of possibilities. It is here, of course, that we find openly admitted a thought that we labored to extract from the account of call and response that appears in *Totality and Infinity*: in the lecture on metaphor, speech, as the expression of meaning, is elementally the act of a creative subject, and indeed its creativity accounts not only for the novelty and enrichment we are accustomed to recognizing in most discourse, but also for the possibility for us to generate anything new and useful to offer the other person.

As it turns out, this thought is already invested in Levinas's own definition of the very word "metaphor." According to a common etymology, metaphors transfer or carry one meaning over to another. Levinas willingly understands the word differently: metaphor is a "passing beyond" and even a "leaping ahead" of present experience.[35] This only seems to echo Nietzsche's contention that metaphor is not merely *Übertragung* (transmitting, carrying over) but *Überspringen* (leaping over). In Nietzsche's understanding, the leap ahead represents the eruption of a primordial drive (*Fundamentaltrieb*) that is originally physiological.[36] Metaphor would thus occur in a cathartic, even salutary revolt against everything that would limit meaning to the present. It would be liberation, the arrival of subterranean forces wishing only to circulate freely (hence the famous image: "a mobile army of metaphors . . ."). For Levinas, in contrast, the movement that metaphorizes—again, we may say: the movement that speaks—is a movement that "elevates," or "leads toward on high."[37] Those who might hear this claim in isolation from Levinas's major works are bound to be puzzled by it. We have seen more than enough to understand that this understanding of metaphor is in close solidarity with transcendence in the full sense that he wishes to defend, and thus also know that its justification must be found in claims for the priority of the other and the provocation that is his or her face. As for its relation to the position taken by Nietzsche, we note that on another, later occasion Levinas has proven willing to reinterpret the Nietzschean conception as having grasped the original moment of metaphor. The cathartic eruption is the "youth of saying" that rises properly toward the other person. Nietzsche himself will have failed to see this. "Nietzschean word, prophetic word," writes Levinas, "like a flame climbing unknowingly toward heaven."[38]

This claim nonetheless calls for closer inspection on its own terms. Why should we think that metaphor, as a leaping ahead, reaches for anything more than an alteration of previous understanding or the proposal of something new? To speak would simply be to go beyond oneself, to join what is here and now to what is there and not-yet. In this case, or if this were all, speech would not seem to involve anything more than a shift from one simple meaning to another that is perhaps slightly richer or only just discernibly different. Though this is already enough to have refused the limits of the present, it does not seem to express anything other than a change of perspective on the part of the subject, either freely or else as prompted by a shift in the real. Of course, Levinas has pressing reasons to observe that there are exceptions to all of this. What of our encounter with an excess of meaning over any possible words for it? What of shock and astonishment? Unless we take the view that speech is constitutionally unable to say anything that will not immediately falsify or suppress this, we must instead envision words that would take the contradictory form of "apprehending more in less"[39]—that is, words that would give meaning while ceding the absolute right to give meaning. In common speech, there is still analogy or proportion between one meaning and the next. It is not without sense to think that this function does require a certain altitude from which to distinguish and join two points on the same plane, but it seems evident that this kind of speech must soon, as it were, submit to the gravity of immediate concerns. It seems evident, in other words, that in the end, in very many cases, speech submits to what *Totality and Infinity* calls "the sameness of the same" and what philosophy more generally recognizes as immanence. This would not be true of certain extraordinary instances that lie at the center of Levinas's position. In order to say "Other" or "Infinity" without contradiction, speech must move "toward on high," since these words express an inexhaustible "surplus," a "more and more"[40] that transcends the limits that belong to our existence. On this point, Levinas's lecture on metaphor is quite close to *Totality and Infinity*, where, however, the emphasis is on the breaching of horizons. Yet the meaning of the notion of horizon eludes us, if it does not appeal to some form of language. It is one and the same thing to think that the face of the other person does not submit to the horizon centered on the subject's understanding, and to think that it is addressed without belonging to the language by which the subject would interpret it.

This still cannot be everything, even if one is prepared to admit the exception as it has been defined. After all, precisely in that case it must appear that Levinas has established only that there are two distinct sorts of metaphors, which is to say only two distinct sorts of "leaping ahead of" present experience. If we compare them, it becomes clear that in the great majority of instances the so-called leap is necessarily qualified. To say with Van Gogh that "conscience is man's compass" is to unite two things that already have something in common, and indeed to play on it. These metaphors are defined relative to the available context, and to the capacities and inclinations of the subject. As for "available context," Levinas does not hesitate to affirm, in fact quite early, that it is made up of what is "already said."[41] Since, of course, what is already said has been said by others, including perhaps the other who is oneself in a former time, the said is the record and the reservoir of humanity as such, which Levinas plainly wishes to raise beyond itself against every tendency to settle. The prophetic nature of his thinking aims at nothing more than this.

It is different with "the exceptions," which Levinas himself goes so far as to call "privileged." Consider the crucial example of "the other." Though the matter has not been worked out in quite these terms, we know enough to be sure that Levinas is willing to extend the notion of context all the way to include everything that is within reach of every negation. What he thinks we say with the words "other" and "face" must positively exceed even this, and so speech—*meta*phor—would be signification that refuses context. For much the same reason, these words also cannot be subject to the limits of any individual perspective. In keeping with a basic axiom of Levinas's thinking, unless they are names for what surpasses any such limits, they draw everything into the orbit of our own understanding. The real difficulty lies with the undeniable fact that we necessarily find the word "other" itself in a vocabulary where it stands out to us—makes itself available—by its relation with a vastly more accessible term that it both presupposes and negates: the same. Certain questions are unavoidable. Can one say "other" without appeal to any vocabulary (and with it, the tradition in which relations between words are shaped)? What would it mean to think, as Levinas seems bound to do, that in some real sense the word "other" is not simply "already said"?

Religious thought knows one form of this problem. It must be possible—or rather, it certainly is the case, but demands clarification— that words with an absolute extension support a meaning that is at once crucial for an entire way of life and virtually incompatible with ordinary understanding. The unspeakable must in some way be spoken, and so a name is accepted, and then in its history the name is said in one way when it is a matter of common practice (worship, obedience, etc.) and in another way when it is a matter of recognizing authentic depth (contemplation, adoration, etc.). For a long time and still in many communities, this difference expresses nothing more than alternating attitudes within a single way of life. Since Spinoza, the modern philosophy of religion has often construed this difference in terms of an opposition between piety and thought, and raised the latter over the former, even while conceding that the former does serve an important purpose for those who cannot think well. Levinas has a complex place in the vast discussion that this calls for, but there can be little doubt of his commitment to the superiority of intellect. Philosophy sees clearly and deeply into human relations, catching sight of dimensions that are covered by our natural tendencies. It is philosophy that alerts us to the ethical relation revealed to us in the face of the other person, and philosophy that teaches us how to see and respect what that face commands. And thus, it is philosophy that might say words like "other" or "face" without forgetting that they are necessarily more than what is invested in them by a vocabulary and tradition— necessarily more than the meaning that is "already said." In ordinary life, of course, this is far from assured, and indeed it may be a mark of our finitude that we are probably always on the verge of a moral *Gerede* in which it quickly gets lost. But this is not only a question of regrettable tendencies. Just as one often prays in all sincerity and with every good effort to an absolute God whom one nonetheless cannot help but envision in very human terms, so does one often speak with an open heart and for love of justice to another person with whom one nonetheless cannot help but feel great familiarity. This concession to our finitude does not mean that the face of the other could not have shocked the one who now exercises some responsibility, any more than it would rule out the possibility that the absolute God has called the believer into prayer. What it certainly does mean is that everyday practice—moral in the one case, devotional in the other—cannot satisfy its own most profound conditions. But far from counting against claims for a God who is absolute or a neighbor who is infinitely other, the evidence of failure or fault is thoroughly consistent with them. In his *Confessions*, Augustine finds not only that the God who moves his heart has already come and gone, but also, and much more to the point, that this is *how* God moves him. If Levinas is correct, something like this can also be said of the manner in which the other person awakens us to responsibility. His phenomenology of the face has no other purpose than to establish this claim.

All of this leads us to conclude that the "privilege" of some metaphors lies specifically in their potential to call us to the real condition of language, which *Totality and Infinity* has called "discourse" and which other works develop in terms of the relation between "saying" and the "said." Among these works, the metaphor of the face is plainly of unique importance, since as the veritable opening of language, it must be the first condition as well as the central theme of the philosophy that is capable of calling us to justice and the good. According to Levinas, it is part and parcel of this task to free thinking of entanglement in being and appearing. In his lecture on metaphor, we find the convergence of two efforts to that effect. On one hand, reflection on the face of the other comes to understand that it is a form of speech before any question of light and luminosity, or rather that its character as speech constitutes a positive refusal of the latter. On the other hand, a more general reflection on language as such recognizes in the peculiar content of the face the first and necessary condition for all meaning. The face thus secures the primacy of the other in both ethics and language, and indeed in the philosophical case for them. As Cesare Del Mastro has shown in an impressive study of the relevant themes, what is most striking in Levinas's unpublished theory of metaphor is its demonstration that when this philosophy truly escapes the "climate" of Heideggerian thought, it becomes an interrogation of language that must know of its own concepts and claims (whatever their conceptual rigor) that they, too, constitute a response to the initiative of what is met only in concrete singularity.[42] In this much, the theory anticipates some of the major claims that we are more accustomed to finding in other, better-known works.

The Metaphor Par Excellence

The ethical relation is therefore language, and in the movement of language it exhibits both senses of transcendence: the subject transcends itself toward the other person, whose face is the revelation of excess. This approach has the evident advantage of freeing the phenomenology of the face from the conceptuality of the image that we encountered in the interplay of face and form taken up in *Totality and Infinity*. To conceive of the face as entering light, if only to contest its authority, is to invite the thought that this necessarily means surrendering some residue of itself to the subject, which for its part, and drawing as it must on all else that it has experienced and retained, interprets it from a perspective. Even if this comes to no more than a sense that the face is not an object, the subject will have found a basis for the understanding that is a kind of possessing.

The effort to instead think the face in terms of language is effectively an effort to think the ethical without any such ambivalence.

We have already had more than one occasion to recognize what this means for Levinas's conception of ethics. At its greatest depth, it has nothing to do with promoting the cultivation of virtues or defining maxims and laws that should govern our freedom. Unmistakably, Levinas understands the importance of these exercises, but for him they belong to the question of how one is to live in robust community, which requires an apportionment of goods, common rules, unifying aims, and so forth. The ethics of the face must inform all of that, and must become the source of constant critique of every instance where, for example, the aims that would unify instead threaten to marginalize or suppress. In this way, the ethics of the face appears as what Derrida famously characterizes as an "Ethics of Ethics," one seemingly beyond all laws and perhaps even without law, but one in the special sense of prophetic access to the anarchic conditions by which there can be laws at all.[43]

As language, this ethics cannot be particular in any way, whether as the legacy of a tradition or only alongside others that are grounded in a different set of principles. It would have to be language from which to understand and critique any such particular languages—"language of the essence of language, and essence of language taking place."[44] Nor can this language be writing, because by its material condition writing is immediately static, making possible and even depending on iterability, as Derrida has emphasized on many occasions. In this way, the language that is writing lends itself to a shift from the first person who, for Levinas, speaks already in the accusative, to the third-person perspective of one whose words are always, as it were, between quotation marks.[45]

What the third-person relation to language would make possible, any conversation among particular languages would require: mediation, in which the relation between two interlocutors would be secured by appeal to some *tertium quid*. Levinas has addressed this possibility at greatest length and no doubt with greatest consequence for his own position in the form of fundamental ontology. In it, the *tertium quid* is of course what Heidegger calls "being," which can only be thought at the price of suspending or refusing the priority of the other (and, if one accepts Levinas's reworking of a classical term, the good). The same challenge would appear in claims to ground the meaning of all discourse on some extra-discursive principle or structure. There may well be many instances of this among philosophies of language. Rather than go into any of them, it may well be asked whether Levinas himself does not fall into some such version of it if, as we have just had reason to observe, what he proposes is "language as the essence of language." Would the theory of metaphor or its successor in the conceptions of saying and said rest on any extra-discursive principle or structure? To the contrary, we have just assured ourselves that the key concepts, and indeed for Levinas *all* concepts, are secured within the same discourse that they bring to light. This claim returns in some passages of *Otherwise Than Being*, where he contends that the correct way to understand the "drama" of philosophy is to see in the manifest disagreement among philosophers an expression of the ethical relation that every inclination to unshakeable claims and settled theses always threatens to suppress.[46] The radical priority of saying in philosophy is affirmed even when the suspension of discourse makes possible the thought of a "nonhuman" language, from which poetry is sometimes born. Here, Levinas has the later Heidegger in mind, and he characterizes this meditation on nonhuman language as forgetfulness of the ethical discourse that has always already come first.[47] The philosopher who is attentive to this is thus called on in the name of both the good and the true to loosen the grip of being that in Heidegger's thinking has language in its grip. In this way, philosophy is led to unexpected solidarity with skepticism, which according to somewhat different impulses refuses the order and evidence of what is submitted to the light of reason.[48] Just as the skeptic cannot intervene against truth without entering into the regime of truth in its own right, the philosopher cannot urge the primacy of ethical discourse against its suppression by being and truth without itself insisting that what it says is true. Indeed, ethics itself requires this hold that is placed on it by being, or else it could not become intelligible as a teaching. But at the same time, ethics also requires that philosophy loosen this grip in order that the teaching remain faithful to its nature. We know that skepticism is capable of returning time and again to take away what it has itself just affirmed in order to inveigh against truth. Philosophy will have to accept a similar fate if it wishes to remain in the service of justice and the good. As it speaks, in its saying, it must enter into the domain of what is already said, where each new proposition must find a place. But it does so precisely in order to make heard what is stifled by this constant victory of the said. Its saying is "both an affirmation and a retraction of the said." This is not paradox, but the difficulty of a task that can never end.[49] Like the skeptic, the philosopher returns again and again to challenge conditions that begin to claim his or her speech as soon as they become intelligible.

The absence of mediation from both the ethical relation and the philosophy that is its teaching is of a single piece with the refusal of reciprocity in human relations at any level of reflection, for it would only be a thought that claims to suspend and overcome reciprocity that might claim to detect what the subject and the other have in common. The thought of mediation is a thought of symmetry, and thus of a leveling down of differences.[50] But the ethical relation is asymmetrical: the face speaks commandingly, from on high, and the subjectivity of the subject is made up of a responsibility that only intensifies as one recognizes its own deficit. There is only a *saying* that has already begun in the word that is the face of the other, and the *said* where one's own words take their place among others and thus where the service that is born in statements of sincere readiness begins to die. But neither of the two has lasting power over the other. Just as the structure of separation was shown in *Totality and Infinity* to be irreducible, so that no power of the subject can truly insulate it forever from the face of the other and no power of that face can truly prevent the subject from a return to its own interests, so in *Otherwise Than Being* is language irreducible to either saying or said, so that each of them returns to disturb the other. The philosophy that proves consistent with these conditions is without consolation for those who would seek stability in being and thinking, perhaps believing that this would be the condition of peace and justice. It is at first sight startling to reach this conclusion when the philosophy in question is nonetheless intent on establishing the positivity of ethical and religious transcendence, and indeed especially when it also continues to speak of "God" even in its final texts (increasingly there, as it happens). Yet, if we only remind ourselves that it is in saying that the singularity of responsibility remains alive, then we recognize in its tension with the said a new instance of Levinas's conviction that "it is not assured that in the end the good will triumph over evil," and thus also of his conviction that we cannot count on God to come to our aid. In short, if Levinas's conception of saying and the said offers us no consolation in the struggle against evil—if instead we are told once again that it is ceaseless and irreducible—it is finally the outcome of his understanding that God is dead. The true God has never intervened in human history, and has never provided individuals with the power to overcome evil. The true God only orders us to one another in language, in which the working of the good take place.[51]

Does this sense of language permit us to say this word "God" without contradiction? We have already come upon at least two calls for considerable discretion in this regard. (1) In *Totality and Infinity*, Levinas has argued that the relation with God cannot be direct, even if it is constant. If the act of turning toward God, whether in speech or in gesture, occurs at the initiative of the subject, it will have first claimed for itself some comprehension of its aim, and in this way already frustrated its own intention. For Levinas, who appeals forcefully to the idea of Infinity, God cannot be captured in an idea or approached as a theme. One goes toward God only in response to the other, who opens a dimension not available to the subject acting by its own powers. The invisible God is approached only in love and service. (2) This point is reinforced by the philosophy of language informing *Otherwise Than Being, or Beyond Essence*. One does not say "God" in prayer or philosophy except in response to the other person. To take the contrary approach, proposing to address God in a manner that prescinds from the ethical relation, is to submit God to the movement of being which, left to itself, only repeats words that have already been said. This would be true in every experience, in the well-intended invocations of the pious, and in philosophy, which would be limited to refining previous conceptions of the divine or perhaps recasting their relations with one another. To seek the meaning of "God" in responsibility and to insist on the primacy of saying is to propose that it is the other person—his or her face, as trace—that inspires in us the word "God." For it is only in this way that a subject is awakened from his or her self-absorption, called back to an ordering that has been established before the time of its own being, and brought up against the question of the principle for that ordering. The word "God" may come to our lips when we sense that our non-indifference to the suffering of the other person is older and deeper than our very existence, and has an intelligibility that does not depend on it. In such moments, "language would exceed the limits of what is thought, by suggesting . . . an implication of a meaning distinct from that which comes to signs from the simultaneity of systems or the logical definition of concepts."[52] But then, whatever the force that inspires it, the name "God" could not be more precarious. Should one prove to have spoken it like any other name, one will have fallen into idolatry. Should one prove to have claimed perfect speech, to have named God as God truly is, one will have instead fallen into blasphemy.

This is a problem for philosophy, and not for the everyday pursuit of responsibility and goodness, in which the word "God" need not arise. Not that what the word invokes is a matter of indifference there. "God" is implicated and in that sense "at work" (though without causation) in the very possibility of everything that Levinas ascribes to the ethical relation. The philosophical account of the face as trace becomes a teaching about "God" when it is shown that what transpires in the encounter becomes intelligible only when the interpretation arrives at notions such as anarchy and non-indifference, and then is led to wonder at the appearance of agreement between them. Can philosophy do without a name for this? Would the name be gratuitous? Only if one is prepared to think that the nature of the ethical relation neither rests on nor is a condition of anything else at all. And this would mean disavowing the conception of Infinity by which plurality is distinguished from sheer atomism without suppressing the singularity of the subject. If, from this perspective, the idea of Infinity now appears as the leading edge of a refusal to think that our sense of debt to one another is only a matter of contingency or only the result of some complex material process, it becomes clear that what is most deeply invested in the word "God" is the possibility of honoring that refusal as the expression of a profound truth.

None of this can mean that for Levinas, the call of the other person which is already a saying unassimilable to the said is in itself the self-communication of God. Discourse only testifies to the transcendence of what "passes by" experience and understanding, and yet it invites the word "God" and a sense of companionship because it is by this passing that we are capable of responsibility and goodness. Tradition, the said considered in its historical and cultural extension, has preserved the word "God" among and alongside other words, and in that way given it a meaning that is only relative to the meanings of other words. According to Levinas, it is possible to regain this word's proper, elevated meaning only if thinking will permit itself to be instructed by the face of the other person—that is to say, only if thinking will catch sight of the fact that its pronouncements, too, have the original character of saying. And this means, at bottom, that thinking would have to also recognize in the saying an ordering that is prior to being. To say "God" would then become an attempt to give meaning to conditions already established before one may pretend to grasp them. Can one do justice to everything that this implies? One would have to relinquish one's own right to a prior understanding of what the word "God" truly means, or as the encounter with psychoanalysis has taught us to put it, one would have to safeguard from the word any definition by the investment of one's own interest. The fact that this is all but impossible reminds us that an extraordinary word is still indeed a word. There is something miraculous about the word "God," as there is about the idea of Infinity that it so closely resembles. It is the presence in language of an opening beyond the very possibility of language, the one word by which to understand the authentic function of all the others. We take this to be what Levinas means when in the lecture on metaphor he writes that "God is the metaphor of metaphors."[53]

The One God and the Other: Levinas and Christian Theology

The prophetic impulse in Levinas's thinking appeared to us first as an implication of his indictment of being as violent and his claim that peace is nonetheless possible. In political philosophy, this shifts the good outside the reach of what can be accomplished by agreement and legislation, which for their part are still the achievements of free beings whose capacities are entangled in self-interest. It is thus an immediate aim of this philosophy to identify a relation with the good that would transcend our attachment to being, however unbreakable that attachment may be. In *Totality and Infinity*, the pursuit of this aim is concentrated on descriptions of the face of the other person and on the life of the subject that it awakens and commands to responsibility. When in the course of this argument Levinas's claim for the priority of the other person reveals itself to also be speech about God, and when both the other person and God are said to transcend history, being, and language, he commits philosophy to prophecy. The face of the other person is the advent of the good, coming in its own time. It is also the opening up of a way to meditate on relations that are secured immemorially, according to the passing of God before any possible measure.

In order for these claims to be heard, they must be brought into the present and its conditions—again, history, being, and language—if only to challenge the hold that these have on us. It must be possible to find, on the surface of the present, indications of relations that do not become present without ceasing to be themselves. This task is given to phenomenology in Levinas's texts. Transformed in this way—for it is an assignment that neither Husserl nor Heidegger could have imagined—phenomenology testifies to matters resembling those of theology, yet without ever wishing to become a theology itself. Indeed, it will even be necessary to engage theology in order to make certain fundamental differences clear: God does not intervene according to any causality, admits of no analogy between the divine and the human, and relates to us without any mediation. If this engagement with theology leads free, thinking subjects to the truth, then it is criticism in the best sense, and it is teaching.

It is well known that an entire branch of Levinas's work is committed to precisely this sort of teaching within the Jewish community. We have investigated some of its origin in the exceptionally difficult circumstances during the Second World War, when antisemitic persecution highlighted the proper definition of what Levinas grasped as Jewishness. What followed, aided by the phenomenological method and an extraordinary facility with texts and the tradition, presents itself as a prolonged call to embrace the rational and prophetic character of a life defined by fidelity to the Torah and Talmud. But if in the end what one is thus to learn is that the divinity of God is consistent with a responsibility that is at once singular and unlimited,[1] then this teaching for Judaism closely resembles what is also offered to a culture and indeed a way of life that is, at least in Levinas's own time, permeated by fidelity to Jesus Christ. When he adopts some of the terms and thought patterns of Christian Europe, it is not merely because he wishes to be understood by those to whom he feels closest, but much more so in order to open them to a teaching that would cleanse religious thought from contamination by philosophies of being and appearing.

The Primacy of Philosophy

We have come to the view, certainly with some simplification, that much of Levinas's philosophical work is organized around two claims. He makes a phenomenological case for ethics as first philosophy, and proposes that this ethics is also religion. There are at least three evident ways to an understanding of what he means by "religion." As we have already seen, a good deal of it rests on his conception of Infinity (chapter 3) and the specific conception of the Good that is associated with it (chapter 4). Further specifications are made in the course of a theory of language able to understand the word "God" in a manner that does not contradict what has been argued concerning ethics and Infinity (chapter 5). This still leaves the question of Levinas's relation to theology. Here, too, there are evident difficulties. Philosophy is not theology, even if each of the two forms of thought does draw concepts and thought patterns from one another. This is at least minimally the case for the philosophy that defends ethical metaphysics. What are we to make of Levinas's use of biblical terms like "creation," "election," or "messiah"? Or his notion of a desire that transcends being toward supreme goodness? If our philosophical use of these terms is originally Greek, it is nonetheless also Jewish and Christian in the meantime, and it would be difficult to contend that Levinas's philosophy is nothing more and nothing less than a reinvigoration of Plato or Plotinus.[2] Still, before one goes in search of a Jewish or Christian supplement to Levinas's Greek (and, let us not forget, German) sources, one should take note of the fact that some key features of his thinking do open a significant distance from the theological principles that are at the very least familiar and recurrent, and perhaps even essential. When it is said that Infinity so completely transcends finite understanding as to rule out any positive grasp of its meaning except through the face of the other person, there is no longer reason or room to think that God would appear directly in human experience or history. Of course, the record suggests that Levinas's turn against this God may well be partly motivated by personal and historical events, but in that case, it was a matter of God's silence and the appearance of inaction (chapter 2). The existence of a God who intervenes in human lives was not at all evident in the *stalag* or the *Lager*, and Levinas's understanding of what that has meant is registered in his interpretation of Infinity. Now, one must certainly honor the moral and spiritual authority from which such claims are made, but one is still permitted to wonder about their implications for the practice of faith rooted in prayer to a personal God and in participation in rituals and sacraments where God is thought to be present—and about the considerable theological tradition that accepts these things on the authority of a revelation that unfolds in time. If these are the necessary roots of theological language, then that language has a particularity that renders it obscure and at least partly inaccessible to those who do not belong to that tradition, though nothing prevents them from appropriating it in a new way. Such efforts would be required in order to sustain the universality that Levinas has sought in his claims for the Jewish character of our subjectivity and, along a different line, the ethical metaphysics that grounds a humanism of the other person.

We have established that the question of God is never far from Levinas's thinking, even if it is sometimes only in the background of other concerns. Not unexpectedly, it is defined in part by an intention to break from Heideggerian ontology. Of the earliest efforts, it is less important to determine quite what sort of God Levinas might have in mind than it is to catch sight of the role it plays in his challenge to Heidegger's conception of being in the world. Expressions such as "savor for the absolute" and "urge for the Creator" signal a dimension of what will later be called our "subjectivity" that Heidegger famously excludes.[3] The first intervention, then, is in the name of challenging the limits of our attachment to being, which however must be understood properly and in detail. Levinas's books published shortly after the end of the Second

World War are committed mainly to this latter task, but in the meantime the notebooks he kept while imprisoned by the Germans exhibit considerable interest in all of the themes surrounding God and religion. Moreover, a conviction that our subjectivity includes a savor or urge for God is not absent even from those early books, though it is not until God is understood as Infinity and Infinity is aligned with exteriority that it becomes possible to defend the thesis of a desire that does not in any way possess what is desired. This metaphysical desire seeks Infinity, the God who positively transcends any possible comprehension, whether kataphatic or apophatic, and whose passing, before any past that would be recuperated by memory as a beginning,[4] orders each one of us to the other. Whatever sense Levinas has of God as creator must be found here. The ethical relation, the relation by which the other is never a matter of indifference to the subject, is the trace of a God who has never been present and yet, so to speak, has a decisive influence on us. In *Totality and Infinity*, the word "creation" stands only for this: our orderedness to one another, without any imputation of an ultimate cause. In short, creation is the ethical ordering of each one to the other, and the God who is its principle has absconded from it.[5]

It is proposals such as these—and as we will see, there are more of them—that put Levinas at a significant distance from theology, or at least a familiar kind of theology (personal God, ontological articulation). If he is at all a theologian in his own right, then the matter rests heavily on a narrow reception of the etymological sense of that word: a theologian gives an account of the gods or God.[6] This Levinas surely does, insofar as he makes a forceful case for God as Infinity and as Good, and militates against conceptions that fall into idolatry and totalization. Still, before one approaches these charges—asking what constitutes them, or, to put a fine point on the matter, asking in what sense theology could be considered guilty of them—there are the transcendental conditions of the discourses themselves to consider. The theology which accepts that God truly *is* necessarily subjects itself to the same conditions that are observed in the relation of the believer to that God such as are present in specific doctrines and practices. The theologian does not produce doctrines but only discovers them or clarifies their meaning, and does not cease to practice alongside the others who have faith. Theology of this sort thus does its work without pretending to an external perspective, so that the exercise of what another school of thought might wish to call "right reason" is also pious and devotional reason. One theologizes on the authority of revelation, and one thinks first in the mode of praise for that God who offers the revelation.[7] Levinas seems to think differently about revelation when he identifies it with the face of the other, and replaces the theme of fidelity with that of an ethical respect that one takes up on pain of otherwise reverting into egocentrism. Moreover, as we have seen, these conditions must be imposed by a subject who philosophizes, even if this means thinking that the entirety of a philosophy thus becomes a teaching inspired by the other person.[8] When Levinas tells us, quoting the eleventh-century Jewish poet Jehuda Halevi, that "God speaks to each man in particular,"[9] he means to remind us that we are turned toward God by the call of the other person for help. The philosopher who would speak of God, and teach us with that saying, must first hear it in the human call for help and must ensure that his or her speech does not depart from the conditions of responsibility. Where the theologian's speech about God must submit to the criterion of praise, the philosopher's speech is subject to the demands of justice.

These differences bring into clear view the basis for Levinas's criticisms of theology. It is philosophy and not theology that attends to the relation with the other person, and given all that this means, it is also philosophy and not theology that attends to the relation with God as Infinity and as Good. By now, we know well what this means within the argument for ethical metaphysics. Theology such as Levinas understands it fails to meet its requirements in either of two ways. Arrested by the beauty of an image[10] or taking comfort from the alleged stability of an incarnation,[11] it proposes to satisfy metaphysical desire with an ultimate theme or an end. A universal mediator is thus installed, or if one prefers, a common locus. The God who is accessible in this way is a God to whom all human relations are referring, and from whom all would receive their true meaning. In this way, the signification of the other person and the witness of a subject who welcomes it are inscribed in a "system of language" that has not yet been opened to the movement of speech that responds first to genuine transcendence (a transcendence that is not merely the counterpart of immanence).[12]

The charge of idolatry is familiar enough, at least in its broad lines. It has been commonly understood since Feuerbach that the heart of every idolatry is auto-idolatry.[13] In the philosophy of Levinas, this receives an ontological clarification: in order to escape the restlessness of our being (which is really restlessness "for the other person"),[14] believers will have projected and then believed in a God who has all of the self-sufficiency that we would like to have for ourselves. But then *only* "like to have," since self-sufficiency would have to be sealed in a pure self-relation that violates what Levinas finds to be the irreducible condition of our existence. This is betrayed at the most fundamental level by the pulse of lived time, which does not cease even when the effort of existing becomes a gift to the other and a hope for peace and goodness.

These last few remarks also reinforce another facet of Levinas's critique. When theology claims to identify an eternal source and center for our being, it thinks from a place that is withdrawn from the temporality that oscillates between being-for-oneself and being-for-the-other person. Throughout Levinas's work, for reasons that hardly need recounting here, such a place is the essential condition of a thought that totalizes. In order to acquire a vision of the whole of which everything and everyone is a part, thought pretends to stand outside its limit, claiming for itself a gaze that would be neutral. So, likewise, would it be timeless in the empty sense defined by Hobbes, *nunc stans*.[15]

The Critique of "Negative Theology"

The reduction of theology to a form of thought that exempts itself from the fundamental conditions of our being and time is associated first with Heidegger. The Heideggerian resonance in Levinas's relation to theology is evident enough, but it does not prevent him from submitting Heidegger himself to some of the same criticism. Whereas Heidegger deconstructs the onto-theological constitution of metaphysics in order to awaken the question of the meaning of being, Levinas proposes to extend that same effort until also freeing thought from its ordering to being and beings. And whereas Heidegger considers philosophy, both in deficient mode and as fundamental ontology, as unsuited to pose the question of God, Levinas wishes to open philosophy to the proper conception of God that has been suppressed by ontology, and with it, theology. As for the convergence of these last two forms of thought, it will not do to claim only that fundamental ontology totalizes by submitting the plurality of separated subjects to the primacy of the concept of being, and that theology does the same with the concept of God. To be sure, this comparison does support the idea that a same logic is at work in each, but when Levinas identifies it—the "logical privilege of totality"—he is careful to suggest that this has entered theology from elsewhere, which is to say specifically when it treats the relation with God "in terms of ontology."[16] Given what we already know of Levinas's understanding of our being/existing and his characterization of the Heideggerian interpretation, this can only mean one thing: Levinas might well agree that there is in theology a sincere wish to articulate our relation with God, but he clearly thinks that any attempt to do so in the categories or concepts of being immediately distorts it with a vision of the whole or sum, and that any attempt to promote that vision has all of the violence of totalization. Not even Heidegger's reflective and critical investigation of being and beings can avoid this outcome, because so long as one thinks only within the horizon of being and time, the most one can do is to seek some account of order in its relation to a more primordial difference. Has Heidegger attempted anything other than this? Let us concede that much to Levinas. What is meant by the "end of metaphysics" is precisely metaphysics gaining clear insight into itself as the thought of beings in relation to their ground, which is to say, in Heidegger's own terms, its coming into place (*das Ende*).[17] It will be possible to see it as a whole, even through its historical permutations, which is to say *from a perspective that is no longer entirely subject to the conditions of the whole.* The later Heidegger does strive to think even this new thinking historically—being is historical, as must be the thinking of being—but without doubting the primacy of the *Seinsfrage*, and according to an insight, a freedom, and a calling that he considers previously lacking in philosophy.[18]

At this particular point, one might want to insist on an important nuance. Heidegger's later works do not simply withdraw into unconditioned thought, but undertake something closer to its opposite. Thoughtful thinking would seem to be much closer to embracing its own contingency than to projecting anything like an embracing whole or sum. Yet it remains the case both that the topic of this newly chastened thinking is itself conceptually fixed in the word *Sein*, however removed this may be from promoting any *ultima ratio*, and that one must approach it meditatively, which is to say individually. It is true that there is something kenotic about thoughtful thinking, as it endeavors to welcome and then meditate on the manifestation of being, but this only underscores the fact that it begins in the efforts of the thinker rather than in the call of the other, and this is enough for Levinas to detect an antecedent claim to place. Thoughtful thinking is stabilized by an effort to keep in view a same and abiding source of meaning.[19]

Now, Heidegger's later thinking does not constitute a theology,[20] but the foregoing review of Levinas's relation to it prepares us to recognize the point at which to assess the critique of theology that must come from ethical metaphysics. After all, theology, too, and for analogous reasons,[21] has often displayed considerable humility about the limits of its own claims concerning the ultimate relation with God. Perhaps this is not evident everywhere. Alongside the hortatory and propositional claims that belong to preaching and the elaboration of scripture and doctrine, there is also the mystical and apophatic current of theology, in which the theologian tempers positive statements about God with negations that signal a clear and constant sense that our understanding is necessarily situated and therefore limited. Levinas's argument is unmoved by this shift from *kataphasis*: "The idea of the perfect and of infinity is not reducible to the negation of the imperfect; negativity is incapable of transcendence."[22] What, then, of the desire that the believer would follow beyond the limits of imperfection to union with perfection? "God always calls us to Himself too soon; we want the here below. In the horror of the radical unknown to which death leads, is evinced the limit of negativity."[23] This second passage is remarkable for its reversal of a common understanding. Where the mystics would go straightaway to God (and make considerable progress), Levinas detects a limitation in their most effective tool or stratagem: since negation remains an act of the subject, negativity can proceed no farther than the inner frontier of being. And this is not due to simple exhaustion or digression; what Levinas suggests here—horror at death, flight into negativity—is rather that apophasis is prevented in advance from final achievement. In his view, it has never been about anything other than the relation to existence, which of course he does not doubt is imposed as an anchor and a burden. Mysticism would then appear as a failed evasion, in Levinas's sense of that word, and apophatic theology would repeat this at the level of discourse.[24]

As an interpretation of mysticism, these few thoughts move too quickly over a crucial point. At the peak of his or her desire, the mystic surrenders even the desire itself to God. This is also said of prayer: at some point along the way, the mystic no longer directs or controls the act, but instead undergoes it, and according to a rhythm that no longer awaits his or her initiative.[25] Between the labor of the mystical path and the intimacy of elevated faith, there is a moment of assent to God that would be difficult to attribute to a power of the subject. The assent that truly is surrender does not project a result (though to be sure, the demons of pride and vanity are close at hand). To what then does the subject surrender? If it is to a known cause or principle, then as far as Levinas is concerned all is indeed lost, since in that case what passes as "God" is really only an idol of the mind, or else is submitted to the logic of totalization by which *explanandum* and *explanans* are present together and at once. And such a thought, let us note, would be the mark of a thinking, at work even where theology is at its most self-critical, that has withdrawn from the conditions of its own finitude. In short, theology, even mystical theology, would claim for itself the stable position within being that Levinas calls "place."

Is this evidently the case? Much depends on how we are to understand the nature of the God to whom one assents. The idea that this can be withdrawn from the charges of idolatry and totalization that are embedded in suspicion of ontology leads inevitably to the early work of Jean-Luc Marion. There, too, philosophy is called to the service of rehabilitating religion both with and against Heidegger—with his critique of foundational metaphysics, but against his restriction of the question of God to vulgar conceptions associated with ontotheology. Marion comes closest to the matter at hand in his effort to show that Pseudo-Dionysius's understanding of God as "cause," or as he prefers, "Requisite" (*aitia*), cannot be submitted to a finite gaze or contained within a totality.[26] This sense of cause has nothing do with the causes at work in the knowable world or, one is tempted to say, within what Levinas calls "being" (or, especially in his early works, existence and existing). It is meant to express our relation to an origin or source that cannot itself be submitted to the categories by which anything else would be known because all else is already given from it. The least that can be said about any such source or origin is that it is not merely a cause like all of the others. And in the case that it nonetheless appears all too plainly accessible to human understanding, one must then consider whether this use of "cause" truly designates only the apex of that understanding and not instead the superabundance of this one "object," God.

This argument has most often been received as the means to revive an entire metaphysics developed especially by Aquinas and his school.[27] Let us instead attend to its immediate interest for the phenomenology of religious life. From the notions of a source for all beings, including in their powers, it follows that all such beings are given, and that those who are free and conscious must know themselves as indebted to their source. Religious debt is not yet guilt. Dependence on a God who is absolute and who gives from love, cannot be reduced to economic debt, as Nietzsche, for one, might have us think.[28] There can be no exchange with an interlocutor who already gives what one might wish to place in trade. Nor can religious debt be taken to designate a place from which thinking might exempt itself from its own essential limits, as Levinas might contend. The humble theologian knows that everything he or she says proceeds from capacities and depends on resources that, again, are given. But religious debt does designate another sort of place that would compromise the primacy of the relation with the other person. This is the "place under the sun" given to me by God, according to Pascal, and understood by Levinas as the origin of usurpation.[29] This yields a great many things one frankly misses in ethical metaphysics and, in its line, what one expects Levinas to understand as mature religion: play, wonder, and enthusiasm. It is also the necessary—and necessitating—condition of the praise that we have found some thinkers to consider as the proper character of theology. The theologian begins each day in thanks to the God who gives everything, and ends each day in praise for the God who makes all things possible.

These last determinations do not spare theology from ethical critique, but only uncover its deepest source. In the end, gift, debt, gratitude, and praise all belong to a relation with God who, one believes, *provides*. Levinas's first and final reason for resisting all of this lies not with his conception of a subject that exhibits no natural telos and no conformity to natural law, and not with his defense of an exteriority that cannot be reached by any analogy, but with the conception of God that is supposed by all of those concepts, and by piety that is articulated in good theology. The God who provides, or whom one believes to provide, remains a God who we can "count on." The philosophy of Levinas is strictly opposed to this thought, according to both the force of profound experience and the essential nature of an entire range of important concepts. If the world stands in need, it is for humankind to do the work.[30] This is the religious condition of ethics.

Creation, Election, Messianism

The religion of ethical metaphysics is certainly not theology in the sense we have just explored, but Levinas does frequently appeal to biblical terms that have long been part of theological discourse. Let us now investigate their meaning in his works. Three of them lie especially close to the center of his position: *creation* (which we have already touched on more than once), *election* (which is already important in the wartime writings), and *messianism* (which, it will become clear, has been close at hand almost constantly).

Plurality as Creation

Levinas's reformulation of the theological concept of creation appears in full detail late in *Totality and Infinity*, but it is sketched or strongly implied elsewhere. There are also nontheological instances of the concept, as when the effort of existing is said to involve repeated creations of oneself out of nothing that make up the pulsation of lived time. This may be an inheritance from Sartre, whose conception of radical freedom requires him to think that one's possibilities must be created ex nihilo in order to become truly present, though of course Levinas is intent on showing that these notions are entirely forgetful of the primary relation with the other person. But this still means first agreeing with Sartre that there is no single principle that would mediate that relation. The first step in this direction must be to sever any notion of divine causation from the Cartesian notion of time that is embedded in the ontology of effort. Levinas finds strictly ontological reasons for doing so. Heidegger's distinction between "that which exists and its existence" helps clear up certain equivocations by which one would start out with existing and end up at God.[31] This would be the error of Descartes himself as well as Malebranche, who attempt to ground the possibility of consistency from instant to instant with the idea of *creatio continua*.[32] This idea itself is the occasion for some theological turbulence. On one hand, it appears to submit God, as creator, to the principle of sufficient reason by which to address a difficult problem in ontology. On the other hand, it also risks conflating the expression of God's will with a movement that does not of itself exhibit any telos. For his part, Levinas understands the ontologization of a God who acts in concert with lived time as only a symptom of the debatable thought that consistency from instant to instant can be provided only by some ground or foundation. He thus takes away from the entire theory only its admission that the existent is not sufficient unto itself. If one interprets our being in the world without bringing in a notion of God that serves only to explain away its original situation, one catches sight of existential dispossession and, in its fullest extension, a plurality of subjects.[33]

Dispossession, or non-self-sufficiency, is interpreted by Levinas as dependence and as passivity. One is dependent on Infinity insofar as it is by the relation with Infinity that one is separated, uniquely oneself in the effort of existing, and yet susceptible to the call of the other person. This is not owed to any prior cause, but is a structure of the relation itself. Most often, this relation is affirmed phenomenologically, as the various features of our subjectivity are followed from simple givenness to the discovery of irreducible relations that Levinas calls "anarchic" in order to indicate their anteriority with respect to being and appearing. Creation, especially ex nihilo, becomes a name for a dependence that could not be caused because it is prior to the difference between cause and effect. This dependence is specifically a passivity, prior to any affectivity, because the relation with Infinity, of creature and Creator, is antecedent to any feeling or mood that may arise in response to the face that touches on it.

This does not mean that the relation cannot be thought, and the non-causal understanding of creation justified, from the side of Infinity. In the passages that *Totality and Infinity* reserves for an interpretation of "Filiality and Fraternity," it is shown that the relation with a source for one's being takes the form of a dependence that does not exclude freedom.[34] Levinas's ostensible theme is human kinship above and beyond the evident biological indications. Parents are antecedent to their children, but their relation cannot be reduced to biological or psychological determinants, which after all would be strictly causal. To insist on these, which is always possible, would be to forget or cancel out the unicity that belongs to separate existence. The identity of the child both is and is not received from its parents; the child receives itself from them but without belonging to them. And any nullification of these conditions would, in a manner that is not only metaphorical, bring about the end of the child as child and the parents as parents, even if the people involved were all still living together. Psychologists will recognize a theory of abuse in this scenario. Levinas offers us an interpretation that is fundamentally ethical. To take away the dependence of the child, or for him or her to deny it entirely, is to promote a solitude consumed by futile efforts to cover up every sign of a vulnerability one has never learned to surrender to the other person. To take away or deny the child's freedom is to suspend the approach of future generations, without which ethics and religion dissolve.[35]

These thoughts are easily applied to the relation with Infinity.[36] The subject's relation with Infinity is one of dependence that does not contradict freedom, and any proposal that either the dependence or the freedom are to be suspended would require the violence of causality. God would then have withdrawn wholly into a deistic indifference that betrays the original relation, or else moved to cancel the freedom in which responsible subjects seek justice and the Good. It is not clear that Levinas has ever associated the problem of divine causality with this particular violence, but there can be no doubt that in his conception of the religious relation he has avoided it. Infinity is consistent with freedom even as it is also consistent with dependence. The face of the other necessarily implies both of these at once—reaching all the way beneath self-interest and the pretense of autonomy, to touch a primordial heteronomy that awakens the freedom to choose for it. This heteronomy, we know, is the condition of the subject's relation with Infinity. It is installed in each of us prior to any attempt to place it in a general account of being human. Each of us has his or her own relation to Infinity, just as each of us is answerable uniquely to the face who calls us to responsibility. It would be my dependence and my responsibility, or rather these make up my mineness, which I alone can exercise without the possibility of exchanging it for that of anyone else.

Call as Election

If the allowable use of "creation" would be to designate a freedom and a dependence that have not been caused, the implications for our ipseity permit recourse to the word "election,"[37] in order to signify its implication for our subjectivity. The ethical sense of "mineness" we have just caught sight of may be heard as a response to Heidegger's *Jemeinigkeit*, the primordial relating to oneself and belonging to oneself that defines the unicity of Dasein's care.[38] Levinas comments on it often. In his original philosophical works, of course, he is intent on overturning the priority that Heidegger claims for the self-relation that is invested in it. In doing so, he does not contest the basic lines of Heidegger's claim that each of us is being-toward-my-own-death so much as recast it within a more primordial relation. According to the initial conditions of my being, my death certainly is my own, but this fact is not impervious to the correction that comes in the face that calls me to anarchic responsibility. The real meaning of my "mineness" thus appears in the form of affairs that only I can undertake, and from prior to any expectation that the other person might respond in turn.[39] Most deeply, I am responsible for the entirety of the I that faces me, all the way to including his or her death. The priority of the other person over me is established in a face that reveals this morality and the suffering in which it shows itself. Even if I do not actually give up my own life for him or her, still, in a deeper sense my death, no less than my being, is for-the-other. Just as I exist in the ambiance of the other, so too do I die in the ambiance of the other. Radical responsibility entails the conversion of one's own death as if solely a private affair into a dying that would be for the other that takes precedence over what Heidegger calls "authentic" death.[40] Death as solitude, and philosophy as ontology, are broken up by the mercy that awakens in one who is called uniquely to care for a suffering that is endless because it is coextensive with life itself. This mercy, which seeks more than justice alone would require, is the sign of our election.[41]

We know that Levinas has associated suffering and election since his wartime writing, when he was preoccupied especially with the possibility of establishing a distinctly Jewish way of existing, a Jewish "facticity,"[42] that would nonetheless also bring to light features or conditions that are universal. This has not vanished behind his emphasis on responsibility for the other person. To the contrary, he considers the latter to be the "essence of human conscience" as known best in Jewish experience. And as for its content, Levinas likes to cite Dostoevsky: "all of us are responsible for one another, and I more than anyone else."[43] There is of course an expansive theory of community and extended responsibility in this claim. In the face of the other, all of the other others also call for help. According to the logic of interiority and exteriority at work in Levinas's conception of the separated subject, it is one and the same thing for the narcissism of the subject to be broken open to the suffering of this other person here and now, and for it to be broken open to the suffering of all of the others.[44] *Totality and Infinity* does not often refer to election, but on the essential point it is clear. The singularity of responsibility, which comprises the very mineness of the subject, makes possible a justice that is guided by the demands of concrete suffering, without which even the deliberation and calculation that are needed for concerted action might otherwise decline into a reasoning that is merely formal.[45] To be elected to responsibility for this other person who faces me is to be led back to the concrete singularity not only of my own existence, but also of the one who suffers before me. Properly speaking, election is anterior to the generalization that is nonetheless required in order to name.

This is not yet everything. As is the case with the claim that the face is a trauma, the claim that it delivers ethical election requires an account of its anterior conditions in the subject. This can be said in plain language: one wants to know how it would be that the face of the other person singles me out for a unique responsibility—me alone, without possibility of substitution or evasion—rather than only presenting me with one possible identity among others (and, since it is a matter of plain language, an identity that I may not be inclined to recognize). Of course, this has everything to do with Levinas's claim for the anarchic relation with what is variously called "Infinity," the "Good," and "God." In the terminology of trauma, there is a "first time" always already installed but awakened only by the "second time" that is the shock of the face. In the terminology of law, there is a heteronomy prior to any pretended autonomy and unknown until that autonomy is broken up by the face. Now, in terms of election, one will have been chosen before and outside of any choice made on one's own part, though choosing on one's own part is all that one may know until one is taught otherwise by the face of the other. To be sure, it belongs to the heart of Levinas's argument to claim that the call of the other person constitutes an election that cannot be declined. But if this claim is left only at the level of the everyday life in its concrete occurrence, it is evidently false. Unfortunately, human beings do see faces of others, feel a strong call to responsibility, and yet summon both the means and the reasons to choose otherwise. Yet this already tells us where the indeclinable truly lies: one cannot *not* be altered in one's consciousness by the call of the other person. Election is thus also a name for the notion of non-indifference which we have come upon more than once. Can one be entirely indifferent to the presence of another person, even in the silence between strangers who give no sign of actually asking one another for anything at all? The discomfort that has not yet found words or a gesture is already a response, before one arrives at an interpretation that might, in turn, suggest a course of action (a smile, a frown, a shiver, etc.). This discomfort is Levinas's evidence for a susceptibility prior to preparedness or expectation, and of a passivity that cannot be annulled by any activity: the other person *always* comes as a surprise, and its first meaning is suffering and need. We should hear Levinas on this at some length. In welcoming the other who suffers,

> the subject finds himself committed to the Good in the very passivity of supporting. The distinction between free and non-free would not be the ultimate distinction between humanity and inhumanity, nor the ultimate mark of sense and nonsense. To understand intelligibility does not consist in going back to the beginning. There was a time irreducible to presence, an absolute unrepresentable past. Has not the Good chosen the subject with an election recognizable in the responsibility of being hostage, to which the subject is destined, which he cannot evade without denying himself, and by virtue of which he is unique? A philosopher can give to this election only the signification circumscribed by responsibility for the other. This antecedence of responsibility to freedom would signify the Goodness of the Good: the necessity that the Good choose me first before I can be in a position to choose, that is, welcome its choice. That is my pre-originary susceptiveness. It is a passivity prior to all receptivity, it is transcendent.[46]

The first time of election belongs to an-archy. The claim of the Good is always already the case, before the beginning, and yet it can become known to philosophy as the condition without which the very nature of radical responsibility would be unintelligible (for Levinas, always, the evidence of the anarchical is the things themselves, interpreted in their original exorbitance). It follows from this that election is no more a matter of causality than is what Levinas means by "creation." If creation characterizes the relation of Infinity and plurality, or God and the ethical relation—a dispersion without atomism—then election characterizes the manner in which this is installed or perhaps incarnated in the subjectivity of the subject. We have already seen this more than once: the "choice" of the Good thus without coercion of its own. The Good has always already passed, and the subject is always already susceptible to the face of the other which, to be sure, obliges. The trace of the Good that is susceptibility in the subject is of a single piece with this undying power of obligation in the face of the other. It belongs to the original situation of our subjectivity that the other person "persecutes" (astonishing recuperation of a term!) with a ceaseless and insatiable call for help, and that we must embrace this as the way to goodness.[47]

Messianic Responsibility

The ethical condition of creation is election, whereby plurality is already the responsibility of the singular subject for this other person who calls for help here and now. The subject who is immersed in being, as effort and as self-interest, is already a subject in relation with the other who transcends being. When the face of the other calls the subject back to this relation, it also opens up a transcendence that could not have been recognized or attained from within being. The choice to commit oneself entirely to the other person, all the way to his or her death, is a choice for a Good beyond what is good only for oneself. This rejoins a thought we found at the heart of *Totality and Infinity*: responsibility is the very work of redemption.[48] We also found, in the same text, suggestions that the work originates *only* in responsibility, since there can be no other advent of the Good than in the face that calls and commands. And from subsequent texts, we have learned, though this was only a matter of appreciating an increased emphasis, that this responsibility is most assuredly of a unique subject for a unique other, present here and now, and that this must be the starting point for any consideration of the many necessary generalizations, complications, and qualifications that make up our morality and politics. All of this means that the Good is produced—brought to light, welcomed into the world—at the level of concrete singularity, which is to say by each one of us, but only at the initiative of the other.

The themes of redemption and of salvation from suffering are addressed in the traditions familiar to Levinas in the form of messianism, in which a privileged relation with God supports the undoing of realities that are inherent to worldly existence. In the Jewish and Christian scriptures, the word "messiah" (*maschiach*: anointed) is associated first with kingship and most emphatically with David (1 Sam. 16; 2 Sam. 5:3), whereupon the sense of expectation that is eventually attached to it is represented in terms of the achievement of perfect conditions. The messiah as anointed one becomes the messiah as ideal ruler, one who keeps peace and cultivates social and material well-being (Ps. 72). Already at this point, the messiah, as king, is the mediator of divine blessing, with his beneficent rule in agreement with fidelity to the covenant with God. This representation polarizes hope in a single figure, but is exposed to calamity. A robust eschatological dimension in messianism goes hand in hand with a deep sense of evil and suffering. The prophetic books testify to this. For a long time, Jesus is hesitant to claim the title of messiah, though his work seems to prompt the thought by observers, and Peter even uses the word explicitly (Mk. 8:39). On Palm Sunday, however, his entrance into Jerusalem on the back of an ass seems to invoke the messianic words of Zechariah 9:9, and by the end of his Passion his discussion with the High Priest gives him an occasion not so much to refuse the term as to clarify what it will mean to him: "you will see the Son of Man seated in the place of power at God's right hand, and coming on the clouds of heaven" (Mt. 26:64, see also Ps. 110:1). It is especially in the light of these passages that the tradition speaks with confidence of Jesus as Christ (*christos*, the Greek translation of *maschiach*). Already in the theology of Paul, Jesus is Christ, the one who suffers and dies for us that we might be saved from sin and evil. For those who believe this, the suffering face of Jesus is thus the very promise of salvation, or if the metaphysician insists, our opening toward a goodness we could not give to ourselves. But the way to goodness, it turns out, is not simple and straight. Love of the God who saves us with the sacrifice of His Son is deflected into love of neighbor. The good believer acts *in persona Christi*, in love of those who he loves, without keeping anything first and only for oneself.

When Levinas takes up the question of Jesus Christ, it is in explicitly philosophical terms and with a particular interest in putting a proper understanding of certain dogmas to the work of clarifying phenomenological topics. In his essay "A Man-God?" this is a matter of two points.[49] Christian theologians account for the incarnation in terms of divine "humiliation," the self-emptying by which divine activity submits itself to the unqualified passivity that belongs to a flesh that willingly undergoes sacrifice. This has the appreciable effect of establishing a relation between finite creatures and the Infinite God in which neither ceases to be itself, and thus which Levinas considers to improve upon the pantheist reduction. In the God-Man, the divine crosses over and crosses out any opposition between the two. God is still God even while in flesh among us, and creatures called to God are most assuredly not God. This claim is inseparable from another which considers the relation to be actualized in the "expiatory" nature of Jesus's death. The passion by which this would be accomplished is at once familiar in some degree to those who are to be saved, and yet transcends anything that they are capable of. The passion of Jesus is therefore to be distinguished from that of the pagan gods, whose share of human joys and sorrows marks their divinity with certain limits. But it would be going too far to conclude to the contrary that a perfect passion is the mark of a God who is impersonal. It is rather the knowable superabundance of what we can achieve by our own natures, yet also the source of a call, and even the specification of a way, to be more than this. Whereas with the notion of divine humiliation, Christianity offers philosophy a means to think deeply about what Levinas calls "creation," the notion of divine expiation approaches

what he calls "substitution," the being one-for-the-other of radical responsibility. This is how to understand his remark to some Protestant
theology students that "I say of the face of the neighbor what the Christian says about the face of Christ."[50] It is not that the neighbor is the
messiah, but that his or her face calls the subject to that role.[51] To love
and serve the other person is at once to seek a goodness that the world
alone cannot provide.

Accordingly, the full weight of the concepts of messiah and messianicity is settled on the ethics of call and response, in which, we can be sure,
Levinas proposes to identify its essential and universal meaning. The
essential meaning is retrieved in some of the work we have already considered. Let us recall them, without pretending to repeat them in detail.
(1) The critique of foundational metaphysics learned from Heidegger,
but intensified and then also turned against Heidegger's own ontology,
banishes teleology from the philosophy of God and religion, yielding
ethical metaphysics and its concentration in radical responsibility for the
other person. Whatever salvation is to come from the call and response
cannot consist in any culmination of a necessary process, whether social
or historical. (2) Nor, however, can it be attributed to divine providence or
action, for Levinas has thought since the time of the Shoah, which specified the meaning of the death of God rather than bringing it about, that
the true God is not one who can be leaned on or borrowed from. Divine
transcendence is such that we are left to one another in the trace of God's
withdrawal from experience and understanding. He thus writes, "It is up
to man to save man: the divine way of relieving misery is not through
God's intervention."[52]

As for Levinas's argument for the universal meaning of ethical messianism, we find an evident point of entry in his claim that what makes
up being Jewish consists in a pure or perhaps especially intense form of
what belongs to being human as such. We know that the original form of
this claim centers on the negative experience of persecution, but this is
revised as Levinas pursues the implications of his ontology of suffering
into an understanding of the other person as vulnerable and in need. In
his late works, persecution has a positive meaning of a ceaseless call for
help. One can neither silence it nor escape it. We also know that it is Levinas's view that every human being, as being, suffers, and that precisely
this expresses itself in his or her face. The particularity of the call that
persecutes is thus also the primary encounter with a universal human
fact. Each of us suffers, and each of us is responsible for the suffering of
the other person. Ethical metaphysics consists in an attempt to show that
what occurs in particularity, at what we have characterized as the level of
singularity, is already universal. Philosophy renders this reversibility of

the particular and the universal in a teaching that might sensitize all of the living to a truth that eludes them in their ordinary existence.

The words "messianic" and "messianism" appear only rarely in Levinas's philosophical writings, and almost uniformly in order to characterize the temporality of an aspiration that refuses the finality of death and evil without simply denying them. To exist is to be subject to death and evil, and yet at the same time to cherish an inextinguishable dream of overcoming them. Were this dream only a function of our existence, as if it were the expression of an attempt to cheat death and evil by some superior effort, the burden of our suffering would eventually exhaust it. Levinas treats this dream in the same way as he treats evasion, which may well be its original ancestor in his phenomenology. Indestructible and irreducible to anything else, the dream is our opening to salvation—though our attachment to our own existence means that perfect salvation is out of our reach. Messianic time goes toward salvation without reaching it, and in this way "converts the perpetual into the eternal"—that is, into a greater fullness than what would otherwise be defined only by endless repetition.[53]

Who then is the messiah? This question is easiest to answer if one looks first at Levinas's Jewish writings, where he has been explicit. "The messiah is Myself," "the being who says Me," "the Self as Self, taking upon itself the whole suffering of the world," which is to say each of us and any of us insofar as singled out by the call for help that is the face of the person. Who is the messiah? "All persons are the Messiah."[54] Phenomenologically, such a conclusion is evident, and is consistent with what we have found in the strictly philosophical works: the messiah is the self, properly understood.[55] But "properly understood" means according to the teaching of the face of the other, which recalls the subject to its ethical self. Not that there can be any question of a messianicity that is compelled or imposed; one is called to a unique responsibility, albeit with force, and yet everything awaits a free commitment to it. Which means that it is finally the result of an "interior event" by which being for-oneself becomes being for-the-other.[56]

There can be no perfect agreement between these claims and what belongs to the life of faith that Jesus is Christ. Those who have this faith are not the messiah, but only share in the mission that He makes possible. Among Christian theologians, Bonhoeffer probably comes closest to Levinas's position when he defines the vocation to love and justice by a responsibility of radical openness to others all the way to forgetfulness of one's own ego. But this is not fully the Levinasian notion of messianic substitution because it is necessarily guided by the image of Jesus Christ. At the highest point of Bonhoeffer's Christology is the thought of a God who suffers for us in the gift of a son who takes on our guilt in order to defeat it (according to what Levinas has called divine "humiliation"). More immediately, the suffering of the son, Jesus, takes the form of a self-emptying that is the perfection and the model for how we must relate to one another. Perfect substitution, in other words, is reserved for the divine, even if human beings are called to aspire to it.[57]

The fact that Jesus Christ calls equally to all human beings means that the responsibility that he enjoins is immediately a matter of solidarity, whereas for Levinas solidarity is only entailed by the primary encounter with a particular other person here and now. Of course, this makes it all the plainer that the Messiah has a mediating function in the Christian ethic that is prohibited by an attempt to recognize what Levinas understands as ethical plurality. Let us admit the evident question: Would the figure of Christ be part and parcel of totalization? Philosophers have not always been able to avoid that outcome. One should bear in mind the claims made against Hegel, who will have drawn from the figure of Christ, who is God and yet Man, inspiration for his own wish to think a concept (*Begriff*) that is at once individual and general, and the crucial role played by the Christ of the Incarnation in the dialectic of Spirit.[58] Against this, some have wished to argue that Christ enters into human experience and history precisely in order to disrupt any such totalization with a love that cannot be submitted to abstraction or contained in a process. In order for this to come to pass, only one savior is necessary, but what he accomplishes is for everyone and all time. Jesus Christ is thus what Xavier Tilliette has called the "universal singular" (*singulier universel*);[59] he and he alone has made possible the victory over sin and suffering that Levinas instead expects from the work of singular subjects, each one taking up its own responsibility and without end.

One thus sees it. Between the Messiah and the messianic subject there is the question of our assurance that Good may triumph over evil, and beneath that the question of the true virility of evil. And one knows, certainly by this point in the investigation, that for Levinas evil is ineliminable from our humanity because it is rooted in our very existence. The God of ethical metaphysics has given us one another, which is to say our responsibility, and while this is enough to resist the approach of evil, it is without dream of defeating it. This is because there can be no act of charity that does not arrogate for itself the right to choose and the power to move, thereby reasserting a degree of the egocentrism that the helpless face of the other person had just broken up. The idea of a unique and personal Messiah is far from denying that there is evil, but it is unintelligible without the premise that the conditions that would be transformed already contain some seeds of goodness. It is not simply that the world in itself or, if one prefers, being in itself are without God, but rather that they do not yet know God but are capable of receiving God. Levinas's philosophy thinks that this is already too much, and yet it also holds open the possibility of a transcendent goodness that is not forever alien to us. In order to do so, it must contend that the matrix of our relations does not rest in being.

Conclusion

Prophecy and the
Ethical Plot of Humanity

In the end, the philosophy that urges us toward a peace and goodness beyond violence but does not pretend that we can ever fully reach them— philosophy as prophecy, in other words—must claim a basis for itself that does not belong to the order that it criticizes. It is necessary to specify: this would be a basis that does not belong to that order, but is not therefore wholly outside of it or separated from it. It is sometimes said of Levinas's critical enterprise that he attempts to turn the conceptual regime of Western thought against itself, without recourse to concepts that are not already found there. When, for example, "being" is received strictly in its verbal sense, as act and as effort, one must recognize only a partial extraction of the well-known Heideggerian perspective on classical and modern metaphysics. Heidegger has certainly emphasized the ontological difference between *Sein* and *Seiende*, but he has also insisted on the transcendence of *Sein* over *Dasein*, and eventually grants priority to the former in the disclosure of truth. To the degree that these themes come up at all in Levinas's engagement with Heidegger, they are submitted to a singular insistence that they are only projections of the one theme that he does take over. Hence would fundamental ontology at one and the same time initiate a break with previous conceptions of being and yield the possibility of a new position taken up against it. Being is effort, and effort is self-assertion that occurs within the ambit of our relation with the other person. In a similar way, Levinas accepts the modern thought of a free and legislating subject, only to then claim that such thought has been too quick to pass over the importance of its own discovery of a fundamental heteronomy that qualifies separated subjectivity. Certain theologies show acute sensitivity to our heteronomy when they make us think of a suffering so unbearable as to call for the idea of a God whose will and powers would justify it. If we did not exactly need the Shoah to put that notion in question, we can nonetheless be sure that the Shoah made it imperative that we do so. The death of God, according to Levinas, lays bare this heteronomy, as the first word of our subjectivity and thus also as a defining feature of the peace and justice that would respect our genuine plurality. By thus calling our attention to overlooked features in claims for the primacy of being, the original freedom of the subject, and the power of the divine to ensure order, philosophy begins a case for the priority of the other person, a relation with him or her that would precede any understanding we may have of it, and a religion in which God *as God* is not the ground of order and meaning. It would be within this framework, according to this account of our humanity, that one might envision the possibility of a conversion from self-interest into radical commitment to the other person. Such a conversion would necessarily be kenotic in the most radical sense. It would also have to be motivated by a desire which, since it has no purchase on an object, is insatiable. This insatiable desire is concretized in absolute responsibility.

We will not attempt to further summarize these arguments, or the refinements pursued by way of exposing them to the experience of psychoanalysis and some difficulties appearing in the nexus of speech and language. Nor will we propose to return them to their places in a single position. It is enough to underline here the fact that in no case are the themes that Levinas places under ethical pressure simply abandoned. But being is not merely reinterpreted, as if only to propose another ontology that would be more dialogical; what is argued about our subjectivity comes to considerably more than insisting that the ego is also an alter ego, and the God of ethical metaphysics transcends any and every other god. The entire field of ontology, anthropology, and religion, along with innumerable related concepts, is crossed from a different direction than the one that is oriented to identity, grounds, and synchrony.[1] This rejoins what we have already said about philosophy as prophecy: it rests on principles that both do and do not belong to the order of what it criticizes, or as we may now put it, what it reinterprets and redefines. To take up one of Levinas's texts, to be provoked and engaged by it, is to encounter a philosophy that has already entered into the modes of thinking that he wishes to disrupt and reconfigure. If it is a matter of criticism, we have no difficulty finding this philosophy's root in his manner of hearing the call of the other person. But if indeed it is also a matter of interpretation, and therefore of new conceptions of being, subjectivity, language, and religion, then we still want to know more about its original principles. Where is the point of engagement, where is the unity of a perspective that establishes the basis for its essential claims? Where does the prophetic impulse driving Levinas's thinking become *philosophy*?

Levinas's argument has willingly given up any claim to a ground or foundation, if by these is meant a principle that is accessible to the reason that philosophy exercises according to some unique capacity or technique. Everything that belongs to Levinas's association of reason with power and of the privileging of concepts with violence has seen to that. The same argument has also disavowed any claim to an intuition of the whole, since it is intent on a plurality that would be anterior to any such whole. At the same time, his argument also refuses to decline into rhetoric, in which violence is instead inflicted obliquely, by a persuasion that would only submit us to the will of the one who persuades. Levinas's method, straightforwardly phenomenological at least in a restricted sense of that term, attempts to protect the givenness of things from both of these distortions. Yet it is immediately distinctive in its focus especially on "things" that are entirely out of reach of ordinary consciousness. We have known since Husserl, and have been reminded by Heidegger, that phenomenology must not confine itself to what appears. But their intention has been to direct us to a consideration of inner processes, so that we might grasp the genesis of appearing from what does not appear. This is not fully Levinas's claim that what appears must be understood in terms of relations that are prior even to the genesis itself. We have seen time and again that for him, the entire dynamism of being and appearing is posterior to the relation with the other person and with the God whose passing establishes that relation. We have also seen that this does not lead him to simply begin with either God or the other person, and then draw certain conclusions about being, subjectivity, and language. To the contrary, one is to follow his accounts of the latter until his definitions of the former impose themselves. *And these definitions are always relational.* When it is said that the otherness of the other person is infinite or absolute, this is meant to express his or her unqualified priority and unlimited transcendence over the subjectivity of the subject. When it is said that the passing of God is immemorial, this is mean to express the fullness of divinity before our finite freedom and desire. It is not enough to say that God is not present, and not enough to say that God is absent or perhaps is present as absent. God is always already beyond recuperation into any presence, as if thinking or prayer could cross over and improve on divine abscondion. The relation of a finite, desiring subject to the true God is defined by this absolute distance that would be greater than any extravagance.

In this sense, Levinas offers us a phenomenology of relations that are given in events. The face of the other person is not the only case in point. It is striking that desire and responsibility are described in their dynamic occurrence, without any attempt to remand the description to a structure or function of either interlocutor. We should also take seriously the fact that in his language about them, Levinas insists that they are not only insatiable but also ceaseless and unending. The topos of our relations exhibits surges and ripples and disruptions, and the phenomenology that becomes ethical metaphysics does so by following these until arriving at relations about which it can only be affirmed that they are already in place—whereupon it becomes evident that this is so from before and outside enclosure within any ontology, system of language, or theology.

It is here that one comes upon what is likely to be the first word of Levinas's philosophy in its prophetic form. Wherever *Otherwise Than Being, or Beyond Essence*, a work which in this respect goes farther than the others, comes upon relations that for considered reasons it wishes to call anarchic, it invokes a "plot" (*une intrigue*) rather than causes and effects, grounds and predicates, or principles and results. It is in every case a matter of affirming a relation prior to the appearance of first separating the parts and then either reconciling them or opposing them. All of the great themes are established in this way. "Responsibility appears without a beginning, [is] anarchic."[2] This plot "forms in the face of another, trace of an immemorial past," and "binds me to the other before being tied to my own body."[3] It is a matter of "proximity and communication" which do not become a "modality of cognition" or submit to "the vicissitudes of representation and knowledge, openness upon images, or an exchange of information."[4] Communication, relation, occur in a "diachronic plot between the same and the other"[5] that bears witness to infinity and issues in goodness. "This plot," moreover, "connects to what detaches itself absolutely, to the Absolute. The detachment of Infinity from the thought that seeks to thematize it and the language that tries to hold it in the said is what we have called illeity. One is tempted to call this plot religious; it is not stated in terms of certainty or uncertainty and does not rest on any positive theology."[6]

Evidently enough, in all of these instances (and there are more), it is finally a question of characterizing our humanity as ethical without a ground or condition in anything else.[7] Before and outside the pretense of any other order, we belong to one another and to what calls for the name "God." Phenomenology is the exegesis of being and subjectivity that is capable of reading from what appear to be indications leading back to the plot of our responsibility and love of the good. One might well be unsettled by the appearance of this term, "plot," which belongs to narrative and thus to a genre that Levinas has often enough accused of submitting the uniqueness of subjects to the unifying force of a story (a twist in the plot of a play or novel is *une torsion de l'intrigue*).[8] But it is possible to receive this word somewhat differently. It also has a sense of secrecy and enigma, one perhaps close to Levinas's use of the latter word as we encountered it in the course of investigating his philosophy of language.[9] What is enigmatic, we have said, shows itself without coming to light. One knows it through its effects, though the effects cannot be traced back to it as if to a cause. The plot of our humanity does not coincide with the designs sketched by ontology, anthropology, or theology, and does not accommodate itself to them. Phenomenology is led toward the plot by its own interest in extraordinary themes like the face of the other person and metaphysical desire, and by its own refusal to submit them to the limits of what is only ordinary.

It is incumbent on the narrative that wishes to truly recognize the uniqueness of its own characters, to constantly undo the suffocating effects of any story that would be imposed on them. This metaphor of breathing comes to us from Levinas's own text, which in some of its more discrete moments describes the oscillation of being and responsibility in terms of respiration. Inhalation, the spontaneous act of self-concern, necessarily gives way to exhalation, a release and an outpouring for the other, which in turn gives way to inhalation. This is not to model ethics on physiology any more than it is to pretend that compassion and justice are spontaneous. Free and committed responsibility becomes possible precisely when this natural flow is interrupted, when one catches one's breath for a moment, and then either releases it in acquiescence to nature or instead makes of it a sacrifice and a gift for the one in need. The drama of what Levinas calls "the ethical" is born in this disruption of any such alleged necessity. It is played out in actions that refuse any assembly into a system that would dictate the meaning of its events as if from outside and above. To denounce any such attempt is to insist that we live first in our care for one another and our love of the good, and that these can only be pursued in the open air.

Abbreviations

Works by Emmanuel Levinas

AE	*Autrement qu'être ou au-delà de l'essence.* The Hague: Martinus Nijhoff, 1978.
CPP	*Collected Philosophical Papers,* trans. A. Lingis. The Hague: Martinus Nijhoff, 1987.
DEE	*De l'existence à l' existent.* Paris: Vrin, 1947.
DVI	*De Dieu qui vient à l'idée.* Paris: Vrin, 1998.
EDE	*En découvrant l'existence avec Husserl et Heidegger.* Paris: Vrin, 1967.
EE	*Existence and Existents,* trans. A. Lingis. Dordrecht: Kluwer, 1978.
EN	*Entre nous: Essais sur la pensée-à- l'autre.* Paris: Grasset, 1991.
ENT	*Entre Nous: Thinking of the Other,* trans. M. B. Smith. New York: Columbia University Press, 2000.
Escape	*On Escape,* trans. B. Bergo. Palo Alto, CA: Stanford University Press, 2002.
Évasion	*De l'évasion,* with an introduction by J. Rolland. Paris: Fata Morgana, 1982.
GCM	*Of God Who Comes to Mind,* trans. B. Bergo. Palo Alto, CA: Stanford University Press, 1998.
OB	*Otherwise Than Being, or Beyond Essence,* trans. A. Lingis. Pittsburgh: Duquesne University Press, 1998.
OC	*Oeuvres complètes,* vols. 1–3. Paris: Grasset, 2009– . Abbreviation followed by volume and page number.
TA	*Le temps et l'autre.* Paris: Presses Universitaires de France / Quadrige, 1983.
TeI	*Totalité et infini: Essai sur l'exteriorité.* The Hague: Martinus Nijhoff, 1961.

TI	*Totality and Infinity: An Essay on Exteriority*, trans. A. Lingis. Pittsburgh: Duquesne University Press, 1969.
TO	*Time and the Other*, trans. R. A. Cohen. Pittsburgh: Duquesne University Press, 1987.

Works on the Thought of Emmanuel Levinas

LevStudies	*Levinas Studies: An Annual Review.* Pittsburgh: Duquesne University Press, 2005– . Abbreviation followed by volume number, year-date, and page number.
Ox Handbk Lev	*The Oxford Handbook of Levinas*, ed. M. Morgan. Oxford: Oxford University Press, 2019.

Notes

Introduction

1. This, as much as anything else, marks the point of my conviction that Levinas must be read as a philosopher of religion in order to fully understand his important claims about subjectivity and responsibility. Any other reading seems likely only to regard as paradoxical or even contradictory a claim that the text clearly considers essential: subjectivity is always already responsibility to and for the other person. To leave undeveloped Levinas's claim that it is by the infinity of the infinite that each of us is open to the other person before any closure into ourselves (see chapter 3 of this work), is to be led sooner or later to the idea that in his philosophy moral conscience must be both the immediate effect of the call of the other person and equally the condition by which that same call is intelligible precisely as *ethical*. In turn, this paradox would appear only as the complement of another, temporally prior one in the very life of the ego, which both tends to closure into itself and yet is already open to the other person. This reading of Levinas is suggested in Diane Perpich, *The Ethics of Emmanuel Levinas* (Palo Alto, CA: Stanford University Press, 2008), 98—an excellent work which, to be sure, does not fail to raise the question of religious subjectivity (120). But there it is a matter of the Christian notion of sin, and thus of a theology that Levinas has in no way identified with his own conception of "religion." This difference, broadly speaking, is taken up in chapter 6 of this work.

2. Jean-Paul Sartre, *Being and Nothingness*, trans. H. Barnes (London: Routledge, 1991), 784. The line furnishes the proper meaning of Sartre's interpretation of human desire as "desire to be God" (724, 755, 764).

Chapter 1

1. Emmanuel Levinas, "Quelques réflexions sur la philosophie de l'hitlérisme," in *Les imprévus de l'histoire* (Paris: Fata Morgana, 1994), 27–41; trans. S. Hand, "Reflections on the Philosophy of Hitlerism," *Critical Inquiry* 17 (Autumn 1990): 63–71. Unsurprisingly, a different publication venue was also required for this work. The texts on Husserl and Heidegger were with established publishers of academic philosophy. The essay on Hitlerism appeared in the progressive

Catholic journal *Esprit*, which had been founded two years earlier, in 1932, by the Catholic personalist Emmanuel Mounier. Between three and ten issues of *Esprit* appeared each year for a considerable period. Levinas's essay is found in volume 3, issue 26. Noted for its open engagement with politics and culture, the journal had by this time published work by Raymond Aron, Nicolas Berdyaev, Jean Lacroix, Jacques Maritain, and Jean Wahl.

2. It will be necessary to return to this and related matters in chapter 2 of the present work.

3. In a lecture given at the 1973 Castelli Colloquium in Rome, Levinas refers to ideology as "suspect reason" according to this same perspective: from the sincerity of an original protest, there comes a thinking that envelops it in concepts and then forgets it. Only ethics truly holds fast to respect for human plurality. Marxism, for example, has become a science of general classes and sweeping processes. *DVI* 17–18 / *GCM* 4.

4. Levinas, "Quelques réflexions sur la philosophie de l'hitlérisme," 41 / "Reflections on the Philosophy of Hitlerism," 70.

5. Given this conception of Nazism, it is not surprising that Levinas associates it with the thought of Nietzsche, with its affinity for rhetoric and power (see "Quelques réflexions sur la philosophie de l'hitlérisme," 41 / "Reflections on the Philosophy of Hitlerism," 71). And yet, as we will have occasion to note, on a later occasion he will nonetheless find the means to inscribe that philosophy, on essentially the same claims, within a theory of language that is ethical and prophetic. See "The Ethical Relation as Language," in chapter 5 of the present work.

6. Heidegger could not have disagreed, first because fear, like anxiety, befalls us; and second, because it does so in response to menace. In his view, anxiety discloses more about our vulnerability than does fear because the whole of our existence has come into question.

7. Perhaps there is another thread still to pull here in the philosophy of Levinas, and not only in its earliest iterations. One notices that the essay at hand pays little heed to the mental vulnerability that one experiences when thought opens to emotions that are not evidently reducible to bodily sources. To be sure, it is not that such a possibility is excluded, but only that the critique of both Hitlerism and its antipodes does not need to take it up. This kind of mental vulnerability, my vulnerability to myself, internal to the movement of my freedom, is seldom if ever a great theme in Levinas's philosophy, at least where he is intent on defining the necessary conditions of acts by which one does good. This cannot be said of the forms of thought that give him the greatest difficulty: a certain kind of existentialism, psychoanalysis, and theology. Chapters 4 and 6, which take up his relation to psychoanalysis and theology, do not exactly follow this thread, but it is woven into much of what I will emphasize there.

8. Throughout this essay, Levinas's word "spirit" is meant in the phenomenological sense of mind or mentality. As his thinking progresses, it is not always clear whether he sometimes assigns it a more religious sense or understands these two as distinct modalities of consciousness. The question deserves separate attention.

9. Husserl uncovers the phenomenological basis for this insight when he

writes that "the body is not only an organ in general and a thing, but is indeed an expression of the spirit and is at once an organ of the spirit." Edmund Husserl, *Ideas Pertaining to a Pure Phenomenology and a Phenomenological Philosophy, Second Book*, trans. R. Rojcewicz and A. Schuwer (Dordrecht: Springer, 1989), 102.

10. Levinas, "Quelques réflexions sur la philosophie de l'hitlérisme," 36 / "Reflections on the Philosophy of Hitlerism," 68.

11. Levinas, "Quelques réflexions sur la philosophie de l'hitlérisme," 38 / "Reflections on the Philosophy of Hitlerism," 68–69.

12. Descartes seems to recognize this insight in *Passions of the Soul*, article 26, when he says that the reality of our passions is not dependent on being awake and need not respond to any external object. René Descartes, *Passions of the Soul and Other Late Writings*, trans. M. Moriarty (Oxford: Oxford University Press, 2015), 206.

13. Heidegger's term is *Jemeinigkeit*. He introduces it in *Being and Time*, §9, pursues it into the question of the "who" of Dasein beginning in §25, and in §47 concludes that in every case death has the determining character of mineness. The importance of this theme for Levinas is constant. We will take up his own conception of it, worked out explicitly in response to Heidegger, in "Call as Election," in chapter 6.

14. Levinas, "Quelques réflexions sur la philosophie de l'hitlérisme," 36 / "Reflections on the Philosophy of Hitlerism," 68.

15. Emmanuel Levinas, *The Theory of Intuition in the Phenomenology of Husserl*, trans. A. Orianne (Evanston, IL: Northwestern University Press, 1975), 146. This objection is patently phenomenological. Empiricists like Locke conflate empirical and transcendental consciousness, thereby losing access to the structure and categories of the real.

16. If this is correct, we should not hear Levinas's criticism without noting that it did not prevent him from dedicating *Difficult Freedom* to Brunschvicg, and including in that book an essay that expresses great appreciation for his intelligence and humanity. See Emmanuel Levinas, *Difficult Freedom*, trans. S. Hand (Baltimore: Johns Hopkins University Press, 1990), 38–45.

17. See Léon Brunschvicg, *Le progrès de la conscience dans la philosophie occidentale* (Paris: Alcan, 1927).

18. It goes without saying that the philosophical targets here are Hegelianism and ideological Marxism. But Levinas's reasons should not be passed over too quickly. To be sure, and as we will see in some detail, the effort to defend an ethical relation irreducible to symmetry yields a conception of plurality that must be prior to any alleged summary of its meaning. Behind this is the thesis that history begins in violence and indeed is a work of violence, since after all one cannot tell a story without assigning everyone a place in it. As for progress, in Levinas's view, such a notion necessarily deafens us to the singularity of real suffering. None of this means that we are without means to work for a better society. In some of his texts, Levinas urges trust, or at any rate hope, in institutions, but then also vigilance about their propensity to self-interest. See Guy Petitdemange, "La notion paradoxal de l'histoire," in *Emmanuel Lévinas et l'histoire*, ed. N. Frogneux and F. Mies (Paris: Cerf, 1998), 17–44.

19. Levinas, "Quelques réflexions sur la philosophie de l'hitlérisme," 33 / "Reflections on the Philosophy of Hitlerism," 67.

20. Karl Marx, *Grundrisse*, trans. M. Nicolaus (London: Penguin, 1993), 245.

21. In "Transcendence and Evil," Levinas speaks of a sense that evil has sought one out personally, and an outrage that is already the beginning of an insistence on goodness. Emmanuel Levinas, "Transcendence et mal," *Le Nouveau Commerce* 41 (1978): 69–70; "Transcendence of Evil," in *CPP*, 181–82. In the essay on Hitlerism, he is closest to this thought when he writes of the "rebellion" and "refusal" that animate pain even as it afflicts us. Levinas, "Quelques réflexions sur la philosophie de l'hitlérisme," 37 / "Reflections on the Philosophy of Hitlerism," 68.

22. Levinas, "Quelques réflexions sur la philosophie de l'hitlérisme," 37 / "Reflections on the Philosophy of Hitlerism," 68.

23. Emmanuel Levinas, "Martin Heidegger et l'ontologie," in *EDE*, 68–69; translated as "Martin Heidegger and Ontology," *Diacritics* 26, no. 1 (1996): 24. It is Levinas who calls his translation "liberal."

24. Bergo's translation of *"l'évasion"* as "escape" is of course correct, and in any case Levinas's notion is difficult. As he makes clear, there can be no question either of finally escaping or fully evading the ontological conditions that one nonetheless revolts against. When it is a matter of the thing itself, I prefer to keep the word "evasion," though admittedly according to a metaphysical scruple. To characterize our movement against our ontological condition as "escape" can suggest that one strikes out toward what would withhold itself from being, as if it were from beyond and outside—in a word, as what being is *not*. But here it is a question of the absolute, which Levinas is consistently at pains to show transcends the reach of any negation. In short, there can be no question of *escape*. As for the existential dimension of "evasion," it either resembles or is indebted to what Levinas's friend Marcel sometimes calls "metaphysical unease," though he does not clearly formulate that expression until works that appear later than the present essay by Levinas. One nonetheless recognizes its approach in passages where, already in his *Metaphysical Journal*, Marcel traces a sense of existential discomfort to a deep need for grounds that the world does not offer.

25. This is the point of departure for chapter 2 of the present work.

26. Levinas, "Martin Heidegger et l'ontologie," 68 / "Martin Heidegger and Ontology," 24. Levinas's term (*voué à*) is evidently meant to improve our understanding of Heidegger's term *Geworfenheit*. This attempt has attracted some attention. See, for example, Samuel Moyn, *Origins of the Other: Emmanuel Levinas between Revelation and Ethics* (Ithaca, NY: Cornell University Press, 2005), 99, 102, 104, 106–7; and Michael Fagenblat, "Levinas and Heidegger: The Elemental Confrontation," in *Ox Handbk Levinas*, 115–17. The term is also open to some debate. As Fagenblat correctly observes, whereas Levinas is intent on highlighting what can only be affirmed from within its grasp, for Heidegger, Dasein's possibilities are "matters for [its own] freedom, even if always within the limits of its thrownness" (Martin Heidegger, *Being and Time*, trans. J. Macquarrie and E. Robinson [London: SCM, 1962], §69, p. 417).

27. *Évasion* 70 / *Escape* 52.

28. *Évasion* 70 / *Escape* 52, translation modified. I adopt the near-homophone "savor" in order to preserve what I take to be Levinas's sense of an inner hint or prompt that cannot be satisfied.

29. Blondel's position may be the most sophisticated one. In his *Action*, he contends that philosophy conducted solely by its own capacities sees in our nature a movement that would be fulfilled only with the help of grace. Philosophy is thus capable of asserting that our natural desire is evocative of a supernatural fulfillment. What philosophy does not see on its own is what it is that might prepare us for grace or what effects grace might have in the further development of our natures. This insight is provided by faith, or at least the thinking that is guided by faith. Since these are within the provenance of church and theology, they lie beyond the reach of the philosopher. The philosopher works in parallel with the thinking guided by faith, but must conduct his or her work without support from it.

30. The essential passages are well known. See Edmund Husserl, *Ideas Pertaining to a Pure Phenomenology and a Phenomenological Philosophy, First Book*, (Dordrecht: Kluwer, 1982), §58, pp. 133–34; and Martin Heidegger, *Prolegomena to the History of the Concept of Time*, trans. T. Kisiel (Bloomington: Indiana University Press, 1985), §8, pp. 79–80.

31. Given everything we have seen until now, it seems likely that this charge is raised with Heidegger, though perhaps not only him, presently in mind. See also Jacques Rolland's Annotation 11 in *On Escape*, citing the final lines of Levinas's 1935 essay, "L'actualité de Maïmonide": "Paganism is a radical powerlessness to get out of the world. It consists not in denying spirits and gods but in situating them in the world. . . . The pagan is shut up in this world, sufficient unto himself and closed upon himself. He finds it solid and firmly established. He finds it eternal. He orders his actions and destiny according to the world" (*Évasion* 118–20 / *Escape* 91–92). The essay in question appears in *Paix et Droit* 15, no. 4 (April 1935): 6–7.

32. Perhaps it is useful to observe that the foregoing supports only the isolation of a problem to which Levinas responds, and not any claim of the original sources by which he would begin to do so. The latter effort has been attempted, for example, in Moyn, *Origins of the Other*, a historical work that has the merit of highlighting a number of important resonances between Levinas's thinking and various strands of modern philosophy and theology, but which proposes to go farther than this, all the way to claiming that Protestant thought from Kierkegaard to Barth has been the particular source for a conception of absolute otherness (12). Were such a claim about intellectual context to be fashioned as a philosophical argument, it would at least flirt with the genetic fallacy. Whether or not Moyn has avoided it, one is entitled to some frank puzzlement over the fact that he argues with confidence for the influence of a form of thinking that was only in loose circulation in Levinas's milieu, and yet remains quite circumspect about any such claim for the French Hegelianism of which he does not doubt that Levinas was personally aware (109).

33. One thinks, for example, of Kant, whose practical philosophy can be interpreted to observe that the presence of others may call us to suspend self-

interest in favor of the reasoning that discovers the moral law. But whereas Kant thus appeals to a capacity of the subject—who is able to discover and give to itself the moral law—Levinas argues that responsibility originates in a passivity to the face of the other person that calls into question the priority of even such a seemingly disinterested capacity.

34. See Heidegger, *Being and Time*, §74, pp. 434–39. The following paragraphs only touch on the pertinent features of this difficult section.

35. This is made especially clear in *Being and Time*, §59, where Heidegger observes that even in the Kantian morality, an ontology of Dasein is presupposed already in the proposal that we might take an interest in its relation to values and norms (339). For its part, Dasein cannot have a free relation with this or that value until it has come to terms with the fact that it *is*, and that this *is* has the character of care about its own existence.

36. Heidegger, *Being and Time*, 436.

37. Heidegger, *Being and Time*, 437 (slightly paraphrasing Heidegger).

38. Levinas is certainly on the verge much later, when he adds the following prefatory remarks to a republication of his essay:

> The article stems from the conviction that the source of the bloody barbarism of National Socialism lies not in some contingent anomaly within human reasoning, nor in some accidental ideological misunderstanding. This article expresses the conviction that this source stems from the essential possibility of elemental Evil into which we can be led by logic and against which Western philosophy had not sufficiently insured itself. This possibility is inscribed within the ontology of a being concerned with being [*de l'être soucieux d'être*]—a being, to use the Heideggerian expression, "dem es in seinem Sein um dieses Sein selbst geht." (Levinas, "Reflections on the Philosophy of Hitlerism," 63)

39. This is no small thing, since it contains at least the slight possibility that death would, among other things, interrupt allegiance to a people, a heritage, and its heroes. Is this interruption enough to ground critique? This seems doubtful, but nothing prevents us from thinking that it would at least make critique possible.

40. Levinas, "Martin Heidegger et l'ontologie," 74–75 / "Martin Heidegger and Ontology," 30.

41. Levinas, "Martin Heidegger et l'ontologie," 76 / "Martin Heidegger and Ontology" 32. In the English translation, the passage that I have just cited would have Levinas characterizing Heidegger's position as "tragic." I have come to this interpretation of Levinas's reading by another route, but in truth the word does not appear in his French text.

42. Heidegger is famously alert to this misunderstanding. In §38 of *Being and Time*, he takes pains to distance all talk of authenticity/inauthenticity, fallenness, and so forth from any sense of higher and lower status (see especially p. 220).

43. Immanuel Kant, *Critique of Pure Reason,* trans. N. K. Smith (London: Macmillan, 1993), A317/B374, p. 312.

44. The possibility is urged most forcefully by Lacan and his school. See chapter 4 for indications of this.

45. And not only in the area of social and political thought. See the initial pages of chapter 3.

46. Sartre, *Being and Nothingness*, 103.

47. Sartre, *Being and Nothingness*, 440.

48. Jean-Paul Sartre, *Anti-Semite and Jew*, trans. G. Becker (New York: Schocken, 1948), 13.

49. Sartre, *Anti-Semite and Jew*, 42–43.

50. Sartre, *Anti-Semite and Jew*, 105.

51. Sartre, *Anti-Semite and Jew*: "We have attempted to show that the Jewish community is neither national nor international, neither religious, nor ethnic, nor political: it is a *quasi-historical* community. What makes the Jew is his concrete situation; what unites him to other Jews is the identity of their situations." When, for his part, Levinas later addresses the book briefly in an interview, he comes close to touching on this very point. What he finds unconvincing in it is the tendency to approach Judaism as the other of antisemitism. As peculiar as that claim must be, it is one effect of thinking that ways of life are mutually exclusive and in historical struggle against one another. See Emmanuel Levinas, "Quand Sartre découvre l'histoire sainte," in *Les imprévus de l'histoire* (Paris: Fata Morgana, 1994), 156.

52. Roberto Unger, *False Necessity: Anti-Necessitarian Social Theory in the Service of Radical Democracy* (London: Verso, 2004), 279–80. Unger's use of "negative capability"—the expression is of course taken from the poet Keats—rests on a conviction that human beings are always and already more than their historical and social conditions, and an understanding of social and political action (and a good deal else) as motivated by an elemental desire for a better life. It would be useful to determine whether there is in his vast and complex work the resources needed to think that what passes there as a "better life" would meet the religious definition of an "elevated life."

53. See Emmanuel Levinas, "Le mémoire d'un passé non révolu," interview with F. Ringelheim, *Revue de l'Université de Bruxelles* (1987): 18.

54. Levinas sometimes writes of the "Jewish particularism" that is visible in the tension between a commitment to universal norms set by "the family of Abraham" prior to the formation of any state, and a need to establish a state whose laws are inscribed in a more limited order. Emmanuel Levinas, "Judaism and Revolution," in *Nine Talmudic Lectures*, trans. A. Aronowicz (Bloomington: Indiana University Press, 1990), 141–42. In chapter 2 of the present work, we find Levinas negotiating the tension between Jewish particularity and universality on the somewhat different terrain of what he is willing to call "the spirituality of being Jewishness."

55. *DVI* 26 / *GCM* 9.

56. These themes are studied closely in chapter 3 of the present work.

57. I am neither the first advocate of the importance of this conception for Levinas, nor the most persistent in tracing its variants. As many have observed, in its most fundamental instance, at the level of what he will eventually call "an-

archy," prophecy is the essence of one's radical responsibility for the other person, in which meaning is constituted in the relation with a goodness that would enter into being from beyond its reach. To give oneself freely to the other in need is to have already heard and to now affirm this good that Levinas is willing, under extraordinary restrictions, to call "God." In this important sense, every subject is thus a prophet, and if this must be true not least of the philosopher who both recognizes and teaches this vision of ourselves, then such a philosopher must also be prophetic at the level of discourse. This position, however, is far from evident even among Jewish philosophers. Spinoza, for example, opposes an elevated status for prophecy out of a conviction that religious thought must appeal to the intellect and not to will or desire. Before him, Maimonides for essentially the same reason qualifies his own appreciation of prophecy by characterizing it as a distinctive kind of wisdom.

Interestingly, all three thinkers consider it among the central tasks of philosophy to demythologize religion, or if one prefers, to identify its rational kernel. Maimonides brings the philosophy of Aristotle to bear on this task. For Spinoza it is modern science and mathematics. For Levinas, it is phenomenology, now in an effort especially against ontological corruptions. For these affinities and a range of inscribed differences, see R. A. Cohen, *Out of Control: Confrontations between Spinoza and Levinas* (Albany: SUNY Press, 2016), chapter 2 (57–81). The present study has taken shape in an effort simply to follow the manner in which a prophetic discourse of this sort yields and protects a conception of the ethical relation in terms of radical responsibility and desire for the good beyond being. In a work that appears as an important counterpart to this one, Richard Sugarman shows that for Levinas, phenomenology is indispensable for a proper, i.e., demythologized, *rational* reading of the very Torah in which the figure of the prophet takes a distinctive place alongside that of the sage, and in which prophetic discourse claims to see further than any other wisdom. More than a reinvigoration of certain themes, this manner of reading the Torah proposes nothing less than to retrieve those themes in their proper richness, so that the texts may give to thinking more than any thinking could give to itself. See R. Sugarman, *Levinas and the Torah: A Phenomenological Approach* (Albany: SUNY Press, 2019), especially 275–80. It is often observed that this facility with both Greek and Jewish thought, and in remarkably similar terms, constitutes the summary achievement of Levinas's work. It strikes not only in the register of prophecy but also, as we will have occasion to recognize, in that of teaching.

Chapter 2

1. There was never any doubt about this. As early as his 1919/1920 course on *Basic Problems in Phenomenology,* Heidegger seeks a givenness that is covered over by the objectivity of science, decries any *inurare in verba magistri* in phenomenology, and proposes to find the meaningfulness of meaning in a facticity that is preserved in its vitality only poorly unless the phenomenologist takes notice

of them *from within them*. This is not yet a break from Husserl, but it does begin to prepare for one, specifically in the name of seeking fidelity to the things themselves.

2. This theme is Husserlian, and Levinas never forgot it. When in his genetic phenomenology Husserl locates sensibility at the level of pre-predicative givenness, he associates it with passivity. At the same time, however, he also ascribes to it structures of synthesis that Levinas, in his own later work, would contend are posterior to the relation with the other person. The continued importance of Husserl for Levinas, including in his own original works, is established in John Drabinski, *Sensibility and Singularity: The Problem of Phenomenology in Levinas* (Albany: SUNY Press, 2001).

3. One cannot deny that Levinas always had a profound understanding of Heidegger's philosophy, but one can nonetheless regret that he has for the most part left it for his readers to wring it from claims made already from a considerable distance. This is the tendency already in the small books appearing after the end of the Second World War, though not of the nearly contemporaneous essay "L'ontologie dans le temporel" (*EDE* 76–89), which does criticize Heidegger explicitly for having excluded the eternal from philosophy and pursuing the ontological question entirely within the relation of the self to its own being (89). These two criticisms mark the point of departure for the analyses appearing in *Existence and Existents*: it is Levinas's conviction that Heidegger proposes a mistaken account of our own existence. The essay has received too little attention, but for a notable exception, see Jacques Taminiaux, "La première réplique à l'ontologie fondamentale," in *Cahier de l'Herne: Emmanuel Levinas* (Paris: L'Herne, 1991), 275–84.

4. James Mensch has argued at greatest length that Levinas is engaged in proposing a correction of key Heideggerian notions, but he concentrates on *Totality and Infinity*. The initial passages of the present chapter willingly take over his characterization of Levinas the phenomenologist as offering a "counter-analytic." See James Mensch, *Levinas's Existential Analytic* (Evanston, IL: Northwestern University Press, 2015). As will become clear, although the work undertaken in *Existence and Existents* and *Time and the Other* produces insights that continue to inform Levinas's thinking in later works, the consolidation of his claims for the priority of the other person calls for some reframing of them.

5. Here "birth" plainly means the auto-genesis of the subject. It is noticed too rarely that Levinas's early works contain one of the best-developed accounts of this theme in all of phenomenology.

6. See Heidegger, *Being and Time*, §72, 426–27, Heidegger depicts Dasein as stretched between birth and death. The sense of his remarks is not biological but existential. The whole of Dasein, in its temporality, appears in its relation not only with a future but also with a past.

7. To be sure, in *Existence and Existents* the concept appears quite early (*DEE* 26 / *EE* 8), but close analysis is not attempted until the later passages of the book. It will be necessary to return to Levinas's claim that the "there is" approaches in insomnia.

8. Levinas's intention with the word "hypostasis" is clear enough. The

being of the subject distinguishes itself from that of objects by the fact that it is dynamic. A subject comes into a world and takes up a relation with objects according to an effort. This is far from an abuse of the word. Aristotle's term *hypokeimenon* (roughly, "that which is placed underneath") refers to a something that cannot be a predicate of anything else (*Categories* 1.20). Neoplatonic thought conceives of the *hypostasis* of the soul, understood as underlying substance. Levinas's interpretation of the subject includes the idea that it cannot be a predicate of objects, and that it furnishes their meaning.

9. See, for example, *DEE* 133 / *EE* 77: "The present is the terminus and in this sense a stop. *What is essential in an instant is its stance.* Yet this stop harbors an event" (emphasis added). *Existence and Existents* only touches on the theme of eschatological time, and when the theme of the Messiah is broached, it is defined as an impossible object for the existent in its unbreakable attachment to the present ("irreparable"). With the achievement of greater clarity about the priority of the relation with the other ("separation," "proximity," "anarchy," etc.), Levinas is able to contend that our attachment to the present is circumscribed with the temporality of diachrony. For an expanded discussion of this, see J. Rolland, *Parcours de l'autrement: Lecture d'Emmanuel Lévinas* (Paris: Presses Universitaires de France, 2000), 291–322.

10. *DEE* 32 / *EE* 12.

11. Heidegger, *Being and Time*, §§60–62.

12. *TA* 57–58 / *TO* 70–71. When Levinas insists that for Heidegger death is the "possibility of impossibility" and not, as Jean Wahl has proposed, "the impossibility of possibility" (*TA* 92n5 / *TO* 70n43), he grounds his claim by saying that on this point *Being and Time* is a philosophy of virile subjectivity, capable of meeting every challenge, if not overcoming every limit. This reading briefly converges with Ricoeur's complaint that these themes in Heidegger's text yield a theory of temporality with evident "heroic connotations." Paul Ricoeur, *Memory, History, Forgetting*, trans. K. Blamey and D. Pellauer (Chicago: University of Chicago Press, 2000), 304. Whereas Ricoeur resists the hierarchical theory of temporality that results from an overt prioritization of our relation with the future, Levinas proposes a robustly different account of our subjectivity.

13. *DEE* 34 / *EE* 28.

14. See especially *DEE* 44 / EE 20: "What we call the tension of effort is made up of this duality of upsurge [*d'élan*] and fatigue."

15. For this same reason, and until *Otherwise Than Being*, when at last Levinas denies that the responsible subject, strictly speaking, is a *being*, the thought of pure expenditure is necessarily absent from his philosophy. We find it on the verge of that book when, for example, the notion of a responsibility before and beyond our being raises the possibility of a perfect generosity in which "activity and passivity [would] coincide." *AE* 146 / *OB* 115.

16. See Jean-Paul Sartre, *La mort dans l'âme* (Paris: Gallimard, 1949); and E. M. Cioran, *Précis de décomposition* (Paris: Gallimard, 1949).

17. The theme of insomnia never disappears from Levinas's thinking, but in his mature works it is consistently inflected with the argument that prior to any self-relation is the relation with the other person. If, according to a claim that is

at most nascent in *Existence and Existents* and *Time and the Other*, the other is closer to me than I am to myself, then our relation denies me the absolute rest of withdrawal into myself, making possible the insomnia that is neither sleep nor lucid consciousness. The earlier works certainly do have in view what alone, according to Levinas, may lift us from this condition: the approach of the Other person frees me, saves me from the perils of a false solitude (*DEE* 144 / *EE* 86). The following lines are typical of the later, complete position: "Insomnia—the wakefulness of awakening—is disturbed at the heart of its formal or categorial equality by the Other who cores out [*dénoyaute*] all that which in insomnia forms a core as the substance of the Same, as identity, as repose, as presence, as sleep. It is cored out by the Other who tears this rest, who tears it from the hither side of the state where equality tends to settle." See also *TeI* 236 / *TI* 258; *AE* 38 / *OB* 30, and so on, and "Éloge de l'insomnie," in *Dieu, le mort, et le temps* (Paris: Grasset, 1993), 236–41; translated as "In Praise of Insomnia," in *God, Death, and Time*, trans. B. Bergo (Palo Alto, CA: Stanford University Press, 2000), 207–12.

18. There are other passages to this experience. What Lacan calls "the real" (*le réel*) is everything that resists expression in the order of language. As distinct from our ordinary sense of reality, which is accessible to us through the senses and thought, the real is unknown and indeed is in tension with what is known. The brute materiality at the underside of language, what is real in this sense does not emerge as meaningful so much as it breaks through or shows up as an interruption of meaning. In clinical experience, trauma, words missing from a sequence, and the body itself can be associated with the real. They exercise some influence on the subject by expressing an urge that cannot be spoken, so that he or she becomes fixated, and is still hindered or even dominated by a force that is known only in its effects. Psychoanalysis tries to bring the real to light by drawing it gradually into words, or as Lacan increasingly puts it, symbolization. The negative counterpart of this process is collapse, in which the subject would be left entirely exposed to the force of the real, and in this way utterly paralyzed. For a helpful discussion with clinical references, see Bruce Fink, *The Lacanian Subject between Language and Jouissance* (Princeton, NJ: Princeton University Press, 1995), 24–25 and 142–48. We will return at length to Levinas's relation to such notions in chapter 4 of the present work.

19. Heidegger thinks being in relation to "abyss." See Martin Heidegger, "What Is Metaphysics?" trans. D. F. Krell, in Heidegger, *Basic Writings* (New York: Harper and Row, 1977), 104–12. By now, it is clear that Levinas thinks being in relation to suffocating excess.

20. As many have observed, this argument is anti-Sartrean and, more deeply, anti-Hegelian: "We think that existence *for itself* is not the ultimate meaning of knowing, but rather the putting back into question of the self, the turning back to what is prior to oneself, in the presence of the Other. The presence of the Other, a privileged heteronomy, does not clash with freedom but invests it" (*TeI* 60 / *TI* 88). As soon as this is said, insomnia appears as a kind of wakefulness at the underside of subjectivity, beneath relations with objects that can be centered on oneself. What keeps one wakeful is the relation with an other who cannot be centered on oneself because he or she has been present before any such at-

tempt. On the verge of collapse, as everything else falls away until the subject, or existent, is lain bare, there is still the claim and thus the support of the ethical relation—"transcendent in immanence" (*DVI* 46–47 / *GCM* 25–26).

21. This concern is expressed in many of Marcel's works. I cite *Tragic Wisdom and Beyond* (Evanston, IL: Northwestern University Press, 1973), 143. The most extensive case is his *Man Against Mass Society* (Chicago: Regnery, 1962).

22. See "Pain and Evasion," in chapter 1 of the present work.

23. *TA* 20 / *TO* 41, *TA* 56 / *TO* 70. Something of a fault line in the French response to Heidegger opens here. Sartre, for example, works in basic sympathy with the general lines of Heidegger's conception of being-toward-death. Immediately after the Second World War, almost certainly in full cognizance of Sartre's stance, Levinas's emphasis on mystery moves him closer to his friend Marcel, who famously distinguishes between a *problem* that must be addressed with a view to solving it and a *mystery* that can only be admitted and attended (see, e.g., the discussion of mind and body in these two terms, in Gabriel Marcel, *Being and Having* [Glasgow: MacLehose / Glasgow University Press, 1949], 115–17). Marcel's distinction places Heidegger's claims in an interesting light, though Levinas does not seem to have been willing to suggest that in *Being and Time* Dasein's death is only a problem to be solved.

24. *DEE* 171 / *EE* 99. The approach of the other is also a "remedy" (*DEE* 147 / *EE* 86), "salvation" (*DEE* 156–57 / *EE* 91–92), and a "pardon" (*DEE* 144 / *EE* 85).

25. *DEE* 153 / *EE* 91.

26. *TA* 55–56 / *TO* 68–69.

27. Simone Weil also describes a primitive cry that marks the boundary of our existence as subjects, and does not hesitate to recognize in it the minimal condition of our relation with the Good. Simone Weil, *First and Last Notebooks* (London: Oxford University Press, 1970), 233–35. I am grateful to Robert Reed for this reference, and for drawing my attention to many other unexpected points of contact between Levinas and Weil.

28. Levinas is not the only one to recognize a suffering that threatens the integrity of the subject, and those who agree with him give us considerable reason to think that the idea is no mere construction. Drawing on decades of clinical experience, Eric Cassell distinguishes suffering from pain on this very point (unfortunately, Levinas often seems to use the terms interchangeably). Whereas pain wounds some features of our being, suffering can proceed to disable or destroy dignity, autonomy, language, and relation until finally the personhood of the person is at risk. See Eric Cassell, *The Nature of Suffering and the Goals of Medicine* (Oxford: Oxford University Press, 2004), 33–36. As we will soon observe, the hospital is not the only place where one finds terrible reason to contemplate a suffering that outstrips meaning (see "Lessons of Suffering," later in this chapter).

29. Does Levinas think that being is itself evil, or only that it holds within itself the principle of evil? In the essay on Hitlerism, he is close to the former view. The early postwar texts are a more complicated matter, and may even be undecided on this, though for the record, on at least one occasion Levinas writes, "being is evil, not because it is finite, but because it is without limits" (*TA* 29 / *TO* 51). This matter has been submitted to precise study by Didier Franck in "The

Body of Difference," in *The Face of the Other and the Trace of God: Essays on the Philosophy of Emmanuel Levinas*, ed. J. Bloechl (New York: Fordham University Press, 2000), 15–16.

30. *DEE* 96 / *EE* 54: "*le tout c'est ouverte sur nous.*"

31. Levinas emphasizes the greater immediacy of nourishment at *DEE* 65 / *EE* 34: "Not everything that is given in the world is a tool . . . For a soldier his bread, jacket and bed are not 'material'; they do not exist 'for . . . ,' but are ends."

32. As these sentences are meant to suggest, there is a case to be made for understanding insomnia as a form of "reduction," and it is aided by the fact that anxiety already has such a role in *Being and Time*. Unlike Husserl, Heidegger, and now with him Levinas, finds the route to greatest phenomenological insight in events that befall us rather than in acts or exercises that we undertake. This is also evident in Levinas's better-known claim that the face of the Other calls me back to a radical responsibility that I cannot recognize on my own.

33. He makes the point himself, repeatedly, throughout *Existence and Existents*.

34. *DEE* 123 / *EE* 71. This thought is explicitly anti-Cartesian, and arises on the way to engaging a deeper claim that the body is still a being.

35. My interpretation thus differs from that of John Sallis, who emphasizes the otherness of the elements with respect to the being of the one who lives from them. His point is well taken, since for Levinas the elements have none of the being that is reserved for the subject. Sallis's reading also has the merit of pointing out that in no case does Levinas seem to draw forth his notion of the elements directly from nature. In this case, however, Sallis is referring especially to *Totality and Infinity*, and his observation fits together with my contention that the theme of nature is underdeveloped in that book (in "Desire and Excess" in chapter 3). See John Sallis, "Alterity and the Elemental," in *Elemental Discourses* (Bloomington: Indiana University Press, 2018), 84–98.

36. André Gide, *Les nourritures terrestres* (Paris: Mercure de France, 1897), 83. Levinas cites this work on occasion, though to my knowledge not this expression.

37. To date, three volumes of a projected seven of Levinas's *Oeuvres complètes* have appeared. Regrettably, further progress has been suspended by a complex legal dispute over publication rights. The so-called "wartime notebooks" are collected, along with other early texts (essays, fragments), in *OC* I.

38. Sarah Hammerschlag, "Levinas's Prison Notebooks," in *Ox Handbk Levinas*, 23.

39. Emmanuel Levinas, "La spiritualité chez le prisonnier Israélite" and "L'expérience juive du prisonnier," in *OC* 1, 205–8 and 209–15, respectively. A shortened version of the former was published in 1945 (see 205, editor's note a). In point of fact, the latter is the text of a radio transmission, preserved by Levinas in essay form.

40. Levinas characterizes Bloy's position at *OC* 1: 151: "Tout l'homme est logé dans les catégories du catholicisme. Mais tandis que nous autres nous reston à la surface de ces catégories . . . il loge tout ce qui est humain à ce niveau des categories." Lest Bloy's argument be put down only to his antisemitic tendencies, we may add that in its broad strokes it has been anticipated by nearly two millen-

nia, in Tertullian's claim that the soul is Christian and the Christian knows this best (*Apologetics* 17). Levinas and Bloy are taken up at length in Philippe Capelle-Dumont, "Le temps dramatique et son au-delà: Emmanuel Lévinas et Léon Bloy," in *Levinas et l'expérience de la captivité*, ed. D. Cohen-Lévinas (Paris / College Bernardins: Lethielleux, 2011), 95–103.

41. *Way of life*, and not necessarily the historical experience and tradition that express and support it. This is the approach of the phenomenological works, whereas the confessional works are scrupulously attentive to history, tradition, and indeed practice. This manner of proceeding contrasts with that of Franz Rosenzweig, who seeks an account of Jewish facticity in full view of its participation in the liturgical cycle. Levinas was certainly aware of this difference, which did not prevent him from recognizing in *The Star of Redemption* a decisive influence (*TeI* xvi / *TI* 28). Important scholarship on their relationship includes R. A. Cohen, *Elevations: Height of the Good in Levinas and Rosenzweig* (Chicago: University of Chicago Press, 1994); and R. Gibbs, *Correlations in Rosenzweig and Levinas* (Princeton, NJ: Princeton University Press, 1993).

42. See *OC* 1: 208.

43. For remarks on this expression, which appears several times in Levinas's texts, see D. Arbib, "L'élection de la souffrance: La captivité de l'Israélite comme 'schema émotionnel,'" in *Levinas et l'expérience de la captivité*, ed. D. Cohen-Lévinas (Paris / College Bernardins: Lethielleux, 2011), 33–34. My interpretation of Levinas's essays on the experience and spirituality of the Jewish prisoner closely follows Arbib's first few pages.

44. See "Pain and Evasion," in chapter 1 of this work.

45. *OC* 1: 206.

46. Arbib, L'élection de la souffrance," 37, comes close to imputing precisely this view to Levinas. "Judaism thus consists in finding happiness [*bonheur*] in the suffering itself." I would rather say that for Levinas, the Jew must willingly identify with his or her suffering as a defining feature of Jewishness itself, and that whatever "happiness" this brings cannot be the final word on a life that is also defined by hope for divine blessing not for the suffering, but in response to it.

47. *OC* 1: 205.

48. *OC* 1: 210.

49. *OC* 1: 211. Arbib detects another lesson here ("L'élection de la souffrance," 39). The descent into suffering anticipates the kenotic themes of Levinas's later work (persecution, subject as hostage, etc.) and, as regards motive, it grounds acts of radical responsibility in being one-for-the-other. Whatever these terms quite mean—and there is no doubt that in *Otherwise Than Being* they do define an ethics that is at once Jewish and universal—I have already noted my reservation at the claim that Levinas has in view a conception of ethical happiness (see above, note 46).

50. The title of this section is taken from a phrase on the final page of *Otherwise Than Being*, in which Levinas situates his entire project in the wake of "the death of a certain god inhabiting the world behind the scenes." Regarding the term "election" here, see, for example, *TeI* 223–24, 256 / *TI* 245–46, 279; *AE* 19 / *OB* 15, *AE* 67–68 / *OB* 52–53, *AE* 157–58 / *OB* 122–23, and so on. These pas-

sages are taken up at some length in chapter 6 of this work, in the context of exploring Levinas's relation to Christian theology.

51. *OC* 1: 206 and 213.

52. See "Situation and Prophecy," in chapter 1 of the present work.

53. Chapter 3 of the present work takes the view that this task consists in deriving plurality and Infinity strictly from one another, without an anterior ground or *tertium quid*.

54. This argument is not made explicitly by Levinas until his remarkable essay "Être Juif," published in *Confluences* 7, nos. 15-17 (1947): 253–64, and reprinted in *Cahiers d'Études Lévinassiennes* 1 (2003): 99–106; it was translated by M. B. Mader as "Being Jewish," in *Continental Philosophy Review* 40 (2007): 205–10. The response to Sartre, appearing in the last two pages of the essay, calls for a remark. When Levinas argues for the centrality of election for a proper account of Jewishness, he draws attention to a notion that is not merely misunderstood by Sartre's *Anti-Semite and Jew*, but is left entirely without mention.

55. See, for example, his "Nom du chien, or la le droit naturel," in *Difficile liberté: Essais sur le Judaïsme* (Paris: Albin Michel, 1976), 201; translated as "Name of the Dog, or Natural Rights," in *Difficult Freedom: Essays on Judaism*, trans. S. Hand (Baltimore: Johns Hopkins University Press, 1990), 152.

56. Primo Levi, *Survival in Auschwitz*, trans. S. Wolf (New York: Touchstone, 1996), 90.

57. This opens up only half of Levi's field of inquiry. We should not forget that he is as shaken by the actions of the perpetrators as he is by their effects on the victims.

58. Levi, *Survival in Auschwitz*, 87.

59. This idea seems at most a temptation, though certainly a real one. "If for no other reason than that an Auschwitz existed, no one in our age should speak of Providence. But without doubt in that hour [as they heard Allied bombs falling in the distance] the memory of Biblical salvations in times of extreme adversity passed like a wind through all our minds." Levi, *Survival in Auschwitz*, 157–58.

60. Levi, *Survival in Auschwitz*, 9, 136 and 140, 51, 92.

61. Dante is certainly closest. The influence of the *Inferno* is all over *Survival in Auschwitz*, not least in Levi's famous chapter "The Canto of Ulysses." Let us make do with a single passage from Dante. It is Virgil speaking to the poet: "Your wisdom cannot withstand [Fortune]: she foresees, she judges, she maintains her reign, as do the other heavenly powers. Her mutability admits no rest. Necessity compels her to be swift, and frequent are the changes in men's state. She is reviled by the very ones who most should praise her, blaming and defaming her unjustly. But she is blessed and does not hear them. Happy with the other primal creatures, she turns her sphere, rejoicing in her bliss." Dante, *The Inferno*, trans. R. Hollander and J. Hollander (New York: Anchor Books, 2000), VII: 85–96, pp. 135, 137.

62. Thomas Aquinas, *Summa Contra Gentiles* III q. 74; and *Summa Theologiae* I-I q. 116 art. 1.

63. As is, it seems to me, all of Levi's thinking in *Survival in Auschwitz*. The

reader is presented with the facts in the simplest terms possible, and then asked to consider the possibility or impossibility of moving from them to certain conclusions that Levi clearly finds unsupportable (though he does not always say so). The resemblance of this procedure to that of Levinas deserves separate study. We have already seen that Levinas, too, moves from close attention to the facts toward conclusions that cannot be supported by modern reason, though of course in his case this speaks entirely in favor of the conclusions rather than the form of reason they elude. It may be ventured that Levi's commitment to a modern, secular mode of reasoning goes hand in hand with a conviction that the idea of God is irrational, whereas Levinas's commitment to the idea of God goes hand in hand with a conviction that secular reason is incomplete.

64. Most emphatically, in *The Gay Science* §125 and *Thus Spake Zarathustra*, Prologue §2.

65. *EN* 115 / *ENT* 97.

66. This essay, "Useless Suffering," has many layers. Its terminology simultaneously puts Heideggerian philosophy at stake. Levinas's French title is "La souffrance inutile." In the primary instance, Levinas is intent on freeing suffering from what he considers the violent pretense of theodicy, in which everything serves the purpose—and in that sense is useful for—the working out of a divine plan. However, Levinas's claims for the primacy of a suffering that is "*inutile*," useless, also challenge Heidegger's claim for the fundamentally practical orientation of Dasein. Prior to the usefulness of tools and the comfort of a home is the existential suffering that cannot be recuperated into any ontology or theodicy.

67. In this, there is an important difference between Levinas and someone like Emil Fackenheim. Fackenheim's God is present in every moment of the history of his people, including the Shoah, which in all of its horror must be grasped as a new revelation and a new commandment: to survive without despair of God or world, and without forgetting the martyrs of the Holocaust. See Emil Fackenheim, *To Mend the World: Foundations of Future Jewish Thought* (New York: Schocken, 1982), 213.

Chapter 3

This chapter constitutes an expanded and slightly modified version of my essay "Excess and Desire: A Commentary on *Totality and Infinity*, Section I, Part D," in *The Exorbitant: Emmanuel Levinas between Jews and Christians*, ed. K. Hart and M. Signer (New York: Fordham University Press, 2010), 188–200.

1. This position is developed in these terms for the first time, and with explicit reference to a crisis in modern thought and the inadequacies of a religion reduced to theodicy, in "The Ego and the Totality" (1954). In the ethical relation, Levinas finds the truth of our subjectivity and the necessary approach to God. Emmanuel Levinas, "Le Moi et la totalité," in *EN* 31–31, 33–35 / "The Ego and the Totality," in *CPP*, 29–30, 32–33.

2. On Levinas's manner of negotiating this difficulty in a manner defined by his deeper philosophical themes, see Fabio Ciaramelli, "Levinas's Ethical Discourse between Individuation and Universality," in *Re-Reading Levinas,* ed. R. Bernasconi and S. Critchley (Bloomington: Indiana University Press, 1991), 83–105.

3. *Tel* ix / *TI* 21.

4. As Michael Morgan points out, Levinas was clearly thinking seriously about Kant by the early 1950s, though his interest in the priority of the ethical was of course complicated by a convergent interest in upholding a metaphysics that is irreducible to ontology (and thus, broadly speaking, a Platonic complication). See Michael L. Morgan, *Discovering Levinas* (Cambridge: Cambridge University Press, 2007), 62–71. As for the essential point, Adriaan Peperzak puts it most concisely. "The face is the simultaneity of a fact and a command" that arrives from outside the entire life of the subject and exercises the authority of a law. Adriaan T. Peperzak, *Beyond: The Philosophy of Emmanuel Levinas* (Evanston, IL: Northwestern University Press, 1997), 222. The difference between command and law is thus the difference between fact and implication. The word "law" is called for when addressing the proper nature of our freedom as ethical subjects.

5. This calls for an important programmatic remark. The present work is self-consciously restricted to Levinas's *philosophical* texts and says almost nothing about his Jewish denominational writings, which as a matter of fact proliferate during the same period when the mature philosophical position is achieved. The reason for this decision is strictly phenomenological: it has seemed to me that a text, even one that is profoundly religious, cannot have the same concretion as does the human face. The denominational writings turn on the acceptance of a form of revelation that has not been exhausted by over two millennia of interpretation, and indeed, interpretation of interpretation conducted at the highest intellectual level. The philosophical texts appeal with increasing intensity to a face that astonishes, shocks, and even traumatizes from beyond any preparation by a tradition, and uncover profound existential conditions by which we not only survive this but are thereby converted to the Good.

6. This objection is of a single piece with the sort of criticism raised by Hilary Putnam, for whom Levinas's notion of the ethical, driven by his conception of otherness, would direct us to living a "one-sided life"—one that is committed too exclusively to the other person as good, and not enough to other goodnesses. See Hilary Putnam, "Levinas and Judaism," in *The Cambridge Companion to Levinas,* ed. S. Critchley and R. Bernasconi (Cambridge: Cambridge University Press, 2002), 55–57.

7. I borrow this use of the word "responsive" from the writings of Bernhard Waldenfels and Adriaan Peperzak. See, for example, Bernhard Waldenfels, *The Question of the Other* (Hong Kong: Chinese University Press, 2007), 21–35; and Adriaan T. Peperzak, *Elements of Ethics* (Palo Alto, CA: Stanford University Press, 2003), 93–94. Neither author restricts himself to the work of Levinas, but both are fully aware of his position.

8. Sartre, *Being and Nothingness,* 364–65. For a penetrating investigation of the unexpected similarities and crucial differences between Levinas and Sartre,

see Rudi Visker, "A Sartrean in Disguise?" in *Levinas: The Face of the Other, The Fifteenth Annual Symposium of the Simon Silverman Phenomenology Center* (Pittsburgh: Duquesne University Press, 1998).

9. In *Totality and Infinity*, the word "anarchy" appears to have the negative sense of the chaos and injustice that are in need of command and teaching (*TeI* 40 / *TI* 70; *TeI* 71 / *TI* 98). In *Otherwise Than Being, or Beyond Essence*, Levinas draws from the word's etymology (*an-arché*) the positive sense of an ordering that is prior to being and appearing (*AE* 125–30 / *OB* 99–102).

10. *AE* 155 / *OB* 121.

11. This sense of a plot or schema anterior to the being of the figures in play suggests a late appeal by Levinas to narrative theory, and an unexpected affinity with that feature in the thought of Paul Ricoeur. I will return to this feature of Levinas's later work in my conclusion.

12. *AE* 127 / *OB* 101. One is not wrong to conclude from this claim that what is structurally anterior must be phenomenally posterior—that is, it must appear, come to light, only afterwards. In order to better understand this, we sometimes appeal to the phenomenological distinction between what is initial, in the sense of first in the order of experience, and what is originary, in the sense of conditions already covered up by the initial. Levinas himself often uses "originary" in this way.

13. *TeI* 77 / *TI* 104: "*la contraction créatrice de l'infini.*" There is no fail-safe translation of this expression. Lingis has "contraction creative of Infinity," which has the merit of avoiding the thought that Infinity itself either causes or originates, but the drawback of seeming to propose that Infinity would result from something else, or worse, be the other of something else. My translation is meant to convey the sense—I think Levinas's own—that finitude and for that matter all distinctions are exceeded by Infinity. As for the alleged event of "contraction," it is best understood either structurally or as myth.

14. There has been steady interest in Levinas's relation with Kabbalah. Early investigations include Charles Mopsik, "La pensée d'Emmanuel Lévinas et la cabale," in *Cahier L'Herne: Emmanuel Levinas* (Paris: L'Herne, 1991), 378–86; and at greater length, Marc-Alain Ouaknin, *Méditations érotiques* (Paris: Belland, 1992). See also Jacob Meskin, "The Role of Lurianic Kabbalah in the Early Philosophy of Emmanuel Levinas," in *LevStudies* 2 (2007), 49–77; and Elliot Wolfson, "Secrecy, Modesty, and the Feminine: Kabbalistic Traces in the Thought of Levinas," in *The Exorbitant: Emmanuel Levinas between Judaism and Christianity*, ed. K. Hart and M. Signer (New York: Fordham University Press, 2010), 62–73.

15. *AE* 64 / *OB* 50.

16. *TeI* 269 / *TI* 293. Needless to say, Levinas's sense of this word ("situated") is far from the Sartrean sense that we have already seen him oppose.

17. *TeI* 19 / *TI* 48.

18. *TeI* 19 / *TI* 48.

19. The *Meditations* contain numerous instances of this expression for Infinity, understood as God: "most perfect being, that is, God," "God, or a being who is supremely perfect," and so on. René Descartes, *Meditations on First Philosophy* (Cambridge: Cambridge University Press, 1996), 51, 54. For authoritative

commentary, see Jean-Luc Marion, *On Descartes's Metaphysical Prism* (Chicago: University of Chicago Press, 1999), 240–44.

20. Hence the remark in the Third of the *Meditations*: "my perception of the infinite, that is, God, is in some way prior to my perception of the finite, that is, myself." Descartes, *Meditations on First Philosophy*, 31.

21. As it happens, this is not certain, at least if one takes seriously the remarkable reading of the *Meditations* proposed by Michel Henry in the first chapters of his *Genealogy of Psychoanalysis*. Henry's reading concentrates especially on the First and Second of the *Meditations*, which he interprets as a search for the being of the ego centered on auto-affection. Such a reading effectively ends where Levinas wishes to start, which is to say with the resources for a philosophy that is intent, instead, on hetero-affection.

22. Here again, we are indebted to the illuminating analysis by J.-L. Marion. See Marion, *On Descartes's Metaphysical Prism*, 249–50.

23. René Descartes, "Letter to Mersenne," January 28, 1641, in *Oeuvres de Descartes, Correspondances III*, text established by C. Adam and P. Tannery, vol. 2 (Paris: Vrin, 1970), 293: "car je n'ai jamais traité de l'infini que pour me soumettre à lui, & non point pour déterminer ce qu'il est, ou < ce > qu'il n'est pas." Levinas cites this letter in his *Encyclopaedia Universalis* article, "Infinity," reprinted in Emmanuel Levinas, *Alterity and Transcendence*, trans. M. Smith (New York: Columbia University Press, 1999), 76.

24. *OC* 1: 69, 134, 162, 185, and 440, 181, 135.

25. The theme of respect opens the problem of language. See *TeI* 41 / *TI* 69: "The claim to know and to reach the other [*Autre*] is realized in the relation with the other person [*autrui*] that is cast in the relation of language, where the essential is the interpellation, the vocative. The other is maintained and confirmed in his heterogeneity as soon as one calls upon him, be it only to say to him that one cannot speak to him, to classify him as sick, to announce to him his death sentence; at the same time as grasped, wounded, outraged, he is 'respected.'" Chapter 5 of the present work takes up Levinas's sense in which speech is both the origin of responsibility and, precisely in the free delivery of contents, its failure. For the moment, let us anticipate this much: language is activated in a movement of self-transcendence that is provoked by the face or word of an other person, and that is drawn inevitably back to itself by the weight of a subjectivity that is anchored in existence. As we will see in chapter 5, in some unpublished notes and a neglected essay, Levinas calls this movement "metaphor." In his later works, he calls it "saying."

26. *TeI* 177 / *TI* 202. We may forgo the vast and complicated effort that would be required to first ask whether there is a single form or essence of either mysticism, prayer, rite, or liturgy, and then whether Levinas's characterization applies to all of them. To be sure, liturgy, for example, always stands in need of ethical critique, but nothing truly prevents us from insisting on a liturgical critique of ethics.

27. See Emmanuel Levinas, "Lévy-Bruhl et la philosophie contemporaine," in *EN* 53–67 / "Lévy-Bruhl and Contemporary Philosophy," in *ENT* 39–52. A similar reference to Lévy-Bruhl, but condensed, appears in *Time and the Other* (*TA*

21–22 / *TO* 42–43). It is worth noting that an analogous conviction runs through Levinas's Jewish writings and indeed seems to have been part of his formation. This tendency has deep historical roots in the conflict between Hassidic Judaism as it moved east from Poland into Lithuania beginning in the late eighteenth century, and the intellectual approach favored by those who came to be known as the *mitnaggedim*: opponents. Levinas retraces his relation to some of this in "Judaïsme et kénose," in *A l'heure des nations* (Paris: Minuit, 1988), 138–51; translated as "Judaism and Kenosis," in *In the Time of the Nations*, trans. M. Smith (Bloomington: Indiana University Press, 1994), 114–32.

28. *TeI* 3 / *TI* 33–34.

29. For example, *AE* 72 / *OB* 56; see also *AE* 99 / *OB* 79.

30. Francis Bacon, *The Great Instauration*, in *The New Atlantis and the Great Instauration*, ed. J. Weinberger (Oxford: Wiley Blackwell, 2017), 28 and 32. The word "vexation" is lifted from Bacon's expression "vexations of art" (*vexationes artium*). Other readings of Bacon's Latin render "vexation" as—implausibly, it seems to me—"torture."

31. *AE* 56 / *OB* 43: ". . . imposed with a good violence."

32. This characterization of the modern perspective and use of the word "amoral" is taken from Rémi Brague, *The Wisdom of the World: The Human Experience of the World in Western Thought* (Chicago: University of Chicago Press, 2003), 185–98.

33. That said, there is considerable scholarship rising in defense of unsuspected resources in Levinas's thinking for a positive relation to other animals, other animal suffering, and other animal rights. As for Levinas's own stated position, Atterton's conclusion is fair and correct: our ethical obligations extend beyond human beings to include all sentient animals, though the latter are of lesser moral status, and indeed the suffering of animals is permitted if it is to serve a legitimate human interest (Peter Atterton, "Levinas's Humanism and Anthropocentrism," in *Ox Handbk Levinas*, 724–25). For an excellent collection of perspectives on this and related matters, see Peter Atterton and Tamra Wright, *Face to Face with Animals: Levinas and the Animal Question* (Albany: SUNY Press, 2019).

34. About this, we may be succinct. There is no doctrine of analogy in Levinas's metaphysics, and this comes at a price that shows up most clearly in the problem of nature.

35. Emmanuel Levinas, "Langage et proximité," in *EDE*, 222–23; "Language and Proximity," in *CPP*, 113–15.

36. Applying himself to this point, Laszlo Tengelyi therefore risks invoking an "experience" of Infinity. See Laszlo Tengelyi, "Experience of Infinity in Levinas," in *LevStudies* 4 (2009), especially 117–21.

37. *AE* 199, 201–2 / *OB* 156, 158.

38. Levinas invokes the "non-indifference" of Infinity for the finite especially in some passages of his essay "God and Philosophy." See Emmanuel Levinas, "Dieu et la philosophie," in *DVI* 105–6, 108–9 / "God and Philosophy," in *GCM*, 62–63, 65–66. In *Otherwise Than Being, or Beyond Essence*, "non-indifference" is also said of the Good (*AE* 157 / *OB* 122). The expression "non-indifference"

is meant to characterize relation without causation, which is to say, in Levinas's terms, election.

39. *TeI* 122–23 / *TI* 148–49. The notion that an infinity produces heteronomy in the subject without in any way entering into it is at once indispensable for the argument and unsustainable on its own terms. Levinas does not conceal this problem. Interiority would be breached by the idea of infinity, but it would be closed entirely into itself and yet "not prevent egress": "the door to the outside must be at the same time open and closed," and it must be possible both for the subject to pursue egoist atheism without refutation and yet also possible that it be incited to another destiny.

40. *AE* 158 / *OB* 123.

41. As Levinas acknowledges in many places, this strand of his thinking draws on the Platonic notion of a divine desire (*Phaedrus* 244a ff.) for the Good that is by definition beyond being and appearing (*Republic* VI). This is neither a sufficient basis to examine Levinas's adaptation, nor the occasion for interrogating various defenses of his idiosyncratic Platonism, but it can fairly be said that the specifically ethical inflection to his own conception of a desire without self-interest is difficult to find in the dialogues from which he takes inspiration. These matters are pursued more deeply in Jean-François Mattei, "Levinas et Platon," in the collection *Emmanuel Lévinas: Positivité et transcendence* (Paris: Presses Universitaires de France, 2000), 73–87.

42. In this context, "originary" is evidently another name for "an-archic." (See note 12 of this chapter.)

43. This is not necessarily to deny that the understanding of desire that Levinas has in view does not infiltrate his description of the encounter. As many interpreters have noted, it is a great difficulty of *Totality and Infinity* that the phenomenological work on separation and the face appears only after the account of desire that seems to presuppose it. See Mensch, *Levinas's Existential Analytic*, 41–46, and for indications of the difficulties that this and related matters impose on how to read the text, 3–10.

44. *TeI* 257–58 / *TI* 281–82.

45. *AE* 118–20, 183–85 / *OB* 93–94, 144–45. This claim informs Levinas's definition of the "glory" of Infinity.

46. TeI 77 / *TI* 104: "Man redeems [*rachète*] creation."

47. This implication guides Michel Haar, in "L'obsession de l'autre," in *Cahier de l'Herne: Emmanuel Levinas* (Paris: L'Herne, 1991), 444–53.

48. This marks the point where Levinas and Lacan are opposed at greatest depth. Chapter 4 of the present work returns to this at some length.

49. An entire series of questions unfolds from this point. I will only formulate some of them. What does it mean to conceive of procreation as the sole proper end of sexual desire? This claim is hardly new, though it deserves notice that Levinas reaches it without reliance on teleology or biology, and thus without appeal to any natural law. And what of female pleasure, beyond and apart from everything that he says elsewhere about Woman, the Feminine, and so forth? Nothing in the passage from erotic relations to procreation requires that a woman enjoy the experience or the relation. What finally of homosexuality and

of other sexualities? In the analyses making up the entire fourth part of *Totality and Infinity*, these are not merely underdeveloped. They are a matter of indifference. The implications here are vast and complex. It seems quite possible that admitting that a non-procreative end for sexual relations is good in its own right, admitting the independent and essential nature of female pleasure in them, and qualifying the heteronormative dimensions of Levinas's position would each require, at the very least, significant adjustments.

50. This claim about a relation with Infinity that would be "withdrawn from any possible representation or comprehension" becomes both necessary and indispensable the moment Levinas associates being with violence and nonetheless upholds the possibility of peace. Without it, the subjectivity of the subject would be closed into itself before any openness to the other person, who would there stand outside and over against it. Levinas, of course, defends an openness prior to closure. Chapter 4 of the present work reviews the claim starting from an investigation of subjectivity and desire.

51. This is a central theme of chapter 6 of the present work.

Chapter 4

1. The few references that one finds in Levinas's works seem to be entirely a matter of *Freudian* psychoanalysis. As for proper names, Levinas refers almost exclusively to Freud, except for a single mention of Jacques Lacan ("prolongation of Freud"), and this only in the course of assessing the interests of his friend, the Belgian philosopher Alphonse de Waelhens. Emmanuel Levinas, *Outside the Subject*, trans. M. B. Smith (Palo Alto, CA: Stanford University Press, 1993), 106.

2. *AE* 75 / *OB* 59: "The suspicions engendered by psychoanalysis, sociology, and politics weigh on human identity such that we never know to whom we are speaking and what we are dealing with when we build our ideas on the basis of human facts. But we do not need this knowledge in the relationship in which the other is a neighbor, and . . . for whom I am responsible." A complementary criticism appears in the important essay "Ego and Totality." By conceiving of language as being infiltrated by impulses that are unconscious and thus inaccessible even to oneself, psychoanalysis contributes to the "destruction of the I" and "casts a basic suspicion on the most unimpeachable testimony of self-consciousness." Emmanuel Levinas, "Le Moi et la totalité," in *EN* 36–37; / "The Ego and the Totality," in *CPP*, 34. Were this only a matter of calling attention to the human capacity for self-deception, even Levinas might agree that psychoanalysis contains a morality. But he has the acuity to understand that at least a certain dimension of psychoanalytic thought—emphasized by the Lacanians more than by the ego psychologists—calls into the question the original integrity of the ego itself.

3. *TeI* 176 / *TI* 202; see also *TeI* 60 / *TI* 88. Chapter 5 of the present work takes up Levinas's philosophy of language.

4. See "Revising the Existential Analytic" in chapter 2.

5. *DEE* 118–19/ *EE* 66.

6. *DEE* 57 / *EE* 28–29.

7. The boundary is clearest where Heidegger recognizes drives (*Triebe*) that function before or prior to care, but argues that phenomenology does not have access to them. Heidegger, *Being and Time*, 238.

8. In *Totality and Infinity* (*TeI* 112 / *TI* 138), Levinas situates the unconscious in relation to the sincerity of sensation, in which the subject is immediately and spontaneously contented by the elements. This is a sincerity prior to the difference between honesty and deception and indeed prior to the movement of the will. The unconscious promoted by "contemporary psychology" would infiltrate and complicate sensation with a tension and a conflict which, for Levinas, "fails to recognize" a contentment that is not gratification.

9. This stands to reason, if we only recognize the fact that not only do we not know what we are repressing, but often we also do not know *that* we are repressing. It can even be the case that when others point it out, we still feel no connection with it. In Freud's terms, the superego does much of its work outside of consciousness.

10. *TeI* 250 / *TI* 272.

11. *AE* 156n26 / *OB* 197n26. Here Lingis translates *non-conscience* as "unconsciousness." I have supplied the literal translation, since Levinas is clearly intent on a different conception than would be associated with a word such as "repression."

12. The classical formulation can be found in Sigmund Freud, "A Special Type of Choice of Object Made by Men," in *The Standard Edition of the Complete Psychological Works of Sigmund Freud*, vol. 11 (London: Hogarth, 1953–73), 171: "[The boy] begins to desire his mother herself in the sense with which he has recently become acquainted, and to hate his father anew as a rival who stands in the way of this wish; he comes, as we say, under the dominance of the Oedipus complex."

13. Further steps must include careful study of the important work by Philippe Van Haute, Tomas Geyskens, and Herman Westerink, which, on the basis of careful readings of Freud's early texts, compel serious reconsideration of the idea that psychoanalysis emerged especially from a formative commitment to the Oedipus complex, notwithstanding Freud's own later efforts to change the published record. See especially Philippe Van Haute and Tomas Geyskens, *A Non-Oedipal Psychoanalysis? A Clinical Anthropology of Hysteria in the Works of Freud and Lacan* (Leuven: Leuven University Press, 2012); and Philippe Van Haute and Herman Westerink, *Reading Freud's Three Essays on the Theory of Sexuality: From Pleasure to the Object* (London: Routledge, 2020).

14. This took time. As early as 1913, Freud rejected Jung's notion of an analogous "Electra complex," but it was not until his own late essay on "Feminine Sexuality" that Freud felt able to say that although there is no clear analogy between male and female, the encounter with a law that influences object-choice is formative in both sexes. See Sigmund Freud, "Female Sexuality," in *The Standard Edition of the Complete Psychological Works*, vol. 21: 223–43.

15. See the section "The Ethical Relation" in the present chapter.

16. Emmanuel Levinas, "Leçon talmudique: Sur la justice," in *Cahier de l'Herne: Emmanuel Levinas* (Paris: L'Herne, 1991), 133.

17. This has been the focus of a previous essay of mine closely related to this chapter. See Jeffrey Bloechl, "The Difficulty of Being Two: Subjectivity and Otherness according to Lacan and Levinas," in *Psychology and the Other*, ed. D. Goodman and M. Freeman (Oxford: Oxford University Press, 2015), 146–59.

18. Lacan interprets *"sujet-supposé-savoir"* both as the analyst (the subject who is supposed by the analysand to know) and as a kind of knowledge (the supposed subject of knowledge, i.e., of what the analyst knows). To my mind, his best concise discussion of this occurs in his *Seminar XI: The Four Fundamental Concepts of Psychoanalysis*, trans. A Sheridan (New York: W.W. Norton, 1998), 230–34.

19. Sigmund Freud, "Fragment of an Analysis of a Case of History," in *The Standard Edition of the Complete Psychological Works*, vol. 7: 43–44.

20. Hence Freud's expression "death-drive." This concept is justified most substantially in the course of Freud's reflections concerning certain difficulties in the therapy that have deep roots in his thinking. The occasional claims that the concept was essentially a product of Freud's reaction to a confluence of experiences after the First World War threaten to give the impression that there may be a complete Freudian psychoanalysis that could do without it (as some analysts have not hesitated to suggest). There is no doubt that the death of Freud's daughter Sophie and his attempts to understand soldiers suffering from "traumatic neurosis" were important aggravating factors, but it remains the case that Freud was aware of Sabina Spielrein's case for a *Todestrieb* as early as 1912 (he alludes to it in a footnote in *Beyond the Pleasure Principle*), and only two years later his growing interest in aggression is well underway in the paper "On Narcissism: An Introduction." Moreover, in the first pages of section 6 of his *Civilization and Its Discontents*, he himself traces much of this metapsychological trajectory from narcissism and aggression to the death drive. Sigmund Freud, "On Narcissism: An Introduction," in *The Standard Edition of the Complete Psychological Works*, vol. 21: 117–19. In the meantime, some of the historical record is settled by Ilse Grubrich-Simitis's discovery of a draft of Freud's *Beyond the Pleasure Principle* that was completed in April 1919, thus fully nine months before Sophie Freud's death. See Ulrika May, "The Third Step of Drive-Theory: On the Genesis of *Beyond the Pleasure Principle*," *Psychoanalysis and History* 17, no. 2 (2015): 205–72.

21. No analyst would deny these things, though most and maybe all would consider them ancillary to the therapeutic goal of reducing suffering.

22. See Freud's instructive remarks to this effect in his "Recommendations to Physicians Practicing Psychoanalysis," in *The Standard Edition of the Complete Psychological Works*, vol. 12: 116–17.

23. Is the therapy that is intent on making use of transference and on redirecting pathology therefore an extended exercise of power? Levinas seems to think so, and not only because he thinks the liberation of our subjectivity must come from the face of the other person. He also suspects psychoanalysis of begging its own question of an unconscious that would truly be without order, precisely where the therapy is conducted on the premise that engaging it might yield self-knowledge. In that case, "the unconscious [*l'inconscient*] remains a play of consciousness, and psychoanalysis means to ensure its outcome, against the troubles that come to it from repressed desires, in the name of the very rules of

this game. The play of consciousness does indeed involve rules, but irresponsibility in the game is declared to be a sickness" (*AE* 130n6 / *OB* 194n6). Read out of context, one might assume that these lines were written by the early Foucault in the pursuit of aims that are at best orthogonal to those of Levinas. In his *History of Madness*, when Foucault is not on the verge of aligning Freud with Sade, Hölderlin, Van Gogh, Nerval, and Nietzsche—prophets of transgression, intent on hearing madness in its own voice—he instead upbraids him for having absorbed all of the moral structures developed by Philippe Pinel and William Tuke entirely into the authoritative figure of the doctor. Michel Foucault, *History of Madness*, trans. J. Murphy and J. Khalfa (New York: Routledge, 2009), 339 and 510–11.

24. Jacques Lacan, *The Seminar of Jacques Lacan: Book VII, The Ethics of Psychoanalysis*, trans. A. Sheridan (New York: W.W. Norton, 1992), 319. There is also a negative formulation: "from an analytical point of view, the only thing one can be guilty of is having given ground relative to one's desire" (321).

25. This is worked out with some care in his *Three Essays on the Theory of Sexuality*, which Van Haute, Geyskens, and Westerink have argued is in fact the founding text for psychoanalysis (see note 13 of this chapter). If they are right, Freud's original thought was of a "polymorphously perverse disposition" (Freud's expression) of our sexuality before *and through* any accommodations made to the law or any of its avatars—most prominently, of course, everything belonging to the Oedipus complex. On "polymorphous perversity," see Sigmund Freud, *Three Essays on the Theory of Sexuality*, in *The Standard Edition of the Complete Psychological Works*, vol. 7: 191.

26. *TeI* 46 / *TI* 74.

27. This expression is taken up in "Restlessness and Enjoyment," in chapter 2 of the present work.

28. For a richly detailed study, see Peter Atterton, "From Transcendental Freedom to the Other: Levinas and Kant," in *In Proximity: Emmanuel Levinas and the Eighteenth Century*, ed. M. New, R. Bernasconi, and R. A. Cohen (Lubbock: Texas Tech University Press, 2001), 327–54.

29. A sketch of this argument appears at *TeI* 182 / *TI* 207. In *Otherwise Than Being, or Beyond Essence*, "dis-interested" reason is for-the-other, operating under the severe conditions of a movement that simultaneously seeks justice for the other person and already opens itself to ethical correction (*AE / OB* 16, 130, 160–61). Further discussion of this theme between Levinas and Kant leads beyond the scope of the present work, but see Etienne Féron, "Intérêt et désintéressement de la raison: Levinas et Kant," *Levinas en contrastes*, ed. M. Dupuis (Brussels: De Boeck University, 1994), 83–105. This conception of speech is a central theme of chapter 5 of the present work.

30. *TeI* 23 / *TI* 52: "The immediate is the face to face." In point of fact, Kant makes a similar claim for our relation with the moral law, when he claims that it determines the will immediately. See Immanuel Kant, *Groundwork of the Metaphysic of Morals*, trans. M. Gregor (Cambridge: Cambridge University Press, 1997), 58.

31. Jacques Derrida, "Violence and Metaphysics," in *Writing and Difference*, trans. A. Bass (Chicago: University of Chicago Press, 1978), 129–33.

32. This conclusion agrees with Salanskis's more general contention that the entire argument depends on the affirmation of unqualified "straightforwardness" (*la droiture*) in both call and response. Jean-Michel Salanskis, *Lévinas vivant* (Paris: Belles Lettres, 2006). This interpretation is supported by a number of passages to the effect that "nothing is more direct than the face to face, which is straightforwardness itself" (*TeI* 51 / *TI* 78).

33. See chapter 3 of the present work.

34. We have come to a moment for an informed retrospective remark. It should not be assumed that Levinas has had this conception of the face in hand from the beginning or that its meaning is univocal throughout his texts. In *Existence and Existents* and *Time and the Other*, it appears only a handful of times and is generally submitted to a notion of "approach" which may invite the sort of interpretation that we have just rejected, or perhaps appear to have Sartrean overtones that Levinas would be eager to dispel. It is only in *Totality and Infinity*, or rather in the texts preparing it and then informing it, that the face of the other is associated robustly with Levinas's conception of exteriority, and only then that it is said with emphasis that the otherness of the other is absolute. All of this speaks against a monism of Levinas's oeuvre and in favor of a living philosophy. And to be sure, this philosophy does not die after *Totality and Infinity*. In *Otherwise Than Being, or Beyond Essence*, Levinas still tells us that the face that "signals for me an unexceptionable responsibility" does so as "the very collapse of representation" (*AE* 112 / *OB* 88). But in this second major book, he takes up the idea of the face most often in the course of further developing his conception of the subjectivity that hears the call, with extensive clarification of the theory of religion that all of this requires.

35. *TeI* 229 / *TI* 251.

36. One thinks especially of Enrique Dussel, whose work Levinas was well aware of. The introductory pages of Dussel's *Ethics of Liberation: In the Age of Globalization and Exclusion* (Durham, NC: Duke University Press, 2013) invoke "the poor, the widow and stranger," and the book engages in a steady dialogue with Levinas. That said, one must wonder how far the rapprochement can go, given Dussel's energetic appeal to myth and his commitment of the ethics of liberation to engage in a micro-politics of power that is frankly indebted to Foucault (see especially chapter 6 of Dussel's book).

37. In an important sense, what we are calling a "fact" is no fact at all, since it is not discovered so much as deduced from an interpretation of conditions that might well count as factual: the spontaneous care of the subject for itself, its non-indifference to the other person, and so on. Moreover, as I hope to have established in chapter 3 of the present work, the concepts of plurality and infinity are present only in their reciprocal confirmation, and in that way they set the conditions by which we are to understand what can and does appear.

38. *AE* 109 / *OB* 87.

39. We have already taken note of this. See note 50 of chapter 3.

40. *AE* 62–63 / *OB* 48–49.

41. We are reminded, not for the last time, of Levinas's polemic with every form of negation. "Negativity presupposes a being established, placed in a site,"

and so on (*TeI* 10 / *TI* 40). The transcendence of the other—human or divine—proposed via negation is a transcendence that is still limited by the perspective of the one who negates.

42. *TeI* 76 / *TI* 102–3 (emphasis in original).

43. This conception of a Good that comes with its own horizon or else exceeds every possible horizon is supported by Levinas's occasional references to what would be its counterpart in consciousness: an "inversion" and "excess" of intentionality; see, respectively, *AE* 77 / *OB* 61 *OB* and "La trace de l'autre," in *EDE* 196. Marion's reading of Levinas concentrates on the importance of this conception, to which his own phenomenology of saturation is indebted. See Jean-Luc Marion, "The Intentionality of Love: In Homage to Levinas," in *Prolegomena to Charity*, trans. S. Lewis (New York: Fordham University Press, 2002), 71–101, especially 82–83; and Jean-Luc Marion, *Being Given*, trans. J. Kosky (Palo Alto, CA: Stanford University Press, 2002), 366–67 n88.

44. This claim is once again best grasped in proximity to Kant. Even in the course of celebrating Kant's discovery of the primacy of pure practical reason, Levinas nonetheless contests the idea that moral willing is simply and strictly obedience to the moral law. Earlier, we took note of Levinas's resistance to the universality that would be the achievement of reason. It may in fact be good to refuse such a universality, and any number of others, in the name of respect for the otherness of the other person. On this, too, see Atterton, "From Transcendental Freedom to the Other," esp. 333–37.

45. *AE* 74 / *OB* 57; see also *AE* 175 / *OB* 138.

46. *AE* 56 / *OB* 43.

47. *TeI* 75 / *TI* 101.

48. See *AE* 158–59 / *OB* 123–24.

49. *AE* 110 / *OB* 87, 83; see also *AE* 104–5 / *OB* 84. In a footnote on this use of the word *frémissement*, or "shuddering" (*AE* 110n22 / *OB* 192n22), Levinas states that he is translating the Greek *phrike*, as he has found it in Socrates's characterization of the response to divine beauty, in the *Phaedrus* (251a). Socrates himself does not hesitate to observe physical manifestations.

50. This idea comes originally from Melanie Klein's observation of the anxiety provoked in an infant by a mother whose desire comes so close and is so unqualified as to provoke fantasies of being devoured. Lacan takes this up in his seminars on object-relations and anxiety on the way to suggesting that subjectivity rests on a lack that must not be filled by any alleged good, or rather that the good, in order to be truly good, must in fact admit of a certain distance from us. This claim opens a complete reading of Levinas under the pressure of Lacanian questions that would take much too long to develop here. One finds it worked out at considerable length in Guy-Félix Duportail, *Intentionnalité et trauma: Levinas and Lacan* (Paris: L'Harmattan, 2005), especially 89–111 and 167–204.

51. Bruce Fink, *A Clinical Introduction to Lacanian Psychoanalysis* (Cambridge, MA: Harvard University Press, 1997), 215–16, 242–43 n43.

52. See *TeI* 5 / *TI* 35. These formulations paraphrase Levinas's appropriation of what Jean Wahl has meant by "transascendence."

53. In different ways, Jean-Louis Chrétien and Jean-Yves Lacoste approach

this theme phenomenologically. See Jean-Louis Chrétien, *The Unforgettable and the Unhoped for*, trans. J. Bloechl (New York: Fordham University Press, 2002), esp. chapter 1; and Jean-Yves Lacoste, "The Phenomenology of Anticipation," in *Phenomenology and Eschatology*, ed. N. Deroo and J. Manoussakis (Surrey, UK: Ashgate), 2009), 15–33.

54. *AE* 106 / *OB* 84.

55. *AE* 158 / *OB* 123.

56. For an important treatment, see Rudi Visker, "The Price of Being Dispossessed: Levinas's God and Freud's Trauma," in *The Face of the Other and the Trace of God: Essays on the Philosophy of Emmanuel Levinas*, ed. J. Bloechl (New York: Fordham University Press, 2000), 243–75.

57. Sigmund Freud, *Origins of Psychoanalysis: Letters to Wilhelm Fliess* (New York: Basic Books, 1954), 310–14.

58. See *AE* 196 / *OB* 154. Recall that this has been Levinas's conception of God at least since his wartime writings.

59. Especially *AE* 196 / *OB* 154, where this thought justifies the concept of God's "illeity," which we have already encountered when exploring Levinas's more general concern with anthropomorphism (see "Desire and Excess," in chapter 3 of the present work). On our relation as the trace of Infinity, see *AE* 149 / *OB* 117; *AE* 178 / *OB* 140; *AE* 189 / *OB* 149.

60. For the psychoanalytic account of psychosis that is closest to this, see Jacques Lacan, *The Seminar of Jacques Lacan: Book III, 1955–1956, The Psychoses*, trans. R. Grigg (London: Routledge, 1997), esp. 143–44. Levinas accepts the word "psychosis" twice in *Otherwise Than Being, or Beyond Essence*: "The psyche, the one-for-the-other, can be a possession and a psychosis" (*AE* 86n3 / *OB* 191n3); and "The psyche, a uniqueness outside of concepts, is a seed of folly, already a psychosis" (*AE* 180 / *OB* 142). This feature of the argument, both in its relation to Judaism and in its affinity with a philosophy of passivity before obligation, has attracted the extended attention of Jean-François Lyotard. See Lyotard, "Figure Foreclosed," trans. D. Macey, in *The Levinas Reader*, ed. A. Benjamin (London: Blackwell, 1989), 69–110, esp. 93–94.

Chapter 5

1. Emmanuel Levinas, "The Name of God according to a Few Talmudic Texts," in *Beyond the Verse*, trans. G. D. Mole (Bloomington: Indiana University Press, 1994), 121–22.

2. Emmanuel Levinas, "Martin Heidegger et l'ontologie," 58-59 / "Martin Heidegger and Ontology," 14.

3. Didier Franck, *L'un-pour-l'autre: Levinas et la signification* (Paris: Presses Universitaires de France, 2008), 24.

4. *TeI* 35–36 / *TI* 64 (italics in original). See *TeI* 70 / *TI* 97: "A relation between terms that resist totalization, that absolve themselves from the relation or that specify it, is possible only as language."

5. This distinction belongs to Aristotle's theory of predication (e.g., *Posterior Analytics* 73a). Levinas often characterizes the face as *kath'hauto*, and in at least one passage does come close to explicitly contrasting it with *pros ti*. "The disclosed being is relative to us and not *kath'hauto*" (*TeI* 36 / *TI* 64).

6. *TeI* 37 / *TI* 65 (italics in original; Lingis translates this as "telling itself to us").

7. Respectively, *DEE* 144 / *EE* 85 and *TA* 81 / *TO* 87.

8. *TeI* 37 / *TI* 66.

9. Heidegger develops this distinction with the German terms *Offenbarung* (revelation) and *Offenbarkeit* (manifestness), and takes care to align the thinking of being with a meditation on the forgotten richness of the latter. See Martin Heidegger, "Conversation with Martin Heidegger: Recorded by Herman Noack," in *The Piety of Thinking*, ed. and trans. J. Hart and J. Maraldo (Bloomington: Indiana University Press, 1976), 64–65. Needless to say, Levinas accepts the distinction, but nonetheless argues that revelation can be admitted to phenomenology in the form of the face of the other person. This proposal agrees with his conviction that the deconstruction of metaphysics is not complete until it has also been applied to fundamental ontology, which continues to suppress ethical plurality. It will be necessary to return to these matters in "The Primacy of Philosophy," in chapter 6.

10. For an illuminating account of Levinas's appeal to different forms of vocal and auditory phenomena and the subtle differences among his accounts of them, see R. Wu, "The Recurrence of Acoustics in Levinas," *LevStudies* 10 (2016), 115–36.

11. *TeI* 37–36 / *TI* 66.

12. *TeI* 64–65 / *TI* 92.

13. This use of the expression "here I am" (*me voici*) is of course biblical. One finds it already in Genesis (22, 31, 46). On at least two occasions, Levinas refers to Isaiah, in which, whether it is God or his people who say the words, the sense is of a futural accompaniment. *Hineni*: "here I am, send me" (Is. 6:8); "you will cry for help, and he will say: Here I am" (Is. 58:9). See *AE* 186n11 / *OB* 198n11, and *AE* 190n17 / *OB* 198n17. Phenomenologically, the expression "*me voici*" designates a sincerity that would be prior to articulation, and an origin of manifestation that would be prior to place or spatial presence. See Franck, *L'un-pour-l'autre*, 195–96.

14. *AE* 186 / *OB* 146.

15. Hence the complex meaning of a well-known claim registered at *TeI* 173 / *TI* 198: "The Other is the sole being I can wish to kill."

16. This rejoins what is said earlier about enjoyment and representation when, however, we did not yet have the means to move from "restlessness for the other person" all the way to discourse. The move is now justified when, in a chapter on enjoyment and presentation, *Totality and Infinity* interprets the alterity of the elemental (which "gives itself away even while escaping," *TeI* 115 / *TI* 141) as our prompt to representation. Representation is itself a heightened attempt at mastery and possession, yet even at this level, possession remains an impossible attempt to maintain the sameness of the same over its prior relation with

the other. Every representation is an expression of meaning that is from and to an interlocutor.

17. Derrida, "Violence and Metaphysics," 147.

18. Derrida, "Violence and Metaphysics," 117, 128–29, 141, 148–49.

19. Derrida, "Violence and Metaphysics," 148.

20. *AE* 151, 22 / *OB* 118, 18.

21. Derrida, "Violence and Metaphysics," 141–42. Levinas uses the Greek expression on occasion, but instances of the phrase "beyond being" are much more frequent in his original works.

22. The impossibility of opposing the good to being is also the impossibility of upholding its original or ultimate purity. Derrida's contention that Levinas's text both must and cannot make such a claim identifies his reading as properly deconstructive. It also identifies deconstruction, at least as Derrida pursues it here, as a philosophy of contamination. In contrast with the prophetic discourse by which Levinas urges ethical metaphysics, the philosophy of contamination denies itself the right to specific concepts that would be withdrawn from the general circulation of all the others. It thus also denies itself the right to positive assertions about an alleged exteriority that would exceed or evade contact with a counterpart interiority. Everything that for Levinas would bind us to the other person and to God without belonging to being provides a structure and a gaze that *Totality and Infinity* calls "eschatological." Philosophy, for Levinas, assures us of the goodness of a good that will always be more than we know of it. If this assurance is undone, we must become considerably more gnostic about any such abundance. This is undoubtedly the case for Derrida's later "messianism without a messiah," which is plainly consistent with the basic position of this early essay.

23. See "Reading Descartes's 'Third Meditation,'" in chapter 3.

24. The shifts in Levinas's arguments for ethics as first philosophy and the particular difficulties accruing to a hierarchical conception are analyzed in Franck, *L'un-pour-l'autre*, 125–26.

25. This concept is defined in the essay that takes it up at greatest length, "Enigme et Phénomène." "This way of manifesting without manifesting itself, we call enigma—going back to the Greek etymology of this term, and contrasting it with the indiscrete and victorious appearing of the phenomenon." Emmanuel Levinas, "Enigme et phénomène," in *EDE*, 208. Alphonso Lingis's English translation of this work reverses the title: "Phenomenon and Enigma," in *CPP*, 66. This use of the concept also appears often in *Otherwise Than Being*.

26. *AE* 178 / *OB* 140: "In the absolute assignation of the subject, the Infinite is enigmatically heard: before and beyond."

27. See "Being as Language" in this chapter.

28. *AE* 14 / *OB* 11–12.

29. *TeI* 38 / *TI* 66.

30. *TeI* 273 / *TI* 297.

31. There are just over forty pages on this theme, the first twenty of which (*OC* 1: 227–42, 329–31, 350–52) are notes that clearly anticipate a lecture given on February 26, 1962 (*OC* 2: 322–47). For reasons of economy, I will refer only to the lecture text and thus only to the second volume of *Oeuvres complètes*. Also of

interest in the second volume are lengthy texts of lectures on "Parole et silence," "L'écrit et l'oral," and "La Signification" (*OC* 2: 69–104, 203–29, 351–82). All of these unpublished texts were written between 1948 and 1960 or 1961, with the lecture on metaphor actually given on February 26, 1962. One should also take note of occasional forays into the topic of language in some of the philosophical essays published during those same years ("Freedom and Command" [1953], "Ego and Totality" [1954], and "Enigma and Phenomenon" [1957]). These forays are sparse, but they do begin to deploy the notions of call, response, and discourse such as are found in *Totality and Infinity*. Together, these various texts suggest, in contrast with what is claimed in some scholarly interpretations of the matter, that far from making a turn to language after *Totality and Infinity*, Levinas was already engaged in a close reflection on that theme for some time before the great book appeared, and indeed there is reason to think that this was already altering the book's general orientation, though not its central argument.

32. *OC* 2: 331.

33. Jacques Derrida, "White Mythology," in *Margins of Philosophy*, trans. A. Bass (Chicago: University of Chicago Press, 1982), 247. Some remarks on the history of texts are in order. The simple fact that Levinas had begun to focus on the problem of language in texts prior to *Totality and Infinity* disabuses us of the hypothesis that this development was in direct response to central theses in Derrida's "Violence and Metaphysics" (1964). To the contrary, if one attends to the appearance of certain resonances (which is not to say convergences) between Levinas's position prior to *Totality and Infinity* and Derrida's position several years after "Violence and Metaphysics," not to mention Derrida's late introduction of footnotes confessing that he encountered Levinas's essays on the trace and language only after it was too late to incorporate them, one must entertain some reason to think that it was Levinas who influenced Derrida. This possibility and any question of its importance for philosophy deserve separate attention. For Derrida's late encounter with "The Trace of the Other" (1963) and "Meaning and Sense" (1964), see his *Writing and Difference*, 311n1.

34. *OC* 2: 332.

35. *OC* 2: 327.

36. Friedrich Nietzsche, "On Truth and Lies in a Non-Moral Sense," trans. D. Breazeale, in *The Nietzsche Reader*, ed. K. Ansell-Pierce and D. Large (Oxford: Blackwell, 2006), 116, 121.

37. *OC* 2: 326, 327.

38. Emmanuel Levinas, *Humanisme de l'autre homme* (Paris: Fata Morgana, 1972), 113; translated as *Humanism of the Other*, trans. N. Poller (Urbana: University of Illinois Press, 2006), 69. This thought runs deep, as Bettina Bergo has shown. In order to uphold a claim that the first word of any subject is already prophetic, and fundamentally hopeful, it will be necessary to interpret sensibility as the intelligence of a body that has never belonged to the world that it nonetheless settles for. See Bettina Bergo, "A Site from Which to Hope? Notes on Sensibility and Meaning in Levinas and Nietzsche," in *LevStudies* 3 (2008): 117–42, especially 125–26. However, this friendly interpretation should not blind us to the fact that Levinas has deeper reasons to keep his distance from Nietzsche. What

has been developed in the present study as Levinas's prophetic discourse is no less opposed to rhetoric, which Nietzsche embraced against metaphysics, than it is to the Western philosophy that for him culminates with Heidegger. When, in the few pages dedicated to rhetoric in *Totality and Infinity*, Levinas speaks of a persuasion that corrupts the freedom to seek goodness and justice (*TeI* 40–42 / *TI* 70–72), he might well have Nietzsche foremost in mind. The lesson is profound. It is within the capacity of being, as power, to undo its own idols *without* opening itself to the good.

39. *OC* 2: 328, 344, 346.

40. *OC* 2: 341.

41. This expression appears already in the notes on metaphor predating the lecture (*OC* 1: 241), and recurs in the lecture itself (*OC* 2: 334). We will not belabor its resonance with what is called "the Said" in later, published works. Cesare Del Mastro draws attention to these matters in his *La métaphore chez Lévinas: Un philosophie de la vulnérabilité* (Brussels: Lessius, 2012), 99.

42. Del Mastro, *La métaphore chez Lévinas*, 133–40. In this context, we cannot ignore the final sentence of Levinas's contemporaneous essay "A priori et subjectivité" (1962), in which he distances himself from the idea that the face is a metaphor. "Absolutely present, in his face, the Other—without any metaphor— faces me" ("A priori et subjectivité," in *EDE*, 186, translation mine). It is no use to immediately dismiss this as a lapse on his part. Levinas's essay, we note, concerns itself with Mikel Dufrenne's attempt, influenced by Husserl, to rethink the a priori in a manner that splits it between structures of external objects and an inner knowledge of these structures attainable in feeling. For Levinas, of course, the face of the other arrives with its own meaning from beyond intentionality, and without submitting to structures that would be knowable according to any inner faculty of the subject. We surmise that a wish to defend the exteriority of the face while insisting that it is intelligible in its concrete occurrence prompts a rejection specifically of what the lecture has understood as *relative* metaphor. The face would deliver its own meaning, without ulterior reference to anything else.

43. Derrida, "Violence and Metaphysics," 111.

44. Didier Franck, "Le sens de la trace," in *Emmanuel Levinas: La question du livre*, ed. M. Abensour and A. Kupiec (Paris: Institut Mémoires de l'Édition Contemporaine, 2008), 22.

45. See A. Cools, *Langage et subjectivité: Vers une approche du différend entre Maurice Blanchot et Emmanuel Lévinas* (Leuven: Institut Supérieur de Philosophie, 2007), 5–6.

46. *AE* 25 / *OB* 20.

47. *AE* 172 / *OB* 135.

48. In an interesting study of this relation, Robert Bernasconi makes a strong case for the possibility that the entire section of *Otherwise Than Being* entitled "Skepticism and Reason" (*AE* 210–18 / *OB* 165–71) is intended in large part as a response to Derrida's argument for contamination in "Violence and Metaphysics." As we have seen for ourselves, skepticism is invited by Levinas into a defense of some of his own key claims, or rather into a demonstration meant to show that they do not belong as securely within the said or, in another register, within

being, as his critics might think. Whether or not Derrida's essay is best read as full-blooded critique or as a sophisticated double-reading—and Bernasconi has done more than anyone to make us ask this question, in all of its importance—it seems clear that Levinas understood it as the former. This is Bernasconi's interest in the presence of skepticism in Levinas's text. Once one becomes alert to the fact that a number of expressions and entire claims made in that context echo points that Derrida had argued, the passage appears as considerably more than a late and gratuitous digression. Of course, the availability of Levinas's previously unpublished work on language gives us a longer perspective on the development of this dimension of his work. In that case, we must still think that it was hastened, and no doubt sharpened, by the encounter with Derrida. Robert Bernasconi, "Skepticism in the Face of Philosophy," in *Re-Reading Levinas*, ed. R. Bernasconi and C. Critchley (Bloomington: Indiana University Press, 1991), 149–61.

49. *AE* 56–57 / *OB* 44.

50. Levinas describes mediation in these terms especially in *Otherwise Than Being, or Beyond Essence*. See *AE* 5 / *OB* 4; *AE* 106 / *OB* 84; *AE* 127 / *OB* 100; and *AE* 156 / *OB* 121.

51. Levinas's understanding of the death of God has been addressed at some length in "Deaths of a Certain God" in chapter 2. Its close relationship with his conceptions of Infinity and plurality are a major theme of "The Linchpin of Totality and Infinity" and "Reading Descartes's 'Third Meditation'" in chapter 3.

52. *AE* 215 / *OB* 169–70.

53. *OC* 2: 346.

Chapter 6

1. See Richard Sugarman, *Levinas and the Torah: A Phenomenological Approach* (Albany: SUNY Press, 2019), 333–35.

2. The nature of that alleged reinvigoration is investigated with scholarly precision by J.-M. Narbonne in *Lévinas et l'héritage grec suivi de cent ans de Néoplatonisme en France*, by Jean-Marc Narbonne and Wayne Hankey (Paris: J. Vrin, 2004), 9–121. The results are much too detailed for review here. For a summary, see Jean-Marc Narbonne, "God and Philosophy according to Levinas," in *LevStudies* 2 (2007), 29–48.

3. *Évasion* 94, 97 / *Escape* 70, 72.

4. "This extravagant movement of going beyond being or transcendence toward an immemorial antiquity we call the idea of Infinity." Levinas, "Énigme et phénomène," in *EDE*, 214; / "Phenomenon and Enigma," in *CPP*, 71. See also *AE* 191n21 / *OB* 199n21, where theology and art are said to "retain" (*retiennent*) the immemorial past.

5. *TeI* 269 / *TI* 293: "To affirm origin from nothing by creation is to contest the prior community of all things within eternity, from which philosophical thought, guided by ontology, makes things arise as from a common matrix. The absolute gap of separation which transcendence implies could not be better ex-

pressed than by the term creation, in which the kinship of beings among themselves is affirmed, but at the same time their radical heterogeneity also, their reciprocal exteriority coming from nothingness."

6. Whether or not Levinas ever contemplated the matter in quite this way, he was explicit about where he stood in the most general sense: "It matters to me that it is not theology that I do, but philosophy." This clarification was offered in response to Jean Wahl during the discussion following Levinas's lecture "Transcendence et hauteur," in *Liberté et commandement* (Montpellier: Fata Morgana, 1994), 96 (to my knowledge, there is no English translation of the discussion).

7. I have specifically adopted these classical definitions in order to foreground an important feature of Levinas's quite different mode of thought. Theology is said to be a discourse of praise by a long range of thinkers, from Augustine and Denys the Areopagite through Bonaventure to Jean-Luc Marion. We will return to some important implications of this practice in the next section, "Creation, Election, Messianism."

8. This theme preoccupies Derrida in his second lengthy essay on Levinas, "At This Very Moment in This Work Here I Am." At the surface of Derrida's reading, Levinas's philosophy necessarily betrays its own intention to argue in a manner that reiterates the conditions of ethical responsibility by setting experiences that would originally be spoken and heard into written texts. Behind this is a more fundamental observation that the coherence of any kind of teaching depends on the stability of an extended moment or sequence of moments, and that the declarative sentences which belong to philosophy (thesis, proposal, claim, counter-claim) cannot but appeal to precisely this moment—even though Levinas has argued a great deal that urges us to identify presence, repetition, and the written text with discursive violence. Jacques Derrida, "At This Very Moment in This Work Here I Am," trans. R. Berezdivin, in *Re-Reading Levinas*, ed. R. Bernasconi and S. Critchley (Bloomington: Indiana University Press, 1991), 11–48.

9. *AE* 232 / *OB* 184.

10. *AE* 191n21 / *OB* 199n21.

11. *TeI* 50–51 / *TI* 78–79.

12. *AE* 193 / *OB* 151.

13. See Ludwig Feuerbach, *Essence of Christianity*, trans. G. Eliot (Amherst, NY: Prometheus, 1989), chapter I, §2, pp. 12–32.

14. *AE* 182 / *OB* 143. This idea is admirably capacious. If this restlessness is unknown to itself, it can trouble existence all the way to suicide (*TeI* 123 / *TI* 149). But properly understood, as a figure of responsibility, it extends all the way to restlessness for the death of the other person.

15. Thomas Hobbes, *Leviathan*, ed. E. Curley (Indianapolis: Hackett, 1994), 4.46.21, p. 475. My reference to Hobbes is only partly supported by context. Hobbes turns against the notion of an eternal presence of God to the human mind, whereas Levinas turns against the somewhat different notion of a thought that would have to remove itself from time in order to contemplate, among other things, such a presence. What *TeI* 269 / *TI* 293 calls "eternity" is associated with totalization, and time is associated with separation (and thus plurality). What

Levinas elsewhere calls "the eternal" would be the deep past of what is irrecuperable and, as we have noted, immemorial.

16. *Tel* 269 / *TI* 293.

17. It is Heidegger himself who understands *das Ende* in this way, that is, according to "the old meaning of the word." Martin Heidegger, "The End of Philosophy and the Task of Thinking," trans. J. Stambaugh, in *Basic Writings*, ed. D. F. Krell (New York: Harper and Row, 1977), 375. The remainder of this paragraph continues to refer to that late essay.

18. At this point, Heidegger distinguishes "thoughtful thinking" from the entirety of "philosophy" descended from ancient Greece, and treats the latter in terms that some may wish to characterize as reductive. This practice, of course, is hardly new in his work. Nor is his claim for a thinking that is capable of justifying it. Has Levinas's own reductiveness about "Western philosophy" been learned from Heidegger? Does one or the other of them proceed with greater plausibility? These questions cannot be dealt with in brief. One thing is certain, and ought to be taken into account by any serious investigation: Levinas did read the later Heidegger. His unpublished works include occasional notes with specific references (e.g., the extended reference to Heidegger's *Holzwege* at *OC* 1: 374), and the attentive reader will recognize many passing references even in his latest major works (e.g., *AE* 70 / *OB* 54: *die Sprache spricht*, and *AE* 172 / *OB* 135: *Geläut der Stille*, expressions appearing in *Unterwegs zur Sprache*).

19. It should be said that the concept of place is scattered throughout Levinas's work, and most often on the noetic level, which, we have given reason to think, is repeated at the conceptual level. The indispensable text on this theme is his essay "Heidegger, Gagarin and Us," which takes direct aim at the implications of a Heideggerian philosophy of "Place," and proposes that a light form of technology might free us from the "seductiveness of [the] paganism" by which we would forget transcendence. The significance of Yuri Gagarin's escape from the Earth's atmosphere lies not in the attainment of some cosmotheoretical command over human life, but in the opening up of new possibilities, in thought and aspiration, that might come to the aid of a philosophy intent on ethics and religion. Emmanuel Levinas, "Heidegger, Gagarin, et nous," in *Difficile liberté: Essais sur le Judaïsme* (Paris: Albin Michel, 1976), 299–303; translated as "Heidegger, Gagarin, and Us," in *Difficult Freedom: Essays on Judaism*, trans. S. Hand (Baltimore: Johns Hopkins University Press, 1990), 231–34. Apart from this, Levinas only rarely approaches the matter of place on the conceptual level, but he is on the verge of doing so at least twice in *Totality and Infinity*. There he writes: "The thinking thought is the place [*lieu*] where a total identity and a reality that ought to negate it are reconciled without contradiction" (*Tel* 99 / *TI* 127, translation mine). And at greater length, with explicit reference to Heidegger, he writes: "In the light of generality which does not exist is established the relation with the individual. For Heidegger, an openness upon Being, which is not a *being*, which is not a 'something,' is necessary in order that, in general, a 'something' manifests itself. In the rather formal fact that an existent is, in the work of exercise of its Being—in its very independence—resides its intelligibility. Thus appear the structures of vision, where the relation of the subject with the object is subor-

dinated to the relation of the object with the void of openness, which is not an object. The comprehension of an existent consists in precisely going beyond the existent, into the open. To comprehend the particular being is to apprehend it out of an illuminated place [*lieu*] it does not fill" (*TeI* 164 / *TI* 189–90).

20. There are many reasons for this conclusion, and the scholarship on them is immense. We will make do here with only a single expansive remark from Heidegger himself: "One could not be more reserved than I at every attempt to make use of Being to think theologically in what way God is God. Of Being, there is nothing to expect here. I think that Being can never be thought as the ground and essence of God, but that the experience of God and his manifestness, to the extent that it can indeed meet us, nonetheless flashes in the dimension of Being, which in no way means that Being might be considered a possible predicate of God." Heidegger offered these thoughts during his Zurich Seminar (1953). Not having access to the German text, I translate from Jean Greisch's French translation, in *Heidegger et la question de Dieu*, ed. Richard Kearney and Joseph S. O'Leary (Paris: Quadrige, 2009), 334.

21. Levinas would not have thought that the analogy is by chance. Among his unpublished writings, we find the following fragment from 1952: "Heidegger–prolongation of Greek thought—Oppose him to Judaism?—But his thought is entirely Christianized." *OC* 1: 467 (translation mine).

22. *TeI* 12 / *TI* 41; see also *AE* 13–15 / *OB* 11–13; *AE* 192–93 / *OB* 151, *AE* 115n31 / *OB* 193n31. There is no scholarly consensus on preferences between "negative," "apophatic," and "mystical" theology. I prefer "mystical" and "apophatic" over "negative," which has connotations that run directly counter to the notion of ascent or, in the thought of the Fathers, that of divination (*theosis*). Levinas uses "negative" almost without exception. He does take up *apophansis* (i.e., propositional judgment) from time to time, but this is not at all the same thing.

23. *TeI* 11 / *TI* 40 (translation mine). I have passed over earlier sentences that are more likely to have been directed at Sartre: "The movement of transcendence is to be distinguished from the negativity by which discontent man refuses the condition in which he is established. Negativity presupposes a being established, put in a place [*placé dans un lieu*] where he is at home" (translation mine).

24. We have alluded more than once to an ethical critique of religious practice. At this point, one sees that it does not stop at insistence on the priority of responsibility and justice. The mystical approach to God would be impossible for reasons that are existential as much as ethical.

25. Is Christian mysticism univocal in its path and practice? It seems not, and so we will settle for invoking only a single form that has approached these matters with especially impressive rigor. In book 2 of his *Dark Night of the Soul*, John of the Cross reports that at a point of great advance the "passion of love" overtakes the free will of action, so that the senses and intellect are darkened and the soul is moved rather than moving itself. In this state the soul reaches the "highest degree of prayer," and is sometimes in divine union with God. But then it is God who visits the soul, and not vice versa. John of the Cross, *Dark Night of the Soul*, in *The Collected Works of John of the Cross*, trans. K. Kavanaugh and O. Rodriguez (Washington, DC: Institute of Carmelite Studies, 1991), II.13.3 and II.23.11,

pp. 424–25 and 453. One has no further difficulty understanding the importance of what is implicit in the Sanjuanist texts from the moment that they are offered specifically to fellow members of the Carmelite community: the ascent of desire that goes all the way to surrendering the right to personal initiative, places the adept in considerable spiritual danger. It hardly needs observing that not every would-be mystic avoids the fusion that Levinas foresees for certain forms of religiosity (on this worry about fusion, see "Reading Descartes's Third Meditation," in chapter 3 of the present work).

26. See especially Jean-Luc Marion, *The Idol and Distance*, trans. T. Carlson (New York: Fordham University Press, 2001), §14, pp. 151–62.

27. Which stands to reason, given the nearness of Pseudo-Dionysius's efforts to elevate divine causality from human comprehension; and the care that Aquinas takes to specify, for example, that the beginning and end of all creatures cannot itself be a being (*Summa Theologiae* I-I, q.2), that God is uncomposed, does not belong to the genus of substance, does not enter into the composition of other things, and so on (*Summa Theologiae* I-I q. 3). But all of this leads far afield, and Marion has stated his relation to Aquinas in an important essay appended to the second edition of his *God without Being: Hors-Texte*, trans. T. Carlson (Chicago: University of Chicago Press, 2012), 199–235.

28. Nietzsche's materialist reduction is undisguised: "the major moral concept *Schuld* [guilt] has its origin in the very material concept of *Schulden* [debts]." Friedrich Nietzsche, *On the Genealogy of Morals*, II.4, in *On the Genealogy of Morals and Ecco Homo*, trans. W. Kaufmann and R. J. Hollingdale (New York: Vintage, 1989), 62–63. Before one objects that Nietzsche says nothing about God in this passage, one might remember that it will not be long before he suggests that the very notion of God is invented as a means to compel certain resolutions of our material strife in terms that are advantageous to some of us rather than others.

29. Blaise Pascal, *Pensées*, trans. A. J. Krailsheimer (London: Penguin, 1995), 112. This is one of five epigraphs for *Otherwise Than Being, or Beyond Essence*. "Usurpation" is Levinas's word.

30. *TeI* 77 / *TI* 104: "The relations that are established between the separated being and Infinity redeem what diminution there was in the creative contraction of Infinity. Man redeems creation." We have commented on these lines in "Ethical Metaphysics," in chapter 3 of this work and will soon return to them in order to understand the messianic strand in Levinas's thinking.

31. *DEE* 15 / *EE* 1.

32. *TA* 128–29 / *TO* 73–74.

33. *TeI* 29 / *TI* 58.

34. *TeI* 255–57 / *TI* 278–80.

35. Child psychologists follow roughly this line of thinking into a theory of the origin of autonomous personhood. What Donald Winnicott calls the "holding environment" postulates an early prenatal relation in which the "good-enough mother" provides the infant with enough love to support the formation of confidence in its own identity, but not so much love as to stunt uninhibited play and the exercise of freedom. According to Winnicott, the mother is for a time her child's entire world, and precisely this experience—or fantasy—must be given up

in order to reach maturity. One easily sees the point at which this developmental theory departs from Levinas. For Winnicott and his school, mature personhood is the result of gradual integration, as the psyche reorganizes itself around the relations between inner life and the external world, *which includes other people.* See Winnicott, "The Theory of the Parent-Infant Relationship," in *The Maturational Process and the Facilitating Environment,* by Donald Winnicott (London: Routledge, 2018), 37–55.

36. In fact, and as is easy enough to see, they repeat many of the themes recorded in the biblical narratives of a relation with the father who is God. One thus cannot avoid the thought that Levinas has taken as his model for a certain form of human relations (filiality, fraternity) possibilities that are recorded in texts whose spiritual intent may raise them beyond what is attainable in ordinary lives.

37. For this confluence of creation and election see, for example, *TeI* 256–57 / *TI* 279. On at least one occasion, Levinas himself recognizes the thought that election, ostensibly unique in each case, might appear as nothing more than a "single articulation in the divine economy . . . that is subject to the play or designs of Infinity" (*AE* 195–96 / *OB* 153)—plays and designs, however, that would imply the sort of causality that we have assured ourselves he rules out of Infinity, properly understood.

38. Heidegger, *Being and Time*, §9, pp. 67–68.

39. Levinas is probably clearest about this in the discussion after the lecture that became his important essay "God and Philosophy." The one-for-the-other that in his later works he calls "substitution" is asymmetrical and prior to any economy. It is already inscribed in me, before any impression that it is also inscribed in the other person. The other person can take the place of anyone and anything except my substitution. This claim is made emphatically at *DVI* 148 / *GCM* 93.

40. *EN* 236 / *ENT* 217. The entire essay cited here, "Mourir pour . . ." / "Dying for . . . ," is dedicated to these claims. As one finds in it, there is reason to think that Levinas has said a good deal more about death than Heidegger, and with greater subtlety. See Richard A. Cohen, "Levinas: Thinking Least about Death—Contra Heidegger," *International Journal of Philosophy of Religion* 60 (2006): 21–39.

41. Levinas does not often use the word "mercy," but it is especially helpful in highlighting the inordinance of the ethical moment. Mercy is not limited by moral or social expectation, and perhaps not even by justice itself. For more on this, see my "Justice and Mercy," *Philosophy Today* 61 (Winter 2018): 137–48.

42. Levinas, "Being Jewish," 208–9.

43. Both of these expressions appear in single response during the interview published as "Philosophy, Justice, and Love," *EN* 125 / *ENT* 107. As many commentators have recalled, Dostoevsky's sentence actually reads, "We are all guilty of all and for all before all, and I more than the others." We can be sure that Levinas knows this perfectly well, as he cites the original sentence earlier in the same interview (123 / 105). Apart from the fact that his version simply fits the terms of his own argument, it may also contain a riposte to Sartre, who has also argued that "I am responsible for all." But this statement turns out to mean

something very like the opposite of what would belong to ethical metaphysics: already before declaring his responsibility, Sartre has said that each of us fashions his or her own image in response to others, and as an expression of who we want all others to be. See Jean-Paul Sartre, *Existentialism Is a Humanism*, trans. C. Macomber (New Haven, CT: Yale University Press, 2007), 24–25, 22.

44. It has not been necessary in the present work to say much about this notion of justice and the other other that Levinas calls "the third party" (*le tiers*). The notion itself is evident: even while one is responsible for this singular other person, here and now, one is also called upon to care for everyone else. In this way, ethical responsibility opens upon considerations of justice. As for its status within the argument, Derrida has on countless occasions given us everything we need to address it as the site of a problem. We should ask not only whether there can be justice without responsibility, but also whether responsibility is possible without justice—since, after all, in Levinas's own account, one would not serve the other person without implications for the relation with other others. Which is to say that a theory of community, a politics, must condition any ethics no less than vice versa. Such an argument is famously Derridean. Simon Critchley's reading of Levinas often appears guided above all by it. See Simon Critchley, *The Ethics of Deconstruction: Derrida and Levinas* (Edinburgh: Edinburgh University Press, 2014), especially the pages on Levinas's political philosophy contained in the chapter entitled, notably, "A Question of Politics: The Future of Deconstruction" (225–36).

45. *TeI* 224 / *TI* 246.

46. *AE* 157 / *OB* 122; see also *AE* 73 / *OB* 57.

47. If one is unsettled by this turn in the argument, one still should take care not to misunderstand it. The persecution to which Levinas assigns positive value, as an irreducible feature of our subjectivity, cannot be conflated with the entirely different sort of persecution that prompted his earliest reflections on Jewishness. At the level of responsibility, which is to say asymmetry, Nazis undoubtedly have faces, and it is a sign of the courage of this philosophy that Levinas has not sought the means to deny it (see, e.g., *EN* 125 / *ENT* 107: "I am responsible for the other person even when he commits crimes"). This does not qualify the evil of their actions, but only furnishes a necessary condition for how to think about it. Levinas is therefore quick to add, without inconsistency, that the same executioner who undoubtedly has a face nonetheless, by his actions, forfeits any claim on our own active and unlimited responsibility. He is a danger to others, and this requires a suspension of responsibility in favor of the decisions that belong to justice. Out of care for his potential victims, and in memory of his real victims, we must treat the executioner as if he no longer has a face (and perhaps insist that this is the responsible thing to do, even for him). But again, this distortion belongs to the exigencies of politics—which, one is certainly entitled to think, weigh heavily on what Levinas calls ethics.

48. See "Ethical Metaphysics," in chapter 3 of this work, commenting on *TeI* 77 / *TI* 104: "Man redeems creation."

49. The remainder of this paragraph summarizes the first few pages of the

essay, before Levinas moves toward a defense of divine transcendence and a case for plurality and proximity already well known to us in the present investigation (*EN* 69–71 / *ENT* 53–55). The words "humiliation" and "expiatory" are his, and as it happens, they are theologically sound.

50. Emmanuel Levinas, *Transcendence et intelligibilité* (Geneva: Labor et Fides, 1984), 51. The lecture by this name appears in *Emmanuel Levinas: Basic Philosophical Writings*, ed. A. T. Peperzak, R. Bernasconi, and S. Critchley (Bloomington: Indiana University Press, 1996), 150–59. Unfortunately, the discussion, which took place one day later has not been included in that book.

51. A final word, then, about Levinas's wartime writings. Earlier, we paused over the fact that in *Existence and Existents* the encounter with the other person is sometimes developed in terms of an "approach" that "liberates" (see "Restlessness and Enjoyment," in chapter 2). At that point, we had reason to wonder whether this conception is truly free of the thought, Sartrean if one wants a contemporaneous name for it, that what is seen coming may not fall immediately under an interpretation projected from one's own situation and concerns. In the present context, we might instead note that the older notions do seem close to investing the other person with a messianic capacity: the other who pardons me saves me from myself, which for Levinas must mean *saves me from the necessary conditions of existence*. When Levinas conceives the face of the other person as trauma and awakening, he takes some distance both from the Sartrean perversion and from a messianism only of the other person.

52. Emmanuel Levinas, "La laïcité et la pensée d'Israël," in *Les imprévus de l'histoire* (Paris: Fata Morgana, 1994), 183; translated by N. Poller as "Secularism and the Thought of Israel," in *Unforeseen History* (Champaign-Urbana: University of Illinois Press, 2004), 117.

53. *TeI* 261 / *TI* 285. This thought is registered only very late in *Totality and Infinity*, which, as Levinas takes care to note, cannot contain it. It is plainly central for *Otherwise Than Being, or Beyond Essence*. For a close and illuminating study of this passage between the two books, see Bettina Bergo, *Levinas between Ethics and Politics* (Dordrecht: Kluwer, 1999), 132–35, 148–49.

54. All of these expressions come from a single page (*Difficile liberté*, 45; *Difficult Freedom*, 89) of the transcription of lectures that Levinas gave to the World Jewish Congress in 1960 and 1961 and later published as "Messianic Texts." The arguments for close agreement between Levinas's Talmudic, Jewish intellectual, and philosophical writings find agreement across the genres on this point, and tend to converge in their understanding of it. The present work has profited especially from Oona Ajzenstat, *Driven Back to the Text: The Premodern Sources for Levinas's Postmodernism* (Pittsburgh: Duquesne University Press, 2001), e.g., 251, "the messiah is me"; and David Plüss, *Das Messianische: Judentum und Philosophie im Werk Emmanuel Levinas* (Stuttgart: Kohlhammer, 2001), e.g., 331, emphasizing the weight of suffering that is taken on by the messianic subject.

55. See Stéphane Lahache, "Le messianisme dans la pensée d'Emmanuel Levinas: Une ethique du pro-nom," in *Emmanuel Levinas: Philosophie et judaisme*, ed. D. Cohen-Lévinas and S. Trignano (Paris: In Presse Editions, 2002), 361.

56. Catherine Chalier, *Levinas: L'utopie de l'humaine* (Paris: Albin Michel, 1993), 146. My consideration of Levinas's conception of messianic subjectivity is greatly indebted to this work.

57. Dietrich Bonhoeffer, *Ethics*, trans. R. Krauss and C West (Minneapolis: Fortress, 2015), 154–55. In Bonhoeffer's vocabulary, the corresponding term for "substitution" is *Stellvertretung*, translated here as "vicarious representative action." A *Stellvertreter* is a "deputy" or perhaps a "proxy."

58. On this, and on other speculative deployments of the *idea Christi*, see Xavier Tilliette, *Le Christ de la philosophie* (Paris: Cerf / Cogitatio fidei, 1990), 93–118, esp. 108–14.

59. Tilliette, *Le Christ de la philosophie*, 248 (gloss on Simone Weil's expression "encompassing subjectivity" [*subjectivité englobante*]).

Conclusion

1. There is at least one important analogue among texts partially inspired by Levinas. Marion's *God without Being* is not only an attempt to free God from the horizon or filter of being (*Dieu sans l'être*—God without being 'it,' that is, a being). It is also at least the outline of an attempt to reenter the field of being from a perspective that is informed by a positive relation with God as God. Hence the deeper significance of his title for chapter 3: "La croisée de l'être": the crossing or intersection of being—evidently, from elsewhere than the *Seinsfrage* alone.

2. *AE* 171 / *OB* 135.

3. *AE* 123 / *OB* 97; *AE* 96 / *OB* 76.

4. *AE* 62 / *OB* 48; *AE* 99 / *OB* 79. See *AE* 60n33 / *OB* 189–90 n33: "plot proper to speaking"; and *AE* 62n34 / *OB* 190n34: "plot of proximity . . . plot of saying."

5. *AE* 31 / *OB* 25. Conversely, "the plot of goodness and the Good, outside of consciousness, outside of essence, is the exceptional plot of substitution," *AE* 176 / *OB* 138.

6. *AE* 188 / *OB* 147. See *AE* 196 / *OB* 154: "The plot of the Infinite is not elaborated according to the scenario of being and consciousness"; and *AE* 115n31 / *OB* 193n31: "plot of infinity . . . not a negative theology."

7. The notion of "plot" is explicitly called "human" twice. See *AE* 206 / *OB* 162 and *AE* 231 / *OB* 183.

8. We will not pursue here the question of whether this late recourse to a prominent feature of narrativity exhibits a debt to Paul Ricoeur. We will note, though, that the manner in which Levinas's concept secures the unity of his argument at least comes close to Ricoeur's sense that plot synthesizes the play of concordance and discordance. Of course, even within that frame, Levinas's understanding of what would be ethical characters and events nonetheless makes great efforts to privilege discordance as the original condition of meaning. This emphasis is of a piece with the reduction of *ipse* to *idem* which has elicited considerable reservation from Ricoeur. We know well enough by now that in order

for Levinas to uphold his claim that the relation with the other person is asymmetrical and that discourse is diachronic, it is necessary to conceive of the subject as *idem,* or as what he calls "the same." For a concise formulation of Ricoeur's reservation, see his *Oneself as Another,* trans. K. Blamey (Chicago: University of Chicago Press, 1992), 335.

9. See "The Ethical Relation as Language," in chapter 5 of the present work.

Bibliography

Ajzenstat, Oona. *Driven Back to the Text: The Premodern Sources for Levinas's Postmodernism*. Pittsburgh: Duquesne University Press, 2001.

Arbib, Daniel. "L'élection de la souffrance: La captivité de l'Israélite comme 'schema émotionnel.'" In *Levinas et l'expérience de la captivité*, ed. D. Cohen-Lévinas, 31–47. Paris / College Bernardins: Lethielleux, 2011.

Aristotle. *Categories*, trans. J. L. Ackrill. In *The Complete Works of Aristotle*, vol. 1. Princeton, NJ: Princeton University Press, 1984.

———. *Posterior Analytics*, trans. J. Barnes. In *The Complete Works of Aristotle*, vol. 1. Princeton, NJ: Princeton University Press, 1984.

Atterton, Peter. "From Transcendental Freedom to the Other: Levinas and Kant." In *In Proximity: Emmanuel Levinas and the Eighteenth Century*, ed. M. New, R. Bernasconi, and R. A. Cohen, 327–53. Lubbock: Texas Tech University Press, 2001.

———. "Levinas's Humanism and Anthropocentrism." In *The Oxford Handbook of Levinas*, ed. M. Morgan, 709–30. Oxford: Oxford University Press, 2019.

Atterton, Peter, and Tamra Wright. *Face to Face with Animals: Levinas and the Animal Question*. Albany: SUNY Press, 2019.

Bacon, Francis. *The Great Instauration*. In *The New Atlantis and the Great Instauration*, ed. J. Weinberger. Oxford: Wiley Blackwell, 2017.

Bergo, Bettina. *Levinas between Ethics and Politics*. Dordrecht: Kluwer, 1999.

———. "A Site from Which to Hope? Notes on Sensibility and Meaning in Levinas and Nietzsche." In *Levinas Studies*, vol. 3, ed. J. Bloechl, 117–42. Pittsburgh: Duquesne University Press, 2008.

Bernasconi, Robert. "Skepticism in the Face of Philosophy." In *Re-Reading Levinas*, ed. R. Bernasconi and S. Critchley, 149–61. Bloomington: Indiana University Press, 1991.

Bloechl, Jeffrey. "The Difficulty of Being Two: Subjectivity and Otherness according to Lacan and Levinas." In *Psychology and the Other*, ed. D. Goodman and M. Freeman, 146–59. Oxford: Oxford University Press, 2015.

———. "Excess and Desire: A Commentary on *Totality and Infinity*, Section I, Part D." In *The Exorbitant: Emmanuel Levinas between Jews and Christians*, ed. K. Hart and M. Signer, 188–200. New York: Fordham University Press, 2010,

———. "Justice and Mercy." *Philosophy Today* 61 (Winter 2018): 137–48.

Bonhoeffer, Dietrich. *Ethics*, trans. R. Krauss and C. West. Minneapolis: Fortress, 2015.

Brague, Rémi. *The Wisdom of the World: The Human Experience of the World in Western Thought*, trans. T. Fagan. Chicago: University of Chicago Press, 2003.

Brunschvicg, Léon. *Le progrès de la conscience dans la philosophie occidentale*. Paris: Alcan, 1927.

Capelle-Dumont, Philippe. "Le temps dramatique et son au-delà: Emmanuel Lévinas et Léon Bloy." In *Levinas et l'expérience de la captivité*, ed. D. Cohen-Lévinas, 95–103. Paris / College Bernardins: Lethielleux, 2011.

Cassell, Eric. *The Nature of Suffering and the Goals of Medicine*. Oxford: Oxford University Press, 2004.

Chalier, Catherine. *Levinas: L'utopie de l'humaine*. Paris: Albin Michel, 1993.

Chrétien, Jean-Louis. *The Unforgettable and the Unhoped for*, trans. J. Bloechl. New York: Fordham University Press, 2002.

Ciaramelli, Fabio. "Levinas's Ethical Discourse between Individuation and Universality." In *Re-Reading Levinas,* ed. R. Bernasconi and S. Critchley, 83–105. Bloomington: Indiana University Press, 1991.

Cioran, E. M. *Précis de decomposition*. Paris: Gallimard, 1949.

Cohen, Richard A. *Elevations: Height of the Good in Levinas and Rosenzweig*. Chicago: University of Chicago Press, 1994.

———. "Levinas: Thinking Least about Death—Contra Heidegger." *International Journal of Philosophy of Religion* 60 (2006): 21–39.

———. *Out of Control: Confrontations between Spinoza and Levinas*. Albany: SUNY Press, 2016.

Cools, Arthur. *Langage et subjectivité: Vers une approche du différend entre Maurice Blanchot et Emmanuel Lévinas*. Leuven: Institut Supérieur de Philosophie, 2007.

Critchley, Simon. *The Ethics of Deconstruction: Derrida and Levinas*. Edinburgh: Edinburgh University Press, 2014.

Dante. *The Inferno*, trans. R. Hollander and J. Hollander. New York: Anchor Books, 2000.

Del Mastro, Cesare. *La métaphore chez Lévinas: Un philosophie de la vulnérabilité*. Brussels: Lessius, 2012.

Derrida, Jacques. "At This Very Moment in This Work Here I Am," trans. R. Berezdivin. In *Re-Reading Levinas,* ed. R. Bernasconi and S. Critchley, 11–48. Bloomington: Indiana University Press, 1991.

———. "Violence and Metaphysics." In *Writing and Difference*, trans. A. Bass, 79–153. Chicago: University of Chicago Press, 1978.

———. "White Mythology." In *Margins of Philosophy*, trans. A. Bass. Chicago: University of Chicago Press, 1982.

Descartes, René. "Letter to Mersenne," January 28, 1641. In *Oeuvres de Descartes: Correspondances III*, text established by C. Adam and P. Tannery, vol. 2. Paris: Vrin, 1970.

———. *Meditations on First Philosophy*, trans. E. Haldane. Cambridge: Cambridge University Press, 1996.

———. *Passions of the Soul and Other Late Writings*, trans. M. Moriarty. Oxford: Oxford University Press, 2015.

Drabinski, John. *Sensibility and Singularity: The Problem of Phenomenology in Levinas.* Albany: SUNY Press, 2001.

Duportail, Guy-Félix. *Intentionnalité et trauma: Levinas and Lacan.* Paris: L'Harmattan, 2005.

Dussel, Enrique. *Ethics of Liberation: In the Age of Globalization and Exclusion,* trans. E. Mendieta, Y. Angulo, and C. Pérez Bustillo. Durham, NC: Duke University Press, 2013.

Fackenheim, Emil. *To Mend the World: Foundations of Future Jewish Thought.* New York: Schocken, 1982.

Fagenblat, Michael. "Levinas and Heidegger: The Elemental Confrontation." In *The Oxford Handbook of Levinas.* ed. M. Morgan, 103–33. Oxford: Oxford University Press, 2019.

Féron, Etienne. "Intérêt et désintéressement de la raison: Levinas et Kant." In *Levinas en contrastes,* ed. M. Dupuis, 83–105. Brussels: De Boeck University, 1994.

Feuerbach, Ludwig. *Essence of Christianity,* trans. G. Eliot. Amherst, NY: Prometheus, 1989.

Fink, Bruce. *A Clinical Introduction to Lacanian Psychoanalysis.* Cambridge, MA: Harvard University Press, 1997.

———. *The Lacanian Subject: Between Language and Jouissance.* Princeton, NJ: Princeton University Press, 1995.

Foucault, Michel. *History of Madness,* trans. J. Murphy and J. Khalfa. New York: Routledge, 2009.

Franck, Didier. "The Body of Difference." In *The Face of the Other and the Trace of God: Essays on the Philosophy of Emmanuel Levinas,* ed. J. Bloechl, 3–29. New York: Fordham University Press, 2000.

———. "Le sens de la trace." In *Emmanuel Levinas: La question du livre,* ed. M. Abensour and A. Kupiec, 15–24. Paris: Institut Mémoires de l'Édition Contemporaine, 2008.

———. *L'un-pour-l'autre: Levinas et la signification.* Paris: Presses Universitaires de France, 2008.

Freud, Sigmund. *Civilization and Its Discontents.* In *The Standard Edition of the Complete Psychological Works of Sigmund Freud,* vol. 21, trans. J. Strachey. London: Hogarth, 1953–73.

———. "Female Sexuality." In *The Standard Edition of the Complete Psychological Works of Sigmund Freud,* vol. 21, trans. J. Strachey. London: Hogarth, 1953–73.

———. "Fragment of an Analysis of a Case of History." In *The Standard Edition of the Complete Psychological Works of Sigmund Freud,* vol. 7, trans. J. Strachey. London: Hogarth, 1953–73.

———. *Origins of Psychoanalysis: Letters to Wilhelm Fliess,* trans. E. Mosbacher and J. Strachey. New York: Basic Books, 1954.

———. "Recommendations to Physicians Practicing Psychoanalysis." In *The Standard Edition of the Complete Psychological Works of Sigmund Freud,* vol. 12, trans. J. Strachey. London: Hogarth, 1953–73.

————. "A Special Type of Choice of Object Made by Men." In *The Standard Edition of the Complete Psychological Works of Sigmund Freud*, vol. 11, trans. J.Strachey. London: Hogarth, 1953–73.

————. *Three Essays on the Theory of Sexuality*. In *The Standard Edition of the Complete Psychological Works of Sigmund Freud*, vol. 7, trans. J. Strachey. London: Hogarth, 1953–73.

Gibbs, Robert. *Correlations in Rosenzweig and Levinas*. Princeton, NJ: Princeton University Press, 1993.

Gide, André. *Les nourritures terrestres*. Paris: Mercure de France, 1897.

Haar, Michel. "L'obsession de l'autre." In *Cahier de l'Herne: Emmanuel Levinas*, 525–38. Paris: L'Herne, 1991.

Hammerschlag, Sarah. "Levinas's Prison Notebooks." In *The Oxford Handbook of Levinas*, ed. M. Morgan, 21–34. Oxford: Oxford University Press, 2019.

Heidegger, Martin. *Basic Problems in Phenomenology, Winter Semester 1919–1920*, trans. S. Campbell. London: Bloomsbury, 2012.

————. *Being and Time*, trans. J. Macquarrie and E. Robinson. London: SCM, 1962.

————. "Conversation with Martin Heidegger: Recorded by Herman Noack." In *The Piety of Thinking*, ed. and trans. J. Hart and J. Maraldo. Bloomington: Indiana University Press, 1976.

————. "The End of Philosophy and the Task of Thinking," trans. J. Stambaugh. In *Basic Writings*, ed. D. F. Krell. New York: Harper and Row, 1977.

————. *Prolegomena to the History of the Concept of Time*, trans. T. Kisiel. Bloomington: Indiana University Press, 1985.

————. "What Is Metaphysics?" trans. D. F. Krell. In *Basic Writings*, ed. D. F. Krell. New York: Harper and Row, 1977.

Henry, Michel. *Genealogy of Psychoanalysis*, trans. D. Brick. Palo Alto, CA: Stanford University Press, 1993.

Hobbes, Thomas. *Leviathan*, ed. E. Curley. Indianapolis: Hackett, 1994.

Husserl, Edmund. *Ideas Pertaining to a Pure Phenomenology and a Phenomenological Philosophy, First Book*, trans. F. Kersten. Dordrecht: Kluwer, 1982.

————. *Ideas Pertaining to a Pure Phenomenology and a Phenomenological Philosophy, Second Book*, trans. R. Rojcewicz and A. Schuwer. Dordrecht: Springer, 1989.

John of the Cross. *Dark Night of the Soul*. In *The Collected Works of John of the Cross*, trans. K. Kavanaugh and O. Rodriguez. Washington, DC: Institute of Carmelite Studies, 1991.

Kant, Immanuel. *Critique of Pure Reason*, trans. N. K. Smith. London: Macmillan, 1993.

————. *Groundwork of the Metaphysic of Morals*, trans. M. Gregor. Cambridge: Cambridge University Press, 1997.

Kearney, Richard, and Joseph S. O'Leary, eds. *Heidegger et la question de Dieu*. Paris: Quadrige, 2009.

Lacan, Jacques. *The Seminar of Jacques Lacan: Book III, 1955–1956, The Psychoses*, trans. R. Grigg. London: Routledge, 1997.

————. *The Seminar of Jacques Lacan: Book VII, The Ethics of Psychoanalysis*, trans. A. Sheridan. New York: W.W. Norton, 1992.

————. *Seminar XI: The Four Fundamental Concepts of Psychoanalysis*, trans. A Sheridan. New York: W.W. Norton, 1998.

Lacoste, Jean-Yves. "The Phenomenology of Anticipation." In *Phenomenology and Eschatology*, ed. N. Deroo and J. Manoussakis. Surrey, UK: Ashgate, 2009.

Lahache, Stéphane. "Le messianisme dans la pensée d'Emmanuel Levinas: Une ethique du pro-nom." In *Emmanuel Levinas: Philosophie et judaisme*, ed. D. Cohen-Lévinas and S. Trignano, 349–92. Paris: In Presse Editions, 2002.

Levi, Primo. *Survival in Auschwitz*, trans. S. Wolf. New York: Touchstone, 1996.

Levinas, Emmanuel. *A l'heure des nations*. Paris: Minuit, 1988. English translation, *In the Time of the Nations*, trans. M. B. Smith. Bloomington: Indiana University Press, 1994.

————. *Alterity and Transcendence*, trans. M. B. Smith. New York: Columbia University Press, 1999.

————. *Autrement qu'être ou au-delà de l'essence*. The Hague: Martinus Nijhoff, 1978. English translation, *Otherwise Than Being, or Beyond Essence*, trans. A Lingis. Pittsburgh: Duquesne University Press, 1998.

————. *Beyond the Verse*, trans. G. D. Mole. Bloomington: Indiana University Press, 1994.

————. *Collected Philosophical Papers*, trans. A. Lingis. The Hague: Martinus Nijhoff, 1987.

————. *De Dieu qui vient à l'idée*. Paris: Vrin, 1998. English translation, *Of God Who Comes to Mind*, trans. B. Bergo. Palo Alto, CA: Stanford University Press, 1998.

————. *De l'évasion*, with an introduction by J. Rolland. Paris: Fata Morgana, 1982. English translation, *On Escape*, trans. B. Bergo. Palo Alto, CA: Stanford University Press, 2002.

————. *De l'existence à l' existent*. Paris: Vrin, 1947. English translation, *Existence and Existents*, trans. A. Lingis. Dordrecht: Kluwer, 1978.

————. *Dieu, le mort, et le temps*. Paris: Grasset, 1993. English translation, *God, Death, and Time*, trans. B. Bergo. Palo Alto, CA: Stanford University Press, 2000.

————. *Difficile liberté: Essais sur le Judaïsme*. Paris: Albin Michel, 1976. English translation, *Difficult Freedom: Essays on Judaism*, trans. S. Hand. Baltimore: Johns Hopkins University Press, 1990.

————. Discussion following "Transcendence et hauteur." In *Liberté et commandement*, 110–11. Montpellier: Fata Morgana, 1994.

————. *Emmanuel Levinas: Basic Philosophical Writings*, ed. Adriaan T. Peperzak, Robert Bernasconi, and Simon Critchley. Bloomington: Indiana University Press, 1996.

————. *En découvrant l'existence avec Husserl et Heidegger*. Paris: Vrin, 1967.

————. "Enigme et phénomène." In *En découvrant l'existence avec Husserl et Heidegger*, 203–316. Paris: Vrin, 1967. English translation, "Phenomenon and Enigma," in *Collected Philosophical Papers*, trans. A. Lingis, 61–73. The Hague: Martinus Nijhoff, 1987.

———. *Entre nous: Essais sur la pensée-à-l'autre*. Paris: Grasset, 1991. English translation, *Entre Nous: Thinking of the Other*, trans. M. B. Smith. New York: Columbia University Press, 2000.

———. "Être Juif." *Confluences* 7, nos. 15-17 (1947): 253–64; reprinted in *Cahiers d'Études Lévinassiennes* 1 (2003): 99–106. English translation by M. B. Mader, "Being Jewish," *Continental Philosophy Review* 40 (2007): 205–10.

———. "Heidegger, Gagarin, et nous." In *Difficile liberté: Essais sur le Judaïsme*, 299–303. Paris: Albin Michel, 1976. English translation, "Heidegger, Gagarin, and Us," in *Difficult Freedom. Essays on Judaism*, trans. S. Hand, 231–34. Baltimore: John Hopkins University Press, 1990.

———. *Humanisme de l'autre homme*. Paris: Fata Morgana, 1972. English translation, *Humanism of the Other*, trans. N. Poller. Urbana: University of Illinois Press, 2006.

———. "Infinity." In *Alterity and Transcendence*, trans. M. B. Smith, 53–75. New York: Columbia University Press, 1999.

———. "Judaïsme et kénose." In *A l'heure des nations*, 133–51. Paris: Minuit, 1988. English translation, "Judaism and Kenosis," in *In the Time of the Nations*, trans. M. B. Smith, 101–18. Bloomington: Indiana University Press, 1994.

———. "Judaism and Revolution." In *Nine Talmudic Readings*, trans. A. Aronowicz, 133–68. Bloomington: Indiana University Press, 1990.

———. "La laïcité et la pensée d'Israël." In *Les imprévus de l'histoire*, 177–80. Paris: Fata Morgana, 1994. English translation, "Secularism and the Thought of Israel," in *Unforeseen History*, trans. N. Poller, 113–25. Champaign-Urbana: University of Illinois Press, 2004.

———. "La philosophie, la justice, et l'amour." In *Entre nous: Essais sur la pensée-à-l'autre*, 121–39. Paris: Grasset, 1991. English translation, "Philosophy, Justice, and Love," in *Entre Nous: Thinking of the Other*, trans. M. B. Smith, 103–22. New York: Columbia University Press, 2000.

———. "La souffrance inutile." In *Entre nous: Essais sur la pensée-à-l'autre*, 107–19. Paris: Grasset, 1991. English translation, "Useless Suffering," in *Entre Nous: Thinking of the Other*, trans. M. B. Smith 91–102. New York: Columbia University Press, 2000.

———. "Le mémoire d'un passé non révolu," interview with F. Ringelheim. In *Les Juifs entre la mémoire et l'oubli*, 1–2, 11–20. Brussels: Editions de l'Université de Bruxelles, 1987.

———. "Le Moi et la totalité." In *Entre nous: Essais sur la pensée-à-l'autre*, 25–52. Paris: Grasset, 1991. English translation, "The Ego and the Totality," in *Collected Philosophical Papers*, trans. A. Lingis, 25–45. The Hague: Martinus Nijhoff, 1987.

———. *Le temps et l'autre*. Paris: Presses Universitaires de France / Quadrige, 1983. English translation, *Time and the Other*, trans. R. A. Cohen. Pittsburgh: Duquesne University, 1987.

———. "Leçon talmudique: Sur la justice." In *Cahier L'Herne: Emmanuel Levinas*, 120–33. Paris: L' Herne, 1991.

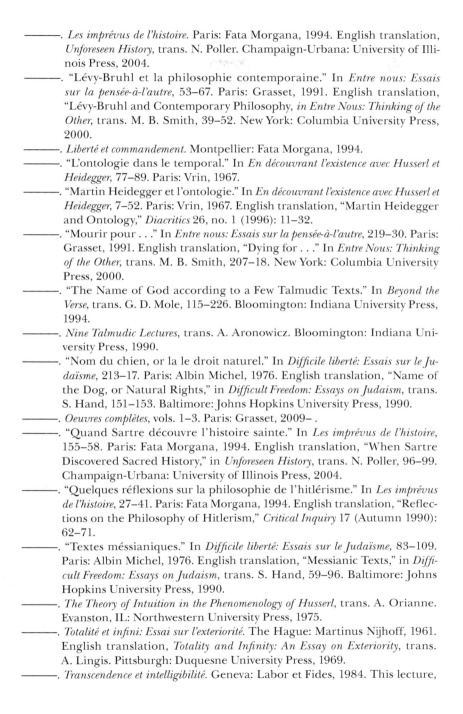

———. *Les imprévus de l'histoire*. Paris: Fata Morgana, 1994. English translation, *Unforeseen History*, trans. N. Poller. Champaign-Urbana: University of Illinois Press, 2004.

———. "Lévy-Bruhl et la philosophie contemporaine." In *Entre nous: Essais sur la pensée-à-l'autre*, 53–67. Paris: Grasset, 1991. English translation, "Lévy-Bruhl and Contemporary Philosophy, *in Entre Nous: Thinking of the Other*, trans. M. B. Smith, 39–52. New York: Columbia University Press, 2000.

———. *Liberté et commandement*. Montpellier: Fata Morgana, 1994.

———. "L'ontologie dans le temporal." In *En découvrant l'existence avec Husserl et Heidegger*, 77–89. Paris: Vrin, 1967.

———. "Martin Heidegger et l'ontologie." In *En découvrant l'existence avec Husserl et Heidegger*, 7–52. Paris: Vrin, 1967. English translation, "Martin Heidegger and Ontology," *Diacritics* 26, no. 1 (1996): 11–32.

———. "Mourir pour . . ." In *Entre nous: Essais sur la pensée-à-l'autre*, 219–30. Paris: Grasset, 1991. English translation, "Dying for . . ." In *Entre Nous: Thinking of the Other*, trans. M. B. Smith, 207–18. New York: Columbia University Press, 2000.

———. "The Name of God according to a Few Talmudic Texts." In *Beyond the Verse*, trans. G. D. Mole, 115–226. Bloomington: Indiana University Press, 1994.

———. *Nine Talmudic Lectures*, trans. A. Aronowicz. Bloomington: Indiana University Press, 1990.

———. "Nom du chien, or la le droit naturel." In *Difficile liberté: Essais sur le Judaïsme*, 213–17. Paris: Albin Michel, 1976. English translation, "Name of the Dog, or Natural Rights," in *Difficult Freedom: Essays on Judaism*, trans. S. Hand, 151–153. Baltimore: Johns Hopkins University Press, 1990.

———. *Oeuvres complètes*, vols. 1–3. Paris: Grasset, 2009– .

———. "Quand Sartre découvre l'histoire sainte." In *Les imprévus de l'histoire*, 155–58. Paris: Fata Morgana, 1994. English translation, "When Sartre Discovered Sacred History," in *Unforeseen History*, trans. N. Poller, 96–99. Champaign-Urbana: University of Illinois Press, 2004.

———. "Quelques réflexions sur la philosophie de l'hitlérisme." In *Les imprévus de l'histoire*, 27–41. Paris: Fata Morgana, 1994. English translation, "Reflections on the Philosophy of Hitlerism," *Critical Inquiry* 17 (Autumn 1990): 62–71.

———. "Textes méssianiques." In *Difficile liberté: Essais sur le Judaïsme*, 83–109. Paris: Albin Michel, 1976. English translation, "Messianic Texts," in *Difficult Freedom: Essays on Judaism*, trans. S. Hand, 59–96. Baltimore: Johns Hopkins University Press, 1990.

———. *The Theory of Intuition in the Phenomenology of Husserl*, trans. A. Orianne. Evanston, IL: Northwestern University Press, 1975.

———. *Totalité et infini: Essai sur l'extériorité*. The Hague: Martinus Nijhoff, 1961. English translation, *Totality and Infinity: An Essay on Exteriority*, trans. A. Lingis. Pittsburgh: Duquesne University Press, 1969.

———. *Transcendence et intelligibilité*. Geneva: Labor et Fides, 1984. This lecture,

"Transcendence and Intelligibility," but not the ensuing discussion, appears in *Emmanuel Levinas: Basic Philosophical Writings*, ed. A. T. Peperzak, R. Bernasconi, and S. Critchley, 149–60. Bloomington: Indiana University Press, 1996.

———. "Transcendence et mal." *Le Nouveau Commerce* 41 (1978): 55–78. English translation, "Transcendence of Evil," in *Collected Philosophical Papers*, trans. A. Lingis, 175–86. The Hague: Martinus Nijhoff, 1987.

Lyotard, Jean-François. "Figure Foreclosed," trans. D. Macey. In *The Levinas Reader*, ed. A. Benjamin, 69–110. London: Blackwell, 1989,

Marcel, Gabriel. *Being and Having*, trans. P. Smith. Glasgow: MacLehose / Glasgow University Press, 1949.

———. *Man Against Mass Society*, trans. G. S. Fraser. Chicago: Regnery, 1962.

———. *Tragic Wisdom and Beyond*, trans. P. Jolin. Evanston, IL: Northwestern University Press, 1973.

Marion, Jean-Luc. *Being Given*, trans. J. Kosky. Palo Alto, CA: Stanford University Press, 2002.

———. *God without Being: Hors-Texte*, trans. T. Carlson. Chicago: University of Chicago Press, 2012.

———. *The Idol and Distance*, trans. T. Carlson. New York: Fordham University Press, 2001.

———. "The Intentionality of Love: In Homage to Levinas." In J.-L. Marion, *Prolegomena to Charity*, trans. S. Lewis, 71–101. New York: Fordham University Press, 2002.

———. *On Descartes's Metaphysical Prism*, trans. J. Kosky. Chicago: University of Chicago Press, 1999.

Marx, Karl. *Grundrisse*, trans. M. Nicolaus. London: Penguin, 1993.

Mattei, Jean-François. "Levinas et Platon." In *Emmanuel Lévinas: Positivité et transcendence*, 73–87. Paris: Presses Universitaires de France, 2000.

May, Ulrike. "The Third Step of Drive-Theory: On the Genesis of *Beyond the Pleasure Principle*." *Psychoanalysis and History* 17, no. 2 (2015): 205–72.

Mensch, James. *Levinas's Existential Analytic*. Evanston, IL: Northwestern University Press, 2015.

Meskin, Jacob. "The Role of Lurianic Kabbalah in the Early Philosophy of Emmanuel Levinas." In *Levinas Studies*, vol. 2, ed. J. Bloechl, 49–77. Pittsburgh: Duquesne University Press, 2007.

Mopsik, Charles. "La pensée d'Emmanuel Lévinas et la cabale." In *Cahier de l'Herne: Emmanuel Levinas*, 428–41. Paris: L'Herne, 1991.

Morgan, Michael L. *Discovering Levinas*. Cambridge: Cambridge University Press, 2007.

Moyn, Samuel. *Origins of the Other: Emmanuel Levinas between Revelation and Ethics*. Ithaca, NY: Cornell University Press, 2005.

Narbonne, Jean-Marc. "God and Philosophy according to Levinas." In *Levinas Studies*, vol. 2, ed. J. Bloechl, 29–48. Pittsburgh: Duquesne University Press, 2007.

Narbonne, Jean-Marc, and Wayne Hankey. *Lévinas et l'héritage grec suivi de cent ans de Néoplatonisme en France*. Paris: J. Vrin, 2004.

Nietzsche, Friedrich. *The Gay Science*, trans. W. Kaufman. New York: Vintage, 1974.
———. *On the Genealogy of Morals*. In *On the Genealogy of Morals and Ecco Homo*, trans. W. Kaufmann and R. J. Hollingdale. New York: Vintage, 1989.
———. "On Truth and Lies in a Non-Moral Sense," trans. D. Breazeale. In *The Nietzsche Reader*, ed. K. Ansell-Pierce and D. Large. Oxford: Blackwell, 2006.
———. *Thus Spoke Zarathustra*, trans. A. Del Caro. Cambridge: Cambridge University Press, 2006.
Ouaknin, Marc-Alain. *Méditations érotiques*. Paris: Belland, 1992.
Pascal, Blaise. *Pensées*, trans. A. J. Krailsheimer. London: Penguin, 1995.
Peperzak, Adriaan T. *Beyond: The Philosophy of Emmanuel Levinas*. Evanston, IL: Northwestern University Press, 1997.
———. *Elements of Ethics*. Palo Alto, CA: Stanford University Press, 2003.
Perpich, Diane. *The Ethics of Emmanuel Levinas*. Palo Alto, CA: Stanford University Press, 2008.
Petitdemange, Guy. "La notion paradoxal de l'histoire." In *Emmanuel Lévinas et l'histoire*, ed. N. Frogneux and F. Mies, 17–44. Paris: Cerf, 1998.
Plüss, David. *Das Messianische: Judentum und Philosophie im Werk Emmanuel Levinas*. Stuttgart: Kohlhammer, 2001.
Putnam, Hilary. "Levinas and Judaism." In *The Cambridge Companion to Levinas*, ed. S. Critchley and R. Bernasconi, 33–61. Cambridge: Cambridge University Press, 2002.
Ricoeur, Paul. *Memory, History, Forgetting*, trans. K. Blamey and D. Pellauer. Chicago: University of Chicago Press, 2000.
———. *Oneself as Another*, trans. K. Blamey. Chicago: University of Chicago Press, 1992.
Rolland, Jacques. *Parcours de l'autrement: Lecture d'Emmanuel Levinas*. Paris: Presses Universitaires de France. 2000.
Salanskis, Jean-Michel. *Lévinas vivant*. Paris: Belles Lettres, 2006.
Sallis, John. "Alterity and the Elemental." In *Elemental Discourses*, 84–98. Bloomington: Indiana University Press, 2018.
Sartre, Jean-Paul. *Anti-Semite and Jew*, trans. G. Becker. New York: Schocken, 1948.
———. *Being and Nothingness*, trans. H. Barnes. London: Routledge, 1991.
———. *Existentialism Is a Humanism*, trans. C. Macomber. New Haven, CT: Yale University Press, 2007.
———. *La mort dans l'âme*. Paris: Gallimard, 1949.
Sugarman, Richard. *Levinas and the Torah: A Phenomenological Approach*. Albany: SUNY Press, 2019.
Taminiaux, Jacques. "La première réplique à l'ontologie fondamentale." In *Cahier de l'Herne: Emmanuel Levinas*, 278–92. Paris: L'Herne, 1991.
Tengelyi, Laszlo. "Experience of Infinity in Levinas." In *Levinas Studies*, vol. 4, ed. J. Bloechl, 111–25. Pittsburgh: Duquesne University Press, 2009.
Tertullian. *Apologetics*. In *Tertullian: Apology and De Spectaculis, Minucius Felix: Octavius*, 2–229. Cambridge, MA: Loeb Classical Library, 1931.
Thomas Aquinas. *Summa Contra Gentiles*. Oxford: English Dominican Province Translation edition, 2017.

————. *Summa Theologiae*, 5 vols. Oxford: English Dominican Province Translation edition, 1981.

Tilliette, Xavier. *Le Christ de la philosophie*. Paris: Cerf / Cogitatio fidei, 1990.

Unger, Roberto. *False Necessity: Anti-Necessitarian Social Theory in the Service of Radical Democracy*. London: Verso, 2004.

Van Haute, Philippe, and Tomas Geyskens. *A Non-Oedipal Psychoanalysis? A Clinical Anthropology of Hysteria in the Works of Freud and Lacan*. Leuven: Leuven University Press, 2012.

Van Haute, Philippe, and Herman Westerink. *Reading Freud's Three Essays on the Theory of Sexuality: From Pleasure to the Object*. London: Routledge, 2020.

Visker, Rudi. "The Price of Being Dispossessed: Levinas's God and Freud's Trauma." In *The Face of the Other and the Trace of God: Essays on the Philosophy of Emmanuel Levinas*, ed. J. Bloechl, 243–75. New York: Fordham University Press, 2000.

————. "A Sartrean in Disguise?" In *Levinas: The Face of the Other: The Fifteenth Annual Symposium of the Simon Silverman Phenomenology Center*. Pittsburgh: Duquesne University Press, 2006.

Waldenfels, Bernhard. *The Question of the Other*. Hong Kong: Chinese University Press, 2007.

Weil, Simone. *First and Last Notebooks*. London: Oxford University Press, 1970.

Winnicott, Donald. "The Theory of the Parent-Infant Relationship." In *The Maturational Process and the Facilitating Environment*, by D. Winnicott. London: Routledge, 2018.

Wolfson, Elliot. "Secrecy, Modesty and the Feminine: Kabbalistic Traces in the Thought of Levinas." In *The Exorbitant: Emmanuel Levinas between Judaism and Christianity*, ed. K. Hart and M. Signer, 52–73. New York: Fordham University Press, 2010.

Wu, Roberto. "The Recurrence of Acoustics in Levinas." In *Levinas Studies*, vol. 10, ed. J. Bloechl, 116–36. Pittsburgh: Duquesne University Press, 2016.

Index

absolute: desire for, 20, 28, 41, 47; God as, 129; plot and, 142; "savor for," 17, 89, 120; as term, 70; withdrawn from order, 58

"absolute I," 75–76

aggression: and fear, 9, 10–14; and freedom, 24; Freud on, 94, 170n20; and insecurity, 41, 58; and moral norms, 31; and otherness, 18

anarchical, the: and election, 132; and language, 106; and law, 113; and plot, 142; and relation of subject to other, 104; and responsibility, 130; and trauma, 93–94, 131

anthropomorphism, 66–67, 174n59

Anti-Semite and Jew (*Réflexions sur la question juive*) (Sartre), 26

antisemitism: and Levi, 50; phenomenological approach to, 4; Sartre on, 26, 27–28, 153n51; in Shoah, 9

Aquinas. *See* Thomas Aquinas, Saint

Aristotle, 65, 154n57, 156n8, 165n5

atheistic, the, 44, 63, 167n39

Augustine, Saint, 65, 111, 180n7

Auschwitz, 50–53, 161n57, 161n61, 161n63

Bacon, Francis, 64, 166n30

being: and beings, 23–24, 33, 40, 97, 123–24, 181n19; and death, 72; Heidegger on, 16–17, 33–34, 59, 120–21; as language, 97–100; Levinas vs. Heidegger conceptions of, 16–19, 181n19; as self-relating, 18–19; and *tertium quid*, 113–14; violence of, 34, 89, 168n50

Being and Nothingness (Sartre), 26, 56–57

Being and Time (Heidegger): appearance in, 74–75; Dasein in, 5–6, 24, 34–36,

74, 98, 152n35, 158n23; on hero, 22, 156n12; Levinas study of, 27; pain in, 15–16; self-relation in, 20; subjectivity in, 156n12

"Being Jewish" (Levinas), 8

beings: and being, 23–24, 33, 40, 97, 123–24, 181n19; conscious, 25; and death, 72; ethical, 64–65; God and, 126; human, 9–10, 13, 34, 53, 57, 82, 84–85, 132, 136–37, 166n33; and self-interest, 118

Bergo, Bettina, 177n38

Bernasconi, Robert, 178n48

Blondel, Maurice, 18, 151n28

Bloy, Léon, 45, 159n40

body: forces emanating from, 12–15; and senses, 43; and spirit, 11, 15, 148n9; vulnerability of, 10–11

Bonhoeffer, Dietrich, 136–37, 187n57

Brunschvicg, Leon, 12, 149n16

"Case of Emma," Freud and, 93–94

Catholics, 18, 45, 148n1

Christianity. *See* theology, Christian

Cioran, Emil, 38–40

community: authentic, 26–28, 30; and ethics, 113; and hero, 22–24; and identity, 19–22; of neighbors, 31; and otherness, 62; and plurality, 46–47; self-justifying, 29; theory of, 130

Confessions (Augustine), 65, 111

creation: as central for Levinas, 128; and election, 48, 133: medieval theologies of, 92

Critique of Pure Reason (Kant), 25

Dasein: anxious, 39–40; Heidegger on, 20–24, 33–36, 74, 97–98, 130, 149n13, 152n35, 162n66; Levinas on, 5–6, 15–

saying (*le dire*) vs. the said (*le dit*), 7, 8, 105–6, 112–17, 165n25
self-interest: being as, 133; conversion from, 140; and evil, 14; and face of the other, 130; of free beings, 118; and good, 3; and immanence, 67; as limit, 79; and metaphysical desire, 69; and presence of another, 19; and psychoanalysis, 86–88; and violence, 5, 15
sexuality, 70, 86, 171n25
Shoah, the, 9, 49, 52, 135, 139, 162n67
Socrates, 76, 107, 173n49
speech: of analyst, 81; in call and response, 86; and face, 99, 117; and God, 7, 118, 122, 140; Heidegger on, 20; in *Totality and Infinity*, 103; and transcendence, 96–117, 165n25, 171n29
Spinoza, Baruch, 111, 154n57
spirit (*l'esprit*): and body, 11, 15, 148n9; dialectic of, 137; Levinas's reticence about, 40; and mental life, 14, 148n8; ontology and, 59
"Spirituality of the Jewish Prisoner, The" (Levinas), 8
stalag (prisoner of war camp), 45, 46, 48, 50, 52, 120
subject: atheist, 44, 63; and ethical relation, 57; and metaphysical desire, 6–7; phenomenology on, 33; and plenitude, 17; and plurality, 19; as *pour-soi*, 25; separated, 44, 54, 57, 62, 68, 104–5, 123, 128, 130–31, 139; subjectivity of, 25, 29, 33–35, 48, 61, 88, 89, 91, 115, 132, 141, 16; temporality of, 106; in *Totality and Infinity*, 61, 63, 97–98; and transcendence, 44; who is supposed to know, 80, 170n18
subjectivity: Heidegger on, 16–17, 24, 156n12; hollowed out in advance, 3–4; inter-, 5–6, 25–26; and the political, 5; and religion, 18, 28–29, 32; Sartre on, 25, 30; separated, 139; as struggle, 16; of the subject, 25, 29, 33–35, 48, 61, 88, 89, 91, 115, 132, 141, 168n50; in *Time and the Other*, 98
suffering: of analysand, 80–81, 170n21; of animals, 166n33; and the body, 13; and death, 36–37; and evil, 42; and God, 6, 139; and Jewishness, 44–53, 130–32, 160n46; and mystery, 41;

of other person, 100, 116; vs. pain, 158n28; salvation from, 133–37; and theodicy, 53, 162n66; and violence, 30
suppression and exclusion, 5–6, 19–20, 27–28, 73–74
sujet supposé savoir (subject who is supposed to know), 80, 170n18
Survival in Auschwitz (Levi), 50–53, 161n57, 161n61, 161n63

Talmud, the, 96, 119, 186n54
teaching: ambivalence and, 99–100; ethics as, 114–16; Jewish captive experience as, 45, 47; Levinas's, 96, 119–20, 154n57; in philosophy, 7, 30, 122, 135–36; as prophecy, 32; theology as, 118–19
temporality: of being, 17; and effort of existing, 39; and messianism, 136; of subject, 106; theology on, 123; of trauma, 93; and the trivial, 23
Tengelyi, Laszlo, 166n36
Tertullian, 160n40
theodicy, 52, 53, 162n1
theology, Christian: and election, 130–32; and ethical metaphysics, 71, 119–22, 124, 126–27, 135–37, 140–42; Heidegger and, 124–25, 182n20, 182n22; Levinas and, 118–38; mystical, 7, 124–25, 182n22, 182n24; onto-, 6, 68; vs. phenomenology, 118–19; and philosophy, 4, 18; and plot, 8; and responsibility, 133–38; as teaching, 118–19; and violence, 124
"Third Meditation" (Descartes), 6, 60–61
third-person relation to language, 113–14
Thomas Aquinas, Saint, 52, 65, 126, 183n27
Three Essays on the Theory of Sexuality (Freud), 171n25
Thus Spoke Zarathustra (Nietzsche), 52
Tilliette, Xavier, 137
Time and the Other (Levinas): call to service in, 41–42; Dasein in, 5–6; insomnia in, 157n17; subjectivity in, 98
Torah, the, 119, 154n57
Totality and Infinity (Levinas): body in, 43; call and response in, 108, 177n31; claims of other person in, 44; crea-